CATULLUS

A Reader's Guide to the Poems

Stuart G. P. Small

UNIVERSITY
PRESS OF
AMERICA

LANHAM • NEW YORK • LONDON

Copyright © 1983 by

University Press of America,™ Inc.

4720 Boston Way
Lanham, MD 20706

3 Henrietta Street
London WC2E 8LU England

Library of Congress Cataloging in Publication Data

Small, Stuart G. P.
   Catullus, a reader's guide to the poems.

   Bibliography: p.
   Includes indexes.
   1. Catullus, Gainus Valerius--Criticism and
interpretation.   I. Title.
PA6276.S64   1983   874'.01   82-20245
ISBN 0-8191-2905-4
ISBN 0-8191-2906-2 (pbk.)

CATULLUS:

A Reader's Guide to the Poems

by

Stuart G. P. Small

iii

To Mary

TABLE OF CONTENTS

CONTENTS

CONTENTS

self-image. Elements of universality. The
sense of human limitation. Some sources of
consolation. The uses of poetry.

PREFACE

This book is intended primarily for readers who are approaching the poetry of Catullus for the first time. Nevertheless, I venture to hope that specialists may find my treatment of the author useful and in some respects novel.

My method has been to concentrate not upon the poet's life but upon his writings. As a glance at the table of contents will show, I have taken up the poems not in chronological order but in terms of subject matter and literary form. I shall assume that the reader has readily available a good Latin text of the poems or a bilingual edition such as that of Cornish (Loeb Classical Library) or Michie or Whigham, or at least a modern verse translation, perhaps that of Swanson or Copley or Gregory or Sisson.

I wish I could take it for granted that all my readers would be able to read the Latin language, but I must reluctantly recognize that this will not be the case. I have therefore provided prose translations for most passages, long or short, which I have quoted from the original. These translations lay no claim to literary merit; they are intended to be close but idiomatic, an adequate crib for the understanding of the Latin text. I have tried to avoid overuse of technical terms, and where an unfamiliar or unusual expression is unavoidable, an explanation is usually provided. Owing to the technical nature of Latin metrics, I have deliberately abridged my discussion of Catullus' versification. The interested reader may consult on this subject the introduction to Quinn's edition, where the essentials are succinctly set forth, or for a more detailed presentation Halporn, Ostwald and Rosenmeyer, *The Meters of Greek and Latin Poetry*.

I have quoted the Latin text of Catullus from the second impression of R. A. B. Mynors' edition, Oxford, 1960, and I have made it my aim to offer no interpretation of the poet's meaning which is incompatible with this text; no. 67, 20 is a unique exception to the rule.

The writer of a comprehensive study such as this is inevitably under an enormous debt to his predecessors. I have tried to give some idea of the dimensions of my own obligation in the footnotes and *List of Works Cited*. But a full annotation at every point would have overwhelmed the text, and I have accordingly had to confine myself to summary indications. If I have inadvertently used the ideas of any scholar without giving proper acknowledgement, or if I have misrepresented the opinions of any, I offer my apologies herewith. My principal debt is to Quinn, Granarolo and Klingner. I must also confess to having taken a short way with doubtful matters. I have scanted certain theories which I regard as mistaken and have refrained from presenting full argument on both sides of some controversial questions. Again I can only plead that a brief survey of this type imposes such limitations on the author. I sincerely trust that I have created no false impressions.

It is a distinct pleasure to thank those colleagues and friends who have read and criticized substantial portions of my typescript: Daniel Garrison, Dennis Groh, Jean Hagstrum, Daniel Harmon, Carl Roebuck and John Wright. I am much indebted to them and to an anonymous referee for a number of corrections and improvements. For the faults and infelicities which remain I assume full responsibility. I am also grateful to Muriel F. Wolff for turning my spidery longhand into flawless typed copy, and to Ann Addis for preparing the typescript for publication.

The most important debt of all is indicated by the dedication.

S.G.P.S.

CHAPTER ONE

Some Preliminaries

We do not know very much about the life of Gaius
Valerius Catullus. Even the dates of his birth and
death are uncertain. Jerome says that he was born at
Verona in 87 B.C. and that he died at Rome in his thir-
tieth year, B.C. 57. Although these dates are presumably derived from Suetonius' *de Poetis*, a respected
source, they must be incorrect. Poems no. 11, 45, 55
and 113 cannot be earlier than 55 B.C.[1] The simplest
solution to the difficulty is to assume that Jerome or
Suetonius has somehow got both dates two or three years
too early. On this view, Catullus was born in 85/84
B.C. and died in 55/54.[2]

His father was a man of some importance in Verona.
Suetonius, *Jul.*73, tells us that he frequently entertained Julius Caesar in his home, presumably when the
great man was governor of Cisalpine Gaul. We know
nothing about the father's occupation, but it is probable that he was a large landowner. In addition to
property in Verona the family seems to have had an
estate at Sirmio on the Lago di Garda (poem no. 31) and
a villa near Tivoli (poem 44).

We have no direct information about Catullus' education or where he received it. His poems show, of
course, that he had a thorough grounding in Greek and
Latin literature. No doubt he had attended the elemen-
tary classes of some local *grammaticus*, conceivably the
scholar-poet Valerius Cato, and a secondary school of
rhetoric. Unlike Virgil and Horace, he seems not to
have studied philosophy. According to poem no. 68,
15-18, he had started to write love poetry by the time
he was sixteen years old.

At some point during his later adolescence,
Catullus' father sent him[3] from Verona to Rome. There
he eventually became acquainted with the *Poetae Novi*, the
New Poets, a group of young writers who were reacting
against the old established traditions of earlier Latin
poetry, especially the long-winded and narrowly nationalistic epics of Ennius and Naevius and their succes-
sors, and were trying to introduce into contemporary
literature something of the polished brevity and sophistication of Hellenistic verse.[4] Many of the

1

literary friends addressed by Catullus in his occasional poems were members of this coterie: Cinna, Calvus, Caecilius, Cornificius, possibly Valerius Cato and Furius Bibaculus.

Uninterested in politics or a career, Catullus gave himself over to literature and love. He says that he led a life of *otium*, "indolence" or "living for oneself" (poem no. 51, 13-16). Eventually he met the woman to whom he gave the pseudonym Lesbia.[5] She was to be the great love of his life. According to Apuleius, *Apol.* 10, her real name was Clodia, which is metrically equivalent to Lesbia, as the convention required. Most scholars[6] identify this Clodia as the second daughter of Appius Claudius Pulcher, consul in 79 B.C., and wife of Q. Metellus Celer, who was praetor in 63 B.C., governor of Cisalpine Gaul in the following year, and consul in 60 B.C.; he died in 59 B.C. She was some ten years older than Catullus. Although she was a proud patrician, her family appears to have lost a good deal of its wealth. Perhaps money problems explain why she married Metellus. Metellus is usually described as a dull and unattractive man, and he was not a patrician; still, he was rich. Clodia was a cultivated and fascinating woman, liberated, independent and unconventional; but she was also ambitious, violent and sensual, perhaps eventually to the point of nymphomania. Because of her unrestrained way of life, she became the most notorious woman in the Rome of her time. She was called *Quandrantaria*, "penny whore," because she had sold herself for the price of a bath.[7] After the end of her affair with M. Caelius Rufus, she had him charged with attempted murder by poisoning (56 B.C.). Rufus was defended by Cicero (according to some, one of her former lovers) in an extant oration, the *pro Caelio*, in which he assaulted her with blistering and unforgettable invective: Caelius was acquitted. After this she drops out of sight. Her brother P. Clodius Pulcher was an extraordinary personality in his own right. He had first achieved notoriety when he was discovered disguised as a woman at the rites of the Bona Dea, a ceremony restricted to females. Clodius was an activist politician--some might say an anarchist gang-leader--who had organized elements of the Roman proletariat into a kind of political party. He managed to bring about the brief banishment of Cicero in 58-57 B.C. His gangs played an important and disastrous role in the politics of the fifties. He was finally slain in 52 B.C. by the bodyguard of a rival demagogue, T. Annius Milo, in a gang fight on the Appian Way.

2

Catullus' love affair with Clodia was mostly unhappy. By 57 B.C., he was ready to turn his back on
her, on *otium* and on Rome. With Cinna (poem no. 10, 30)
and other companions he joined the *cohors praetoria* or
unofficial retinue of the propraetor C. Memmius and
spent a year on staff duty in the province of Bithynia
(western Asia Minor), hoping to enrich himself at the
expense of the provincials. These hopes were not fulfilled, and Catullus blamed Memmius for it (poems no. 10
and 28). While he was in Asia he visited the cities of
Ionia (poem 46). He also visited the grave of his
brother, who had died in the east and was buried in the
Troad (poem 101). For his return to Italy he acquired
a small ship, a *phaselus* (poem 4), in which he sailed back
across the Aegaean and Ionian Seas, up the Adriatic,
then up the Po and Mincius or Adige; somehow or other
he was able to get the *phaselus* over into the Lago di
Garda. His celebrated homecoming poem to Sirmio, no.
31, belongs to this period.

He had only a year or so left to live. To that
final year perhaps belongs the series of poems addressed
to the boy Juventius, a ward of his, for whom he had
conceived a jealous but short-lived passion. Also to
his final months belong the invectives against Julius
Caesar and certain of his satellites, in particular his
praefectus fabrum or chief engineer Mamurra, whom he sometimes calls Mentula (meaning *membrum virile*) in allusion
to his hyperactive sex-life. Caesar himself comes under
direct attack in three poems, nos. 29, 57, and 93. Although these invectives were personally (i.e., not
politically) motivated, we are told by Suetonius that
Caesar felt deeply wounded by them (*Jul.* 73):

> Caesar made no bones about the fact that
> Valerius Catullus had inflicted an in-
> delible stigma on his name by the poems
> against Mamurra; yet when the poet apolo-
> gized,[8] Caesar invited him to dinner the
> very same day and continued his relation
> of guest-friendship with Catullus' father.

Poem no. 11, probably written after the "apology," seems
to show a change of feeling toward Caesar, who is carefully praised in line 10.[9] That poem, however, mentions
Caesar only in passing. It is essentially a farewell to
Lesbia and a rejection of her attempts to win back her
former lover. Within a matter of months after writing
this poem, Catullus was dead. We have no idea what he
died of, but that has not prevented interpreters from

speculating about possible causes. Lindsay, on the basis of a few references to coughing (poem no. 44), imagines that he died "ravaged by consumption." Thornton Wilder, even more extravagantly, depicts him dying in a pool of his own (doubtless symbolic) vomit, utterly disgusted with Rome, the world and life.[10] Other writers have imagined different death-scenes, more or less picturesque; their suggestions must be dismissed. It is enough to say quite simply that Catullus probably died in Rome at the age of thirty, as Jerome laconically notes.

This is the essence of what is known about Catullus' life; it is not very much. And it is important to observe that the little we do know comes almost entirely from the poems and not from external sources. There are only four exceptions to this: (1) the birth and death dates, presumably derived from Suetonius through Jerome, and problematical; (2) the story of the reconciliation with Caesar, given by Suetonius; (3) the identity of "Lesbia," provided by Apuleius; (4) the information about Catullus' father's relationship with Caesar, also from Suetonius. It follows from this that we cannot ordinarily interpret Catullus' poetry from his life.[11] To the contrary, we are obliged to reconstruct his life from the poems. I have set forth the bare facts of the biography here not because I think that the biography supplies a key to his writings, but simply to offer a modicum of orientation and background to the historically minded reader who is encountering Catullus for the first time. But I wish to make clear my own conviction that biography is one thing and poetry is something else.

The text of Catullus' poems as we now know them hangs by a single thread; it has come down to us through one MS called the "Verona archetype," V. This MS was discovered toward the end of the thirteenth century, at or near Verona. A strange little poem by Benvenuto Campesani of Vicenza, copied into two of our earliest surviving MSS, tells us about the finding of V. The poem represents Catullus as speaking to the citizens of Verona:

> Ad patriam uenio longis a finibus exul;
>   causa mei reditus compatriota fuit,
> scilicet a calamis tribuit cui Francia nomen,
>   quique notat turbae praetereuntis iter.
> Quo licet ingenio uestrum celebrate Catullum,
>   cuius sub modio clausa papyrus erat.

Exiled in far-off lands I come back to my
native country; a fellow-townsman was responsible for my return, a man to whom France
gave a name derived from reeds, one who watches
the passage of the transient throng. Praise
your own Catullus with whatever skill you may:
his book was hidden under a bushel.[12]

Sub modio, "under a bushel," is of course a biblical
metaphor; it need mean no more than "in the library of
Verona cathedral."[13] Wherever it was found, the Verona
archetype was soon lost again, but luckily not before it
had been copied several times. The three best surviving
MSS, G (Paris), O (Oxford) and R (Vatican), all written
in the fourteenth century, are derived from it. In addition we possess a ninth century anthology of Latin
poets, the *Codex Thuaneus*, now in Paris, which contains the
hexameter wedding poem, no. 62. All other MSS of
Catullus (there are about a hundred and twenty of them)
are late and of limited value; like G, O and R they are
descendants of the Verona archetype.

The present collection totals nearly 2,300 lines.
Its bulk and variety make it improbable that the collection was prepared by Catullus personally. During
the poet's lifetime, books of verse were brief and more
or less homogeneous. The ordinary vehicle of publication was the *volumen* or papyrus scroll. The Alexandrian
Greeks had standardized the length of the scroll at
about 700-1,000 lines, and the Romans had apparently
followed the same norm (so that each book of Virgil's
Aeneid, for example, would be contained in a single
scroll). We know from poem no. 1 that Catullus himself
published at least one *volumen* of poems, namely the
libellus or "little book" dedicated to Cornelius Nepos,
which contained an undetermined number of *nugae*, short
pieces. Our poem no. 1 was originally the introduction
to this *libellus*. Wheeler[14] thinks the poet may also have
published the *Wedding of Peleus and Thetis*, no. 64, as a
single *volumen*, and a brief selection of his elegiac
verse. By the time of the poet's death there probably
existed at least two published *volumina*, maybe more. In
addition, there must have been scattered poems, known
to be Catullus' work, which had passed from hand to
hand among his friends. These were collected and published by a nameless editor or literary executor. The
poems circulated for some time after this in separate
volumina. It is likely that the collection we now have
was made in the second or third century, when the *codex*
or parchment book with leaves and pages had come into

5

common use. The editor of the *codex* seems to have
gathered together all the poems that he could find
extant in the various *volumina* and to have reordered
them by a system of his own devising,[15] different from
that of the *volumina*; he grouped the poems according to
meter and length, with little or no reference to subject
matter or chronology. His order is the same order we
follow today: poems 1-60 are *polymetra*, short pieces in
various metres, mainly iambic or aeolic; next follows a
group of longer poems, nos. 61-68, in glyconics, hexameters, galliambics, and elegiacs; finally, there is a
group of (mostly) shorter poems, nos. 69-116, all in
elegiacs. These 116 poems make up the collection as it
has been transmitted to us by the medieval MSS. The
ancient *volumina* are lost, no doubt forever. We shall
never know for sure which poems Catullus published in
his own lifetime or in what order he arranged them.

*

One might expect an introductory poem to give the
reader some idea of what the poet is going to write
about and why. But in poem no. 1, Catullus offers us
neither a table of contents, nor any indication of his
views concerning the ends and aims of poetry, nor a
statement about the purpose of his *libellus*. At most he
provides us with an example of the way he intends to
write, or more precisely of one way among many others.

We can scarcely miss the sustained modesty of the
references to his own work: *nugas*, "trifles," v. 4;
quidquid hoc libelli, "this little book, such as it is,"
v. 8; *qualecumque*, "good or bad," v. 9. These expressions
are not to be taken too seriously. Cornelius, the
addressee, does not think the poems are *nugae* (vv. 3-4);
nor does Catullus. His prayer to the Muse in the last
two lines proves this. If he wants his poetry to endure down through the years, he must believe, along
with Cornelius, that it has some merit. Who then consider his poems *nugae*? In all likelihood, conventional
readers with old-fashioned tastes, people who preferred
poetry in the Ennian tradition. There were still many
Romans, a large majority in fact, who expected poetry
to be *polis*-centered, connected with the Roman state, the
gods, and the four cardinal virtues. They wanted poets
to teach and wanted their writings to have moral

6

utility. Catullus is not attuned to the conventional literary opinion of his own age; he is estranged from traditional Roman literary values. His ironic use of the word *nugae* alludes to this disaffection. Though others considered them "trifles" Catullus expects that his poems may well survive and endure *plus uno saeclo*, "down through the years."

There is an accumulation of adjectival expressions modifying *libellum*, line 1; *lepidum*, "charming"; *novum*, "new," "fresh"; *arida modo pumice expolitum*, "just now polished with dry pumice-stone." Several recent interpreters hold that these expressions apply not only to the physical appearance of the scroll, but to Catullus' literary style as well; they provide a first hint as to his esthetic principles.[16] In other words, there is an analogy between the appearance of the scroll and the kind of writing it contains. By this implied comparison, the author is obliquely praising his "trifles" for their grace, modernity and polish. These are the positive qualities that will make them live "down through the ages."

Why did Catullus elect to give a presentation copy of his *libellus* to Cornelius and not to somebody else? Was it because Cornelius was a fellow countryman from Cisalpine Gaul? Catullus makes no allusion to the fact; and he is certainly far from saying that Cornelius was his literary patron, his "Maecenas."[17] The Muse, not Cornelius, was his patron (v. 9). Perhaps he regarded Cornelius as his ideal reader. For some time now Cornelius has taken his "trifles" seriously, has appreciated them at their just worth. In addition, there seems to be a certain affinity between Cornelius' prose and Catullus' verse. Cornelius alone among the Italians had the courage to compress the whole recorded history of the world into a work of only three *volumina*, vv.5-7; Cornelius' writing is preeminently concise, concentrated and distilled; it bears every mark of learning and care.[18] A man who writes this way can appreciate similar qualities in other authors. Catullus' poetry is concise, concentrated and distilled, too; it too is backed by learning and composed with care. Even in the present poem, not one of his most ambitious efforts, Catullus manages to pack a great deal of meaning into the space of a few lines. In sum, he and Cornelius are kindred spirits; Cornelius' prose is comparable to Catullus' verse; he is Catullus' ideal reader.

The diction of this poem is informal, the syntax

7

uncomplicated, the versification light and conversational. It is written in a metre called the hendeca-
syllabic or "eleven-syllabled" line. The pattern is

X X — ∪ ∪ ∪ — ∪ — ∪ — X

The eleven-syllable was a fashionable metre in Catullus'
day, much affected by the New Poets. Except for the
elegiac couplet, it is Catullus' favorite verse form.
He uses it in 43 polymetric poems (552 lines), all
short. It was of course borrowed from the Greeks:[19]
Sappho, Anacreon and the tragedians employ it. It is
also found in the Athenian *skolia* or drinking songs,
including the well-known one in praise of the tyranni-
cides Harmodius and Aristogeiton.[20] During the Hellenistic period it came fully into its own, appearing in
Phalaecus, Theocritus and Callimachus. It was normally
used to treat light or playful themes in independent
short poems. In Catullus the eleven-syllable is often
cheerful and sportive. Certainly it has this effect in
poem no. 1; but it is not confined to light-hearted
verse. Poems no. 38 and 58, both in eleven-syllables,
are among the saddest Catullus ever wrote. More than
a dozen of his invectives are in the same metre.

No. 14b seems to be another preface, or conceivably
an epilogue. In either case it is out of place in its
present position, and we have no way of knowing where
it was originally located. It is obviously only a fragment. Unlike no. 1 it is addressed not to an individual
but to *lectores*, Caullus' readers collectively--if he has
any (*si qui forte...eritis*, vv. 1-2). This is mock apologetic and reminiscent of the tone of poem no. 1; mock-
apologetic too is the term *ineptiae*, "my silly stuff,"
(v. 1) which he uses to designate his writings. The
verb in vs. 3, *horrebitis*, "shrink," "tremble" at the
thought of touching his verses, seems again to acknowledge that a prejudice is working against him. Apparently he is already well-known, not to say notorious.
Notorious for what? For being vituperative and sa-
lacious? Some of his epigrams might easily have won
him such a reputation. But here his writings are merely
ineptiae, silly modernism, in no way formidable. The
exact implication of *horrebitis* therefore is somewhat
elusive. It is much to be regretted that the rest of
14b has perished. It is a most intriguing little fragment.[21]

To return to no. 1 for a moment, we happen to know
that Cornelius was an older, more distinguished man than
Catullus. Nevertheless Catullus does not address him

8

in a deferential tone. Even while praising him he
speaks in a breezy, perhaps faintly disrespectful way.
Catullus shows something of the self-confidence of a
high-born moneyed Roman who expresses his likes and dis-
likes without inhibitions and does not need to flatter.
But above and beyond this, Catullus speaks to Cornelius
as one speaks to a friend. Catullus had an enormous
talent for friendship. He tells us in one passage (no.
9, 1-2, according to one tenable interpretation of the
lines) that he had no fewer than 300,000 friends. Many
of his poems are addressed to friends or are about
friendship. In the next chapter we shall scrutinize
some of these poems.

CHAPTER TWO

Friends

Friendship is without question a basic and indispensable human relationship known and valued the world
over. Classical antiquity is certainly no exception to
this general statement. Examples of ideal friendship
abound in Greek mythology. One thinks immediately of
such famous friendships as that between Achilles and
Patroclus, Orestes and Pylades, Theseus and Peirithous;
there are many more. Hereditary guest-friendship, in
which host and guest are bound to each other in a life-
long relationship sanctioned by Zeus Xenios,[1] is already
an established and venerable institution in Homer. It
continues to be held in honor until late antiquity.
The philosophers, too, set a high value on friendship.
It is prized by the Pythagoreans, by Plato (especially
in his *Lysis* and *Laws*), and by the Stoics and Epicureans.
Theophrastus wrote a treatise *Peri Philias*. Aristotle
devotes two entire books of his *Nicomachean Ethics* to the
subject. At Rome also friendship is esteemed and
written about. Cicero's attractive dialogue *De Amicitia*
is well known. He defines friendship (vi, 20) as "a
common mind (*consensio*) in all things human and divine,
accompanied by benevolence and affection (*caritas*)."
Like Aristotle, Cicero has a forbiddingly idealistic
view of friendship: in its perfect form it can exist
only between morally virtuous men (v, 18). Catullus,
of course, does not theorize on friendship and certainly
attempts no formal definition of it; but a number of his
poems show it in action, dramatize it, so to speak. His
idea of friendship is not so dauntingly moral as that of
the philosophers. It is warmer and more tolerant,
closer to ordinary experience, yet still distinctly
idealistic. Poem no. 9, to Veranius,[2] is a good example
to start with.

No. 9, like many of Catullus' poems to friends, is
a versified letter. Line 6 shows that the addressee has
returned to Rome from Spain, but Catullus has not yet
seen him. The poem is written in anticipation of the
reunion and not spoken in the actual presence of
Veranius. It is worthwhile to observe that a versified
letter is in itself a considerable present: the poet
took time and pains to compose it and perhaps had it
delivered as well. To receive such a letter from his
poet-friend must have been an honor and a pleasure for

Veranius.

In no. 9 Catullus shows none of the traditional
Roman *gravitas*, "restraint." On the contrary, he appears
here as a man of strong feelings openly expressed. This
is dramatized by his emotional questions and exclamations and by the threefold repetition of the strong
adjective *beatus*, "blissfully happy." In line 6 the
three elisions convey the impression of tumultuous
eagerness; Catullus' words tumble over each other in
the vehemence of his joy. The first two lines and the
last two are markedly hyperbolical, and lines 8-9 envisage a kind of hyperbole of action: the poet looks
forward to the time when he will pull his friend's neck
close and kiss him on the face. *Os* means "face" with
especial reference to the mouth.[3] To add to the
impression of uninhibited familiarity he will also kiss
Veranius' eyes. So Catullus' physical greeting to
Veranius will be highly demonstrative to say the least.
To northern Europeans and to many Americans the bodily
expression of friendship by an embrace and a kiss on
the eyes and mouth seems to verge on the sensuous or
erotic, but Catullus' effusive behaviour is not exceptional for an ancient Mediterranean. In Homer's
Odyssey the faithful swineherd Eumaeus greets his master
Telemachus in the same way. What is expressed in both
passages is the joy of reunion after a lengthy and
anxious separation.

Catullus has known Veranius for a long time, and
he knows his family, too. But what is the basis for
their friendship? What do they have in common? It is
hard to say. Indeed, lines 6-8 seem to point to a difference between them. Veranius has a well-known interest in foreign lands which Catullus evidently does not
share. It is a reasonable inference that Veranius has
been playing the conventional Roman "success" game. He
went to Spain as a member of the staff of a provincial
governor, whereas the nonconformist Catullus does not
play that game, stays at home. Why Veranius is such a
good friend--his best, according to lines 1-2--Catullus
does not say. The poem is just not about that. The
fact is that it tells us much more about Catullus, his
capacity for affection and joy, than about what he saw
in Veranius.

The greeting to Veranius is simplicity itself.
No. 13, to Fabullus,[4] is a little more complicated. It
is a mock invitation to a party (line 2 is deliberately
vague). The humor comes mostly from a comic reversal

of the roles of host and guest. Ordinarily the guest
brought a small present such as *unguentum,* "perfume," while
the host supplied the rest. In this instance, because
Catullus' purse is "full of cobwebs,"[5] Fabullus is asked
to supply everything but the *unguentum,* including a *candida
puella* (v. 4). She might be Fabullus' "date," but is
more likely to be a music girl. *Candida* connotes a
dazzling white skin. The *puella* is a beautiful, carefully treated slave who is kept indoors and is not expected to do hard labor under the blazing Italian sun.

Is Fabullus as good a friend of Catullus as
Veranius? Or is he simply a crony, one with whom the
poet shares his grosser pleasures? He is much more than
that. Catullus explicitly praises him for his wit and
humor (v. 5), qualities which he certainly valued. In
line 6 he calls him *venustus,* one of his favorite adjectives, but not easy to bring over into English.
Kroll renders it by *liebenswürdig.* A *venustus* is a "sensitive" person, exactly the opposite of a lout or an oaf
or a clod. Veranius receives no such specific praise
in poem no. 9; as we have seen, Catullus indulgently
refers to certain dissimilarites between Veranius and
himself, even though Veranius is his "best" friend. He
mentions no differences between himself and Fabullus.
Moreover, he seems to want to tell Fabullus something
about his love life. He tries to whet his curiosity
about a new girl friend. For there is a girl (Lesbia,
in all likelihood): she is the one who gave Catullus
the *unguentum* with which he and Fabullus will anoint
themselves at the imagined party. And she received the
unguentum[6] from Venus and the Cupids. By this bit of
whimsy Catullus means of course that this perfume is so
extraordinary that one might think she got it from the
gods, who smell much better than we do to start with,
and have proportionally better perfumes. Furthermore,
she is such an attractive creature that one might sup-
pose she lives on familiar terms with the deities of
beauty, love and desire. So the indirect celebration
of the girl's quasi-divine charm and beauty is an important sub-theme of this poem.[7] Catullus is attempting
to arouse Fabullus' interest in her identity. But the
close returns to comedy; the poet toys with the quaint
idea of Fabullus smelling the perfume and wanting the
gods to transform him into one gigantic nose. The
reader forms the mental picture of an enormous (Roman?)
nose walking about on two little legs.

We turn next to no. 27. This poem is not a versified letter. In fact it is not addressed to anyone in

particular, and strictly speaking it is not a poem of
friendship at all. It is a drinking song and the only
one Catullus ever wrote. (Horace has dozens of them.)
Catullus is at a rather wild party where the guests are
drinking Falernian, known as a fiery wine, expensive and
outstandingly excellent. According to traditional Roman
usage women were not allowed to drink wine, and only
hetairai were present at *convivia*. But in the present case
Postumia, quite possibly a lady of the highest aristo-
cracy[8] whose husband became consul shortly after
Catullus' death (51 B.C.), was not only present but had
been elected *arbiter bibendi* or "mistress of the revels"
by dice-throw, and as such had laid down a stricter
"rule" (v. 3) than ordinary, i.e., she had prescribed
straight wine, unmixed with water. Catullus compares
this emancipated lady to a plump grape (v. 4): she is
filled fuller with wine than the grape itself is full
of grape juice. Maybe she resembled the fat grape in
shape and color as well. Catullus' attitude toward
Postumia is by no means unfriendly. He goes along with
her rule, expressing disapproval of the *severi,* the
"blue noses" (v. 6) who prefer water to wine. He thinks
the Falernian Postumia prescribes is comparable to that
which the god of wine himself drinks: such at any rate
is one possible interpretation of *Thyonianus* in the last
line.[9] It would be a mistake to treat this slight occasional poem as symbolic in any profound sense, but it
is legitimate to point out that it fits very nicely into
the pattern of Catullus' sensibility, his characteristic
emotional and intellectual responses to experience.
Poem no. 27 illustrates the poet's acceptance of modern
emancipated attitudes and his willingness to be carried
away by the joy of life. Yet he does not lose all control. He is still able to sum the moment up in an
ordered and concentrated poem. His sensibility is un-
dissociated. When he feels he does not cease to think,
and when he thinks he still feels.[10]

Banter is not incompatible with friendship. In
some of his poems to friends Catullus adopts a teasing
tone, expecially when the friend has dropped out of
sight in the pursuit of a new love affair. No. 55 with
its pendant 58b (to Camerius) is an excellent example
of this good-natured bantering; no. 6, to Flavius, is
another. No. 100, to Caelius,[11] is somewhat similar
but altogether slighter and need not be analyzed here.

No. 55 is not a versified letter but a kind of
extended apostrophe to his absent friend Camerius
(otherwise unknown). Camerius is nowhere to be found.

Catullus has been looking for him in all the places frequented by young men. He even buttonholes the young ladies of the street and asks whether they have seen him. But all to no avail. So at v. 15 he puts the question to Camerius himself, asks him if he is not spending his time with a girl, or rather with several of them (v. 17). He urges Camerius to let him into the secret. Catullus' concern for his elusive friend is mostly put on, and mock-anxiety is the chief source of the poem's humor. Quinn[12] suggests, however, that the concern may also be partly genuine, in the sense that Catullus does not want Camerius to make a fool of himself.

No. 58b is in the same subvariety of the hendeca-syllabic metre (spondee substituted for dactyl in lines 2 and 9) as no. 55 and is also addressed to Camerius. Hence it is usually regarded as a rejected draft for part of no. 55; very likely it was found among Catullus' papers after his death and preserved by the editor. It is merely an accumulation of examples (mostly mytholo-gical) of swiftness: "Talos or Perseus would not be swift enough to overtake you and find you." This is exuberant comic hyperbole, mock-heroic fun. Granarolo[13] rightly calls attention to the deliberate disproportion between the elevated mythological imagery and Catullus' prosaic search for his vanished friend.

Rather similar to poem no. 55 is no. 6. This is addressed to one Flavius, again an unknown, who is carrying on with another unidentified girl friend. Here the criticism is a little harsher than in no. 55. Catullus concludes that since Flavius will not tell him his "darling's" (v. 1) name, there must be something the matter with her. He suggests that she is *illepida*, "dull," and *inelegans*, "gross" (v. 2), in fact a *scortillum febriculosum*, "a little bitch on fire for men" (vv. 4-5). Nevertheless, Flavius wears himself out making love to her, as is proved by his exhausted physical condition; Catullus sarcastically offers to praise their love to the skies in "charming verse." In interpreting no. 6 the main question is to decide why Catullus adopts such a provoking tone. Is he deliberately trying to anger Flavius, so that he will leap to the girl's defense and inadvertently reveal her identity? Many readers have thought so. Another possibility is that the poet knows perfectly well who the girl is, but does not think much of her: in which case the purpose of his mock severity would be to shame Flavius out of his infatuation with an unworthy slut.

The second interpretation would make Catullus more concerned with his friend's welfare and is perhaps preferable.

*

Of his poems to friends the majority are addressed to fellow poets, and it is to this category that we must now turn. It may be well be begin with no. 56. Unfortunately this insubstantial trifle is not altogether clear. It is perhaps not even addressed to a poet. The recipient is named Cato (vv. 1, 3). This might be Cato the Younger, the austere Stoic who was to take his own life at Utica, a martyr to the Republic. It is more likely to be the scholar-poet Valerius Cato, born 100 (?) B.C., commonly regarded as the dean of the *Poetae Novi*. But the poem certainly is not about poetry, and conventional modern opinion might deem it the most scabrous thing Catullus ever wrote. The poet regards the story of his deviant sexual assault on a child[14] as uproariously funny. What is the point of telling this curious story? Is Catullus trying to embarrass or annoy or anger the addressee? If Cato is the austere Cato of Utica the interpretation might seem attractive; this Cato was certainly one of those *severi* whom Catullus depreciates elsewhere, and the affirmation that the anecdote is "worthy of his ears" (v. 2) would be a distinct provocation. On the other hand if Valerius Cato is the addressee, we must assume that he had a broad-minded sense of humor and could appreciate a cleverly versified epigram of this type. A final possibility is that Catullus is simply showing off to the older man, demonstrating how emancipated and up-to-date he is, both in his use of language and his way of life. (Benedetto Croce saw Catullus as fundamentally immature and boyish.)[15] It is impossible to decide. No. 56 is one of those poems to which we have simply lost the key.

No. 35 offers fewer difficulties. This deft and playful verse-letter is addressed to a poet-friend, not otherwise known, whose name is Caecilius; the epithet *tener*, "tender" (v. 1), suggests that he is a love poet. He is fellow countryman of Catullus and lives at Novum Comum on the Lago di Como. He has a bluestocking girl friend, hyperbolically praised as *Sapphica Musa doctior*, "more accomplished than Sappho" (v. 16-17), who has read with admiration and delight his work in progress, a poem about the great mother of the gods, Cybele; the theme may have resembled that of Catullus' own Attis poem, no. 63. Even though it will mean leaving the girl behind, Catullus urgently invites Caecilius to come to Verona and have a talk with an unnamed friend on an unspecified but important topic (vv. 5-6). It is commonly thought that the unnamed friend is not a third party but Catullus himself, and that the topic to be discussed is the poem Caecilius has in hand: Catullus has some ideas to impart about how Caecilius ought to finish it. The vagueness of Catullus' invitation is intended to tease Caecilius and arouse his curiosity.[16] In any case we need not strive for complete clarity concerning the projected tête-à-tête. Poem no. 35 is only secondarily an invitation; the more important purpose is to encourage Caecilius in his literary efforts and to say something nice about his girl friend. It shows Catullus at his urbane best.

A much more distinguished poet than Caecilius is the C. Helvius Cinna praised in no. 95. Cinna, like Caecilius, was a fellow countryman of Catullus, perhaps from Brescia. As we have already seen, he served with him in Bithynia. Poem no. 113, the little epigram on the adulteress Maecilia, is also addressed to him. He was one of the better known New Poets and also a competent orator. Some of his works were so learned and obscure that commentaries were written on them during the generation following his death. Only a dozen brief fragments of his poetry survive. In the forties he joined Caesar's party and became a tribune; after the funeral of the great man he was killed by a mob, having been mistaken for the conspirator L. Cornelius Cinna. Every schoolboy will recall Shakespeare's version of his last words: "I am Cinna the poet, I am Cinna the poet." (*J.C.* III, 2)

Poem no. 95 celebrates the enduring fame of his masterpiece, the *Zmyrna*. This poem resembled Catullus' own *Wedding of Peleus and Thetis*, no. 64, in that it was a miniature epic on a mythological subject, written with exact and painstaking care. It took nine years to finish. The central character was a woman, the Cyprian princess Zmyrna or Myrrha; the theme was the passion of love, or more specifically a corrupted love, in fact incest.[17] Catullus' imagery in vv. 1-2 shows that he thought of the *Zmyrna* in personal terms as a living creature conceived by, carried in and born of Cinna's mind and heart, sprung (*edita* v. 2 is ambiguous)

17

from the substance of his life after nine years, rather
than the nine months required for an ordinary non-
metaphorical birth. In v. 9 the figure is changed; the
Zmyrna is here a *monumentum* of Cinna, a memorial to his
talent. Perhaps we are to visualize a piece of fine
architecture, a small but elaborate shrine. Catullus
also praises Cinna by contrasting his work with that of
two bad poets, Hortensius and Volusius, who share the
fault of long windedness. Hortensius produced a large
quantity of trash in a short time, whereas Cinna produced a small amount of outstanding work after a long
time. Volusius wrote *Annales,* old fashioned annalistic
verse, probably historical epic in the manner of Ennius,
puffing the traditional Roman virtues. This kind of
writing is no longer believable; patriotism begins to
seem insincere or foolish. Rome is no longer the paragon of all excellence in men's eyes. Paradoxically the
passion of a mythological heroine has more immediacy
and reality than Volusius' poem about contemporary
history. Hence the *Zmyrna* will go far (v. 5) and live
long (v. 6), whereas the *Annales* will go nowhere (v. 7)
and meet an inglorious end: the papyrus it is written
on will be used to wrap mackerel (v. 8). Poem no. 95
shows more clearly than any other Catullus' position in
the literary controversies of his time. It reveals him
as a modernist and an elitist, opposed to the epic
writers of the Ennian school. Yet to Ennius' dramatic
writings Catullus is not altogether unsympathetic.
There are a number of Ennian echoes in his work, especially in poem no. 64.[18]

Mynors hesitantly separates lines 9-10 from what
precedes. In these two lines Catullus contrasts his
own poetical preferences with those of the general
public (*populus,* v. 10). Catullus likes the distilled,
concentrated and demanding art of a (nameless) poet
friend, whereas the common reader delights in the
swollen and bloated style (*tumido,* v. 10) of an Anti-
machus. The couplet thus attacks literary popularity
based on ignorance. But since lines 1-8 say nothing
about the popularity of Volusius' *Annales,* lines 9-10
may reasonably be regarded as a separate but damaged
poem.[19]

No. 95 is our first poem in elegiac couplets (or
"distichs"), Catullus' favorite metre. The pattern is

$$- \overline{\cup\cup} \; - \; \overline{\cup\cup} \; - \mid \overline{\cup\cup} \; - \; \overline{\cup\cup} \; - \; \cup\cup \; - \; X$$
$$- \; \overline{\cup\cup} \; - \; \overline{\cup\cup} \; - \mid - \; \overline{\cup\cup} \; - \; \overline{\cup\cup} \; X$$

The first line is a dactylic hexameter divided into two

elements by a caesura (variously placed but usually as indicated above); the second is a dactylic pentameter divided in two by a diaeresis. The couplet, therefore, has four parts, which are metrically similar yet not identical. Gilbert Murray[20] points out that "each member is an attempt, and a different attempt, at the rhythm which is at last perfected in the fourth member." The resultant distich is remarkably symmetrical and compact; the balanced metrical structure invites a balanced, antithetical "witty" style.[21] Elegy was one of the first Greek meters to be domesticated at Rome. A recent investigator[22] traces it back to the middle of the second century B.C. The same scholar has also established that Catullus' longer elegies, nos. 65-68, differ markedly from most of the shorter epigrams, nos. 69-116, in diction, word order and versification. The long elegies are "Neoteric," i.e., they conform to the practice of the New Poets and have a smooth modern finish. The majority of the shorter distichs follow the metrically rougher pre-neoteric tradition of Roman epigram, going back to the first introduction of elegiac metre into Latin literature. No. 95 happens to be one of the atypical epigrams. Since its subject is neoteric poetry, it is appropriately written in the neoteric style.

Poem no. 65 is addressed to the same Hortensius Ortalus who is unfavorably criticized in no. 95. However, it must belong to a different period, for at the time of writing Catullus and Hortensius are close friends. Hortensius' poetry is not mentioned, nor the florid oratory for which he was also well known. No. 65 is a versified cover letter accompanying a translation of Callimachus' *Lock of Berenice*, which follows as poem no. 66.[23] This translation was intended as a substitute for an original poem which Hortensius had requested and which Catullus had apparently promised to provide. Catullus says that he is too broken up by sorrow over his brother's death to compose original verse. The theme of mourning for the lost brother dominates the first half of the poem (vv. 1-14). That portion of no. 65 will engage our attention in a later chapter. For the present, our sole concern is with the lines dealing with Catullus' attitude toward Hortensius. In vv. 15-24 he says that in spite of his prostrating grief he will remember his promise to his friend. He would be ashamed to go back on that promise, ashamed to have Hortensius think he has given his word lightly, ashamed to have him think he had forgotten his pledge (vv. 15-18). The two ideas of shame and forgetting, the forgetting producing the shame, are expressed in the concluding simile of the rolling apple (vv. 19-24). This simile has an intensifying effect. Catullus is trying to imagine an acutely embarrassing situation, one in which shame is caused by forgetting. He invents the image of a "pure maiden" who has forgotten an apple which she had hidden under a fold of her garment: the apple is a love gift. The girl stands for Catullus. It is not necessary, however, to assume that he compares himself to a girl for complicated psychological reasons. He brings in the girl because women are more subject to shame than men, because young women are more so than older women, and because young women are expecially subject to shame in matters involving love (if they are "pure" and gently reared, as this one is). As her mother enters the room, the maiden rises to her feet; the apple which she has forgotten falls from her clothing and rolls across the floor; her mother sees it and the maiden flushes with shame. So ashamed would Catullus be, if he forgot his promise to Hortensius. But he does not forget; the simile describes a purely hypothetical situation. Despite the distractions of his grief, the poet remembers his promise to his friend. And so Hortensius gets his poem after all, even though it is only a translation from Callimachus and not an original composition.

Despite what he said to Veranius in no. 9, 1-2, Catullus' best friend was unquestionably C. Licinius Calvus, the distinguished "Attic" orator and New Poet. Born of an old and noble Roman family in 82 B.C., son of an orator and historian, Calvus was in background and temperament not far removed from Catullus, and like him died young. Catullus addresses him in three poems, nos. 14, 50 and 96. In a fourth, no. 53, which speaks of his successful prosecution of Vatinius, he makes an amusing allusion to his short stature: *Di magni, salaputium disertum,* "Ye gods, the little cock is an accomplished crower" (v. 5). Later poets like to mention the two friends together. Propertius claims to belong to their lineage:

> haec quoque lasciui cantarunt scripta Catulli,
> Lesbia quis ipsa notior est Helena;
> haec etiam docti confessa est pagina Calui
> cum caneret miserae funera Quintiliae. (II, 34,
> 87-90:
> cf. II,
> 25, 3-4)

These lines may be translated as follows:

Love was also the theme of Catullus' sportive
song which made Lesbia more famous than Helen
herself; Calvus' accomplished pages were also
a confession of love, when he sang of
Quintilia's pitiable death.

Ovid imagines Tibullus meeting them in Elysium:

> obuius huic uenies hedera iuuenalia cinctus
>   tempora cum Caluo, docte Catulle, tuo; (Amores
>   III, 9,
>   61-2)

Accomplished Catullus, you shall go to meet
him, an ivy wreath about your young temples,
accompanied by your beloved Calvus.

Calvus' surviving poetry, despite the paucity and
brevity of the fragments, gives evidence of a sensibility remarkably similar to that of Catullus. He wrote
a miniature epic on a mythological subject, the *Io*,
which must have resembled Catullus' *Peleus and Thetis* (no.
64). He also wrote love lyrics and an elegy on the
death of his wife Quintilia, alluded to in the quotation
from Propertius. Two wedding songs are attested. He
shared Catullus' proclivity for writing invectives
against eminent politicians and chose the same targets,
Pompey and Caesar. From all available indications, the
two poets were linked in an extraordinarily close community of mind and spirit. They seem, in fact, to have
been *unanimi,* one soul in two bodies.

The earliest poem to Calvus must be no. 50. Calvus
and Catullus had spent an idle[24] afternoon extemporizing
in various metres; this poem is a versified letter sent
to Calvus the morning after. Yet as Quinn[25] points out,
the letter is not meant solely for Calvus' eyes; it must
be intended for a wider readership as well, as is proved
by the narrative introduction, vv. 1-6, which Calvus did
not really need, although we do. In lines 7-17 Catullus
goes on to describe the *furor,* "distraction," and *dolor,*
"passion," which he felt after their parting. On fire
with admiration for Calvus' *lepus,* "brilliance," and
facetiae, "wit," he could not eat or sleep; he tossed and
turned all night. One might think of Achilles grieving
for Patroclus in *Iliad* XXIV. He says he wants only to
talk to Calvus and be with him again. The symptoms
listed here are appropriate to a crisis situation in
epic or tragedy or in an exalted love affair. Catullus
may be laughing a bit at his own vehemence, and at the
same time providing himself with a refuge from

21

embarrassment in case Calvus does not wish to continue their friendship: "Of course, I was only concocting a few comic hyperboles."[26] Hyperbolical, certainly, is the mock-threat which accompanies the request for another meeting: if Calvus arrogantly refuses Catullus' request he must expect punishment at the hands of the formidable goddess Nemesis. Nemesis, of course, is the goddess who, in tragedy or early Greek history, brings great sinners low, especially those guilty of *hubris*.

To be a gifted poet is to be one man in a million, or several millions. Such a man is bound to be aware of his own uniqueness, and no matter how many ordinary friends he may have, to be a little lonely. It is easy to appreciate the joy Catullus must have felt when he at last discovered in Licinius Calvus an *alter ego*, a man whose wit, taste and talent equalled his own. It is this joy that poem no. 50 expresses, this discovery that it celebrates.[27] Poetry more than anything else is the basis of their friendship.

Poem no. 14 seems to have been written some time later, after they had come to know each other better. It is another versified letter, written on the Saturnalia. As Frazer tells us in his *Golden Bough*,[28] the Saturnalia was a festival during which normal routine was temporarily suspended or reversed, so that for one day at least the inappropriate might be accepted as appropriate and the irregular as regular. In the spirit of the feast Calvus had sent Catullus a large anthology of spectacularly bad verse, as if he thought it was all first-rate stuff. Catullus, reacting with mock violence and indignation, pretends to think that Calvus has sent this lamentable trash in order to destroy his poor friend by boredom and vexation. He threatens dire retaliation in kind on the very next day, meanwhile sending the anthology back to Calvus. The comic pretenses on both sides are mainly for mutual amusement. They are Saturnalia fun and not (as some have held) a pretext for satirical attack on certain bad poets: that aspect is of secondary importance. Behind their pretenses the two friends are delightedly aware that they like and dislike the same things and are linked by a common mind, a *consensio*. They are two of a kind, kindred spirits. They take the same things for granted, share the same tastes and sensibility, delight in each other's wit and agree about their own superior literary judgment. Those who differ from them, men like Sulla, Caesius, Aquinus and Suffenus, are wrong and inferior, or (not to put too fine a point upon it) tasteless

idiots. Reasons for their inferiority do not need to be
given, for the poem is not an attempt at criticism but
sheer comedy. Catullus' mock indignation has something
in common with the comic pretenses of no. 6, to Flavius,
and no. 55, to Camerius, but the undertone of solicitude
we saw in those poems is, of course, lacking here.
Calvus needs no warning.

In no. 96 the mood shifts radically from Satur-
nalian comedy to pathos: trouble has struck. Calvus'
young wife Quintilia has met an untimely death. He has
written an elegy in which he represents her shade as
reproaching him for his past infidelities.[29] He has
sent a copy of this elegy to Catullus. Catullus replies
in the present poem, in which he strives to alleviate
Calvus' guilt feelings and offers him some consolation
for the loss he has suffered. In line 4 *missas* means
"rejected" or "forsaken," with an allusion to Calvus'
self-accusation; but the first person plurals in lines
3-4 tacitly remind Calvus that he is not the only man
who ever betrayed a wife's love; we are all betrayers.
In holding out consolation to his friend, Catullus
refuses to indulge in sentimentality or falsification.
He does not pretend to believe in comforting theories
about the immortality of the soul, translation to the
Elysian fields and the like. However, he somewhat
abates the bleakly pessimistic views he expresses in
some of his other poems about death, e.g., nos. 5 and
101. As I see it, he does not altogether foreclose the
possibility that the dead have a kind of consciousness
and are aware of the attitudes of the survivors. There
can be little doubt that his first word, *si*, "if," is
deliberately ambiguous. It might be interpreted as
meaning "if the dead feel solace, but they probably do
not," connoting sad doubt.[30] But it could also mean,
"if they feel solace, as is commonly affirmed and as
we may well believe is the case."[31] The first interpretation makes room for Catullus' personal convictions;
the second answers Calvus' present need.[32] On the
assumption that Quintilia still retains consciousness,
she must (*certe*, v. 5) now feel joy as well as pain.
Catullus does not deny that she will grieve over the
brevity of her life, but he insists that there will be
happiness too, a happiness greater than the grief,[33]
since Calvus' present *dolor* and *desiderium*, his "pain"
and "longing," prove that his love for her is real.
Quintilia cares less about her own hard fate than she
does about her husband's love. Poem no. 96 is, therefore, a tribute to Quintilia as well as a consolation
to Calvus. Calvus has a true friend in Catullus, one

who can praise the lost wife and alleviate Calvus' distress of mind without compromising his own integrity. Letters of condolence are notoriously difficult to write; this one is open-handed and loyal, a sensitive expression of friendship.

*

Catullus was nothing if not an idealist in personal relationships. He offered unswerving *fides*, "good faith," to his friends, and he expected no less in return. Predictably, his hopes were often disappointed. Some of his friends were ungenerous and failed to respond to his needs in time of crisis. Some repaid his kindness and devotion with disloyalty and base ingratitude. Some even turned out to be his rivals in love and supplanted him in Lesbia's affections. We shall conclude this chapter by examining a group of poems in which he reproaches several friends who have failed to live up to his notion of *fides*, that bond of mutual trust without which friendship between equals is an impossibility. It will be convenient to take up these poems in order of increasing intensity. We shall start with poems in which the offense is minor and reconciliation is still conceivable; we shall go on to consider others in which the offense is so serious as to deal the relationship a mortal blow; and we shall conclude with a poem in which the very possibility of human friendship is called into question.

Our first poem of complaint is no. 38, a versified letter to Cornificius, who, as we have already mentioned, was a fellow poet, one of the *Poetae Novi*. Catullus begins by saying he is in terrible distress and the suffering gets worse from day to day and hour to hour. We do not know what he is alluding to here. It might be his brother's death, Lesbia's infidelities, or a physical illness. Whatever the reason for his pain may be, he writes Cornificius to reproach him for his want of sympathy. Cornificius has not consoled him with any words of comfort (vv. 4-5); Catullus is really annoyed with him: "Is this the way you repay my friendship?" (v. 6). But it is not too late. Cornificius can still send a "little something" of consolation, a poem sadder than the dirges of Simonides. Why the poem should be sad is not made entirely clear. No. 38 is too

24

elliptical and private to engage the modern reader very deeply.[34]

No. 82 is perhaps not strictly a poem of reproach. Catullus is pleading with his Veronese friend Quintius (who also appears in no. 100) not to rob him of one whom he loves more than his eyes. Presumably Lesbia is meant. There are no threats here; the poet merely promises to be enormously grateful to Quintius if he complies with his request. This, at any rate, is the traditional explanation of the poem. One scholar,[35] however, has suggested that the verb *eripere* in line 3 does not mean "rob me of her" but "save me from her"; if this is correct, Quintius is trying to talk the poet out of his affair with Lesbia. Catullus realizes that Quintius is acting out of good motives but he wishes he would stop.

No. 30, to Alfenus,[36] resembles nos. 38 and 82 in that the precise occasion is uncertain, but the tone of reproach is much stronger. Catullus is involved in some sort of misfortune, *in malis* (v. 5). Although his state is pitiable (*miserum*, v. 5) his false friend Alfenus feels no pity for him. He is indifferent, he withdraws, does not support his comrade in his need, forgets all his promises. And yet it was he who had taken the initiative in the friendship and had given Catullus lavish assurances of his loyalty. Half a dozen stinging epithets are flung in his teeth: he is *immemor*, "unmindful," (v. 1), that is, he has forgotten the obligations which friendship imposes; he is *falsus*, "false," v. 1; *durus*, "hard-hearted," v. 2; *perfidus*, a "traitor," v. 3; *fallax*, "deceitful," v. 4; *iniquus*, "heartless," v. 7. Another half-dozen verbs refer to betrayal and stony indifference. The poem ends with a threat of divine retribution: the goddess of Good Faith and all the heavenly gods will punish Alfenus for failing to keep his word. Despite its vehemence, poem no. 30 is not without art. It is written in the difficult and unusual greater Asclepiadean metre.[37] The opening questions give vivid expression to Catullus' astonishment and consternation at Alfenus' disloyalty, and line 6 suggests that such treachery undermines the very possibility of human trust. Catullus mourns for its passing (*eheu*, "alas," first word). But because the nature and extent of Alfenus' betrayal are kept private,[38] the reader once again feels shut out and unable to respond fully to Catullus' impassioned reproaches.

We move on to no. 77, addressed to his former

friend Rufus, who has robbed him of *omnia bona*, "all his
happiness," v. 4. If Rufus is to be identified with
M. Caelius Rufus,[39] Catullus is presumably alluding to
the fact that Rufus stole Lesbia from him. This poem
is not so much a reproach as a wail of grief. The tone
of voice is signalled by the repeated interjections *ei
misero*, v. 4; *heu heu*, v. 5 and again in v. 6. All of
them mean roughly "alas," so that the keynote would seem
to be lamentation, partly over Catullus' pain and loss,
partly for Rufus' treachery. The metaphors *subrepsti*,
"crept stealthily into my affections" (v. 3), *crudele
venenum*, "cruel poison" (v. 5), and possibly also *perurens*
"burning up" (v. 3) imply that Rufus is like a snake,
sly, guileful and dangerous. His treachery has poisoned
the poet's "life," v. 6, that is, his former happiness.
Pestis in the last line changes the metaphor somewhat.
It means "blight." Rufus has destroyed, as if by plague
the friendship he and Catullus used to share. The rhetorical question with which the poem opens implies (as
does the inerrogative opening of no. 30, to Alfenus)
reproach, disillusionment, shock, astonishment and dis-
may.[40] Catullus can hardly believe that Rufus has betrayed his trust in him so flagrantly. In line 3
intestina perurens, "burning up my inner self," is somewhat
obscure. It may be that the words refer to the fires of
jealousy which Catullus feels toward the viper Rufus,[41]
but there is perhaps also a reference to the burning
sensation produced by the presence of snake venom in the
blood stream.[42] On this view, *intestina* means ultimately
the same thing as *vita* in line 6. [43]

Finally, a word about no. 73. This poem has no
addressee. The poet is either speaking to himself or
more probably to anyone who is willing to listen, i.e.,
the reader. The betrayer's name is not given. Whoever
he was, he once considered Catullus his best friend; but
now, in spite of the many kindnesses he has received in
the past, he treats him as his worst enemy. Our author
is so disillusioned by this transformation that he draws
a general conclusion: ingratitude is all, and people
actually resent kindness. Is the generalization meant
to apply to contemporary Roman society? Or is the poet
saying that this is the way the world has always been,
from the beginning of time? Whichever interpretation we
choose, Catullus as a man of *fides*, a man who honors the
bond of shared trust, feels estranged and alienated
from a dishonest and faithless world. Like the young
Hamlet, young Catullus has discovered the fact of evil,
the hideous discrepancy between what should be and what
is.

For all its force, the language of this brief epigram has been criticized as being awkward and insuffi-
ciently concrete. Imagery is lacking; there is an accumulation of general and abstract expressions, and the
last line contains no fewer than five elisions. The
elisions, however, could be regarded as dramatically
expressive;[44] the speaker seems to trail away into dis-
consolate silence, mumbling the last half-dozen words.
Weinreich[45] points out that in the six lines of this
poem which bewails the passing of a friendship, there is
only a single noun, the next to last word: it is *amicum*,
"friend."

*

We have not analyzed all of Catullus' poems to
friends in this chapter. There are several others, notably no. 68, consideration of which will have to be
deferred to a more appropriate place. In the meantime,
however, it is not too soon to draw some general conclusions from the poems we have examined so far. These
make it clear that Catullus was far from being a solitary misanthrope. He had many friends and took keen
delight in close personal attachments; they are an
important part of his happiness. Yet he was not every
man's friend. His friends are chosen from people of
similar backgrounds and interests, Calvus being an outstanding example of this selectivity. Many of them are
poets. This is no more than we should expect, for we do
not need an Aristotle to inform us that "we like those
who resemble us and have the same tastes";[46] common
sense assures us that this is so. Catullus sometimes
expresses affection in perfervid language and uninhibited actions which by our standards seem to verge on
the amorous but which were perhaps not so exceptional in
his time and place. Although he does not dwell on the
moral dimensions of friendship so insistently as Cicero
and the philosophers, he is perfectly aware that it imposes ethical obligations. Despite the bantering tone
which he occasionally adopts, he is fundamentally serious about his friends. He is solicitous for those who
may be on the point of making fools of themselves. Yet
he does not lecture them, never nags: he retains his
urbanity. No. 56 (to Cato) may represent a unique lapse
in taste and judgment. He offers literary advice to
Caecilius and enthusiastically praises the *Zmyrna* of

Cinna. Even when he is prostrated by his brother's death, he remembers his promises to Hortensius and fulfills them as well as he can. In Calvus' hour of bereavement and self-reproach, he comes to his aid with an honest and truly humane letter of consolation. He is a sensitive and faithful friend.

But he is also, as we have said, an idealist; and this idealism is clearly apparent in the demands he makes upon others. Loyal and sincere himself, he stood ready to give himself to his friends in time of need, and he was cruelly disappointed and disillusioned when they failed to respond in kind. Disillusion led to sad reproach and bitter complaint, rather than to angry indictments. Yet the disloyalty of Alfenus can move him to predict divine retaliation: Alfenus forgets, but the gods will remember his forgetting; *pietas*, "recognition of one's responsibilities," and *fides*, "faithfulness to one's word," are not optional virtues in the gods' eyes. They, too, demand fidelity and honesty in personal relations. When friendship's obligations are broken and betrayed, they are angry; sooner or later they smite the guilty.

Many of the qualities he shows as a friend he will also show as a lover. In fact, he considers love a special form of friendship (no. 109, v. 6). It is to Catullus the lover that we must now turn, and that means, above all, to Catullus as the lover of Lesbia.

CHAPTER THREE

Lesbia

Gilbert Murray once remarked[1] that the favorite
topics of poetry are love and death, the things we care
most about and understand least. The observation is
certainly applicable to Catullus. Love is one of his
basic themes, and he is principally remembered for his
poems to Lesbia. It is true that her name occurs only
sixteen times in his writings, and that only some
twenty-six[2] out of his 116 compositions are addressed
to her or are about her. Nevertheless, what our poet
learned from his experience with this remarkable woman
had an indirect influence on his other writing as well.
She kindled his genius; and it is certain that the exhilaration and pain of the Lesbia affair, more than anything else, made him into a first-rate lyric poet. That
lived experience, that real-life suffering, was the indispensable raw material of his most distinctive literary achievement.

Chronological arrangements of the Lesbia poems are
mostly guesswork, but we shall probably not be far wrong
if we assume that no. 51 was among the earliest he
addressed to her. At first sight this ode seems to be
a rather free translation of Sappho no. 31 (Lobel-
Page).[3] I say free because Catullus omits one stanza of
his original, adds another, and makes a number of lesser
alterations elsewhere.[4] On closer inspection, however,
we discover that the poem is not really a translation
at all, for the speaker is Catullus throughout, not
Sappho; the addressee is Clodia/Lesbia, not Sappho's
Greek girl friend; the situation and the problem are
Catullus' own, not just Sappho's. Catullus has transferred Sappho's poem to his own experience. More than
that, in reliving her experience and recreating her ode
in the Latin language, he in effect becomes a second
Sappho, a Sappho reincarnated as male and Roman; and by
the same token, Clodia/Lesbia is parallel to those girls
of Lesbos whom Sappho addressed in her love poems. As
we have already indicated, this is the probable origin
of the pseudonym "Lesbia."

Ille mi par esse deo videtur: he begins by saying that
anyone who sits by Lesbia, listens to her and gazes at
her, seems to him to be *par deo,* "equal to a god."
Equal to a god in what way? In happiness? This does

not accord with what follows. In lines 5-12 he contrasts his experience with that of the generic *ille* in vv. 1-2, that nameless man who looks at her, hears her sweet laughter, and is apparently unaffected; Catullus looks at her, listens to her, and goes to pieces, blacks out. The nameless man is therefore godlike because of his power to endure Lesbia's overwhelming proximity. Catullus is less than godlike because whenever he looks at her all his senses are affected: he is struck dumb, liquid fire penetrates the marrow of his bones, his ears ring, and his eyes are shrouded with "double" (*gemina* v. 11) night. Clearly the unnamed man is equal to the gods in imperturbability, not in happiness.

Catullus' list of symptoms is ambivalent. It pays tribute to Lesbia's beauty and power to attract, but that beauty produces a pathological reaction in him, a sick and fevered response: in lines 5-12 he seems to be itemizing the symptoms of a disease. Her dazzling presence produces not joy but pain and is grounds for alarm; he senses that he is in danger. Compared to the unnamed man, he is oversensitive to her charm, overreacts to it. Nevertheless, he cannot help himself. He is in the grip of passion; he is like someone coming down with an illness. He feels that he is pathetic, *miser*, "pitiable" (v. 5), because he is held in utter subjection by the power of love. Even though no. 51 may well be his earliest poem to Lesbia, it is not a happy poem.

The last stanza is lacking in the Greek original and seems to be a Catullan addition.[5] In it, he turns · aside from the listing of his symptoms to reflection and generalization. The addressee changes, too. Catullus is no longer speaking to Lesbia; he is speaking to himself. Or, more precisely, a superior self who analyzes and understands confronts an inferior self who agonizes and endures. The superior self is meditating upon the life of *otium*, "doing as one likes,"[6] that Catullus has been leading since he fell in love. Such *otium* will surely destroy Catullus also, as it has already destroyed so many others.

Poem no. 51 is a poem of reflection as well as a poem of passion. Thought and feeling are intertwined in ironic tension here. The coexistence of both is characteristic of many of Catullus' most sucessful love lyrics. Ever the artist in control of his art, he refuses to capitulate to his emotions. He tries to stand aside from them, to view them with discriminating

objectivity ("aesthetic distance"). Many readers will
regard this capacity for detached self-criticism and
objective self-understanding as one of his clearest
titles to artistic preeminence.[7]

The adaptation of Sappho is a carefully written
ode, heavy with presentiments of disaster. Some other
"early" poems about Lesbia are comparatively light-
hearted and informal. No. 86 is an example.[8] In this
epigram, Lesbia is compared with a woman named Quintia,
widely regarded as a ravishing beauty. Catullus dissents from the majority opinion. Quintia is nice to
look at, but she lacks *venustas*, "charm," "grace," "se-
ductive appeal," and she does not have a spark of wit
or personality. Lesbia is liberally endowed with both.
Lines 5-6, paraphrased and expanded, seem to mean that
if you set Lesbia in her vibrant and radiant loveliness
beside any other woman alive, that woman will seem to be
drained of all her attractiveness; she will seem dull,
leached out, insipid. So powerful is Lesbia's dazzling
presence. Poem no. 86 is exceptional in that it is one
of a very few in which Catullus tells us what he admired
in Lesbia.[9]

Nos. 83 and 92 are also informal but a little less
light-hearted. Lesbia has been snarling at Catullus; he
takes this as a sign of growing love. Her husband does
not understand what is going on. The poet dismisses him
as an imperceptive blockhead.[10] What makes both epigrams a little less than light-hearted is Catullus'
awareness of a certain ambivalence of feeling on both
sides. They love each other, but wish they did not.
Lesbia resents (*irata est*, 83,6) the attraction she feels
toward Catullus; her love diminishes her autonomy, makes
her dependent on him, limits her personal freedom.
Catullus, too, feels trapped; *deprecor*, "I wish I could
get rid of her," 92, 3. One is left with the uneasy
suspicion that he may be misgauging Lesbia's reaction.
Khan[11] believes that no. 92 is a deliberate travesty on
logic which has a comic-pathetic effect; Catullus is
mocking his own oversensitivity to Lesbia's moods or
making fun of his tendency to grasp at straws in ex-
plaining away her annoyance with him.

The poems about kissing, nos. 5 and 7, are universal favorites.[12] They seem to belong to an early
period, before he had begun to mistrust her. In no. 5
he asks her for love. She objects, as women are supposed to do: "What will people *say*?" He urges her to
despise the spiteful gossip of old puritans. He reminds

31

her that love is the only compensation for life's brevity:

> soles occidere et redire possunt:
> nobis cum semel occidit breuis lux,
> nox est perpetua una dormienda.

> Suns can rise and set, but when once
> our brief light has set, we must sleep
> through one unending night.

Here he is drawing a familiar contrast between the infinite cycles of nature and the single cycle of man's existence. There is a new sun every morning, and day follows day forever; but man's life has one dawn, one noon, one sunset, followed by an everlasting night. Since life is short and death is forever, let us make the most of the time we have. Let us love while it is still morning: give me kisses. The hyperbolic numbers of lines 7-10, introduced by the urgent monosyllabic imperative *da*, "give," suggest an attempt at squeezing--cramming--an infinity of kisses into finite time. Then in the closing lines, after so much hyperbole and straining after the unattainable, comes a return to the idea of social disapproval. Our happiness is so great that some *malus*, v. 12, some envious and malicious observer, might want to put the evil eye on us, i.e., give us the "whammy." Therefore let us cook our accounts, muddle the sum of our kisses. If the *malus* is one of the *senes seueriores* of line 2, Catullus is suggesting that the criticisms of the older generations are motivated not so much by love of virtue as by simple envy of the young. This is another reason why gossip should be ignored.

Nos. 5 and 7 are obviously companion pieces. Both are addressed to Lesbia, both are about "kisses," both raise questions about the right number of kisses and both bring in the envious person who might cast a spell on the lovers. The situation in no. 7, however, differs somewhat from that of no. 5. There Catullus was asking for many kisses; here Lesbia wants to know how many will satisfy him. I take it that her question is essentially rhetorical. She is suggesting that he is too demanding, indeed that he is insatiable. He freely grants that this is so, answering her in two hyperbolical comparisons, both conventional and verging on the commonplace: only as many kisses as there are grains of sand in the desert or stars in the sky[13] could satisfy him. These hyperboles indicate, not very indirectly, that no number of kisses would be large enough, that it is impossible for him to fix a number, that his desire is limitless. To be fair to the author here we should notice that to each of these rather trite comparisons he adds a certain amount of significant detail that helps to lift them above the level of cliché: he says, as many grains of sand as there are in the *Libyan* desert and as many stars as *look down on the guilty loves of men*. Libyan desert, because that is the greatest known desert; guilty loves, as if in admission that his own adulterous passion for Lesbia is one of those guilty loves. An element of self-criticism appears here and is reinforced at v. 10 where he admits that his love is madness; he is *vesanus*, "not in his right mind." He is aware of the judgments that might be passed upon his affair, and even supports them (referring to himself in the third person singular). Yet he does not act upon them. He does not fight against his unquenchable desires, does not try to control or suppress them. On the contrary, he exults in them, mad though they may be. In this poem, Catullus is altogether happy. His only fear is that his happiness may provoke envy and that envy in turn may provoke the evil eye. Even the reluctance implicit in Lesbia's opening question does not seem to bother him very much.

Nos. 2 and 3, about Lesbia's pet sparrow, are also companion pieces and again amongst the best known and most loved of Catullus' *nugae*. Unfortunately, no. 2 was damaged in transmission, and several readings, especially in lines 7-9, are uncertain. If we follow the text as printed in Mynors' Oxford edition,[14] the poem presupposes that Catullus and Lesbia are in love with each other but are separated for some unspecified reason. Thinking about her bird, he remembers the games she plays with it, how she fondles it, holds it in her lap, makes it "kiss" her with its bill. These games are like love play, in which the bird takes the role of the absent lover; they provide "small solace" (*solaciolum*, v. 7) for her love pain (*dolor*), assuage her painful desire (*gravis ardor*, v. 8). It follows that Lesbia is better off than Catullus: she can allay her longing by playing these little games, but it will take more than a pet bird to quiet the sad cares of his heart (v. 10). He realizes that love has hit him much harder than it has hit her. Poem no. 2 foreshadows the painful course his affair with her will take in the future. Love will be an unassuageable passion for the poet: it will not be that for her.[15] It is almost as if he has a premonition of this from the start.

Pet birds do not live very long. In no. 3 the
sparrow is dead, and Lesbia is inconsolable. Some
scholars hold that his poem is a mock dirge: Catullus
gives vent to hyperbolical grief, calls upon all the
Venuses and Cupids, asks every man of finer feeling in
the whole world to share her sorrow, mourn with her;
all that, for a bird? According to this view, Catullus'
intent in no. 3 is not to mourn the bird but to banter
Lesbia out of her grief, a grief which (as the closing
lines may suggest) is incommensurate with what has
happened; after all, the creature is only a sparrow. I
venture to dissent from this interpretation. It fails
to discern the poet's underlying seriousness. The subject of no. 3 is the grief of Lesbia, but the theme is
the universal power of Orcus, the god of death. What
has happened to the bird is a tiny instance of something
that goes on continuously. All must take that dark
journey (vv. 11-12) from which there is no returning:
the sparrow, Lesbia, Catullus, you and I. In v. 14 the
image changes, grows even more sinister. Death is the
darkness that swallows up and consumes all that is beautiful. *Devoratis*, v. 14 is a strong word: it implies a
hideous maw that eats us alive. This is not pretty
sentimentality, not comedy: it is bleak truth. The
poem is about something very little, a pet sparrow,
which might be sold for half a farthing, but at the
same time it is about something very big, the boundless
power of death over all living things. Universality is
said to be a characteristic of classical literature; if
this is so, and we may well believe it is, then no. 3
qualifies as a classical poem.

In addition to being a poem about death, it is also
a love-poem. The pronoun *mihi* in v. 15 shows this.
Catullus feels Lesbia's grief as his own. He extends
his love to everything she loves. He shows the perfect
empathy of the true lover. His reactions reflect hers,
his language echoes her, he projects himself into her
personality. Yet it is the terror of death which predominates here. It would be a mistake to say that he
is more disturbed by Lesbia's tears than he is by the
sparrow's death--and what it symbolizes.[16]

Eventually there were fallings-out. She grew cool
and indifferent, turned to other interests; he was
deeply hurt. Poem no. 8 may have been written during
an early period of estrangement, at a time when he was
still unaware that he had rivals. Early or not, this
is a tormented[17] and contradictory piece of work. The
convention of self-address, suggesting (as in no. 51)

34

internal conflict, is maintained throughout. The rational self admonishes the passionate self; the thinking and judging Catullus arraigns Catullus *miser* (vv. 1 and 10) and *impotens* (v. 9), the pitiable lover suffering the pangs of rejection and unable to control his emotions. *Desinas ineptire,* the superior self begins: stop making a fool of yourself; face the fact that you have lost her. The superior self admits that there was a period of happiness once, when both of Catullus' selves (*nobis,* v. 5; plural because at that time there was no division in the poet's personality) loved her as no other woman shall ever be loved again. Yet even then he was her helpless dependent; she led and he followed. The desire was his and she merely accepted it, passively allowing herself to be loved. But now the happiness is over and she withdraws. The proper response to this withdrawal is to reciprocate, give her up, refuse to chase after her, cease to be *miser*, learn to be firm. *Obdura*, he cries: "harden yourself;" *perfer*, "be resolute." The superior self then bids her good-bye, v. 12. But he cannot leave it at that. He goes on to apostrophize her in half a dozen rhetorical questions. As he recalls their past happiness, his resolution wavers and is almost overwhelmed; then he recovers and in the last line doggedly resumes the didactic tone. One has the feeling that the struggle will continue and that deep down Catullus is still hoping for a reconciliation.

The rhetorical questions of vv. 15-18 imply that if she rejects Catullus she will be unable to find anyone else to take his place. But that is not really what he intends. Line 5 supplies the key to his true meaning. There he says he is the paragon of all lovers, never to be equalled. Lines 15-18 should be read in the light of this declaration. Catullus is not saying that Lesbia will have no one at all, but that she will not have anyone worth having, compared to the one she has thrown over, a lover whose equal the world shall never see again. Certainly there is no self-effacement here. In spite of the humiliation of rejection, Catullus retains a high and positive image of himself as a lover. That is why he can say to her in v. 14, *at tu dolebis,* "you'll be sorry," a sentiment echoed in v. 15, *scelesta, vae te.* These words are sometimes mistranslated "wicked woman, woe is you," or words to that effect. But Catullus imputes no guilt to her in this poem; he simply finds that she is cold and indifferent (*non volt...fugit,* vv. 9-10; *inuitam,* v. 13). Hence *scelesta, vae te* must mean "poor creature, I feel sorry for you," as Baehrens p. 109[18] saw. But for most readers, it is

Catullus, not Lesbia, who is the pitiable figure in no. 8.[19]

If he was hoping for a reconciliation, his hopes were not disappointed. It eventually came. Perhaps there were several of them. Poem no. 107 celebrates one such occasion. Against all expectation, unaccountably, she comes back to him, of her own free will. He does not ask why, does not reproach her or scold her for having left him; her return is pure happiness to him. Despite his tumultuous emotions, this epigram reads like versified prose. The language is overly conceptual; notable imagery is lacking.[20] The two figures, *carius auro,* "more precious than gold" (v. 3), and *o lucem candidiore nota,* "white day in the calendar" (v. 6), are both commonplace. Still it would be a mistake to conclude that no. 107 is carelessly written. An artful interlace of repeated words and ideas lifts and intensifies the language. Notice in vv. 1-4 the chiasmus of *cupido/ gratum, gratum/cupido,* which links the first couplet to the second. In v. 4 *restituis cupido* connects the line to v. 5, where the same words recur. *Insperanti* in v. 5 echoes *insperanti* in v. 2; *refers te,* v. 5, is synonymous with *te restituis,* v. 4. In v. 8 *optandas* (Lachmann's conjecture) picks up the *optanti* of v. 1. These repetitions reinforce the basic ideas of longing, surprise and superlative happiness at her spontaneous return. After losing Lesbia for a more or less protracted period, he suddenly and unexpectedly gets her back. Joy floods his whole being and no. 107 expresses that joy.

No. 36 is another poem about reconciliation, but it is comic rather than effusive. It revolves around a mock-solemn vow made by Lesbia[21] before they got back together. The details of the vow are controverted and we shall probably never achieve unanimity with respect to all the particulars; but according to the commonest interpretation, Lesbia had promised Venus and Cupid that if Catullus came back to her and stopped writing savage attacks (unspecified, but doubtless aimed against her) she would burn as a holocaust the *electissima pessimi poetae/scripta* (vv. 6-7). By *pessimi poetae* "worst of poets" she presumably meant Catullus; and by *electissima scripta* his "choicest," i.e., most offensive attacks. Now that they are reconciled, Catullus wittily reinterprets her vow, taking advantage of the ambiguities in her language. By *pessimi poetae* he pretends that she must have meant Volusius, the worthless epic poet whom we have already encountered in no. 95; and by *electissima scripta* she must have meant his absurd and uncouth

Annales. Catullus proceeds to offer up this monstro-
sity22 to Venus, first uttering a mock-serious prayer
in the hymnic style, vv. 11-15. In these lines we have
a parodic enumeration of her principal shrines, culmina-
ting in an anticlimactic reference to the seaport town of
Dyrrachium as "general pothouse of the Adriatic." No.
36 has been interpreted as serious literary criticism,
but surely the tone is humorous throughout: a comic vow
is comically reinterpreted, and in consequence the poet
declaims a mock prayer and offers up a mock sacrifice.
This dramatizes the *consensio*, the community of mind and
spirit, which united the lovers at this particular moment in the affair. Lesbia is almost as witty and urbane as Catullus himself (but not quite); she will no
doubt agree with his devaluation of the clumsy old-
fashioned poet Volusius; she will relish his burlesque
invocation of Venus and the amusing sacrifice; she will
smile when he retorts with *pessima puella* to her *pessimus
poeta*; and she will permit him to trump her whimsical
vow with another wittier than her own. This poem provides a concrete example of the *sal* he praised her for
in no. 86. It also presupposes that she can laugh when
he turns her own jokes against her. This is a confident
and exuberant poem.23

The confidence did not last, nor did the exuber-
ance. A whole series of epigrams, nos. 109, 70, 104,
87, 75, 72 and 85, gives expression to his growing
awareness that he cannot trust her assurances of fidelity, that she is incurably promiscuous, and that they
have two different conceptions of what love ought to
be. The simplest procedure will be to take up these
poems individually, beginning with the more hopeful ones
and ending with the more despairing. It must be emphasized, however, that none of them is strictly dateable
by internal evidence and that next to nothing is known
about the order of their composition.

In no. 109 he is still hopeful, but doubts are
starting to arise. He begins by quoting a promise she
has made him to the effect that their love affair will
be long-lasting (*perpetuum*, v. 2) and lots of fun
(*iucundum*, v. 1). To Catullus this is a frivolous and
inadequate view of the relationship. More than that,
he fears that her promise is not serious, that she does
not really mean it. In his anxiety he turns to the
gods in prayer. He asks them to give her the gift of
sincerity. One notices how this idea is stressed by the
accumulation of synonyms in lines 3-4: *vere, sincere, ex
animo*. Finally, he reveals his idea of what their love

ought to be. First, it should be life long: *tota vita, aeter-num*, vv. 5-6. Second, it should not be taken lightly but respected as one would respect a solemn *foedus* (v. 6); a *foedus* is a sworn pact or covenant, any infraction of which would constitute perjury.[24] Furthermore, it ought to be not merely carnal and hedonistic, but also a *sancta amicitia*, v. 6, an "inviolable friendship." Friendship, as we have indicated in the preceding chapter, implies *benevolentia*, mutual well-wishing; it also implies *consensio*, a union of minds. How much *consensio* exists between Catullus and Lesbia? The discrepancy between her promises (in vv. 1-2) and his ideals (in vv. 5-6) shows that already they fall far short of *consensio* on the crucial subject of their own relationship. This bodes ill for the future of the affair, and the poem ends with his doubts and apprehensions unresolved.

No. 70 also opens with a reference to her protestations of love. They are fervent and extravagant; she would rather love[25] him than anyone else, even Jupiter himself. Catullus is aware of the probable discrepancy between what she says now and what she may well do in the future. He reminds himself that women are irremediably fickle and capricious; therefore, write their words on wind and running water. (This is the opposite of writing them on something like marble or bronze; in other words, one might as well forget what they say.) In this poem, Catullus is still in love with Lesbia, although his mistrust of her has advanced a degree beyond no. 109. Still, he does not reproach her or upbraid her for her unreliability. In fact, he excuses it. The generalized statement in 3-4 declares that fickleness is a failing common to all women and not peculiar to Lesbia. She is just no better than her sisters. The poet's tone is affectionately indulgent here: nevertheless, he openly avows his disbelief in her words.

No. 104 is cryptic and the occasion for it is not explained. Perhaps she has done him some injury: he is aware of it, yet loves her so much that he cannot bring himself to speak ill of her. But who is the mysterious Tappo of v. 4? What is his relation to Catullus and Lesbia? Who is the unnamed addressee? And does the last line mean "You and Tappo exaggerate everything," or "You and Tappo stop at nothing, where evil is concerned"? The Latin is highly ambiguous, permitting either interpretation, and the modern reader is again baffled.

In no. 87 he amplifies an idea touched upon in no. 8, line 5, that his love for her is absolutely unique in intensity and fidelity. He pointedly refuses to mention any corresponding intensity or fidelity on her part. This suggests a reproach, and the reproach is all the more scathing in that it is indirectly implied and not explicitly stated.

No. 75 is still darker. In this poem he openly accuses her of *culpa*, v. 1, that is, of carrying on with another man; he contrasts her infidelity with his *officium*, v. 2. *Officium* is the service one owes one's friends and so is closely related to the concept of *fides*, "faithfulness to one's word" or "reliability." Her *culpa* has destroyed the *bene velle*, the "friendly benevolence" (v. 3), which he had once hoped might be lifelong. That friendship can never revive, even if she were to reform completely; yet on the other hand, though she were to sink to the lowest depths of depravity, he could not stop wanting her. In this context *amare*, v. 4, must be interpreted as referring exclusively to physical desire. Catullus no longer has any liking for Lesbia, but he feels sexually enslaved to her.[26]

No. 72 resembles no. 75 but is still more intense. As he frequently does, he begins with a contrast: he sets her exaggerated protestations (vv. 1-2) beside the reality of his love (vv. 3-4). That love had the usual physical component, to be sure; but in addition it had a non-physical dimension which went far beyond the *bene velle* of ordinary friendship. It was like the love that Roman fathers feel for their sons and sons-in-law. The second element in the comparison may sound anticlimactic to modern ears, but the poet's contemporaries had no difficulty in understanding it.[27] Catullus means that he felt a proud, protective and responsible affection for her. Now her *injuria*, v. 7--unspecified, but probably the same as the *culpa* of no. 75--has swept that affection away. He no longer feels any fondness for her whatsoever: *bene velle minus* in v. 8 is interpreted by Quinn (correctly, in my opinion) as deliberate understatement. Since he has found her out, v. 5, he holds her in contempt, v. 6. He goes on to reiterate the same strange admission he made at the end of no. 75: even though she may find it incredible (*qui potis est, inquis*, v. 7), he cannot stop wanting her more than ever (*cogit amare magis*, v. 8, cf. *impensius uror*, v. 5). The divorce between affection and desire is expressed even more emphatically than in no. 75.

It is in the celebrated *Odi et amo,* no. 85, that
Catullus' agony finally peaks. Here he feels racked and
tormented by two vehement and contradictory impulses.
Amo is again used in the sense of physical desire, and
odi of course refers to undisguised aversion: not simply
the absence of *bene velle* with contempt taking its place,
but the direct antithesis of *bene velle,* namely malevolent
loathing. Ordinary opinion would regard these two
feelings as mutually exclusive; it is humanly incon-
ceivable that they should coexist. Catullus is aware
that his experience is extraordinary, and therefore introduces a nameless addressee to act as a kind of
"choral" foil and to ask *quare id faciam,* "why I do it."
The poet answers that he cannot understand or explain
the experience. He can only feel the searing pain of
it happening to him.[28]

Although only two lines long, *Odi et amo* brings the
story of Catullus' alienation from Lesbia to a tremen-
dous climax and expresses his suffering with incomparable force. How is the force generated? Weinreich[29]
points out the prominence of the verb in these two
lines. The verb is unquestionably the most vigorous
and dynamic of the parts of speech. There are eight
verb forms in the poem. On the other hand the adjective, which tends to dissipate impact by fussy qualifications, is totally absent. Catullus' single metaphor, the raw and brutal *excrucior,* is deferred to the
end of the last line. The mental anguish of his experience is so painful that he compares it to the physical
sensation of being torn in two. No. 85 is still another
poem that ends with the tensions unresolved; conflict
continues in full strength, with no way out apparent.
This is a cry of pain uttered out of the depths of despair.

*

We move onward to the poems usually regarded,
though without compelling reason, as belonging to the
very end of the affair with Lesbia: nos. 60, 76, 58,
and 11. In these compositions, disillusionment has not
much farther to go; desire fades, and the pain of inner
division and conflict begins to dwindle. Yet these four
pieces yield little in intensity and bitterness to the
short elegiacs we have just been considering.

One approaches no. 60 with some trepidation. As so often is the case in Catullus, the circumstances are cloudy and the addressee is unnamed; we do not even know whether the poem was written to a man or a woman. These lines are mostly a two-way transaction between the poet and a mysterious second person singular, with the reader left out in the cold. But not entirely so. It is at least plain that no. 60 is a poem of reproach. Catullus is exclaiming against the cruel and hard-hearted inhumanity of someone who has ignored his cry for help in an hour of urgent need. This one-sentence composition is cast in the form of a rhetorical question introduced by the particle *num*. *Num* signals that a negative answer is expected; in English it means "it isn't true, is it, that..." Catullus is therefore saying, in effect, "No, you are not the child of a lioness or a Scylla; if you were a beast or a monster, I could understand your inexorable, inhuman hard-heartedness; but you are a human being. Why don't you act like one?"

Figurative language is confined to the first two lines. The lioness and Scylla are symbols of ferocity, that is, outstanding examples of it. Both will inevitably transmit their inhuman natures to their offspring. It is clear that the images are arranged in climactic order. First the poet names a beast, the most formidable of all beasts, the lion; then *montibus Libystinis* specifies the most formidable variety of lion, the Libyan. The second image is an intensification of the first. Catullus rises from the most formidable beast he can think of to Scylla, who is not a beast but a monster, i.e., an animal combining features of two species: a monster, furthermore, that dwells not in the mountains but in the sea and is even further from humanity than the formidable Libyan lion. An impression of hyperbolical cruelty and brutality is generated.

Is it possible that the hard-hearted addressee was a faithless friend, someone like the Alfenus of no. 30 or the Rufus of 77? Many have thought so. Weinreich,[30] however, dissents from this view. Investigating the ways in which other classical poets utilize the sort of animal/monster imagery we find in vv. 1-2, he discovers that figures of this type are normally employed by one partner in a love affair who is reproaching his or her mate for insensitivity. This is the way the figure is used by Euripides, Virgil and Ovid. Moreover it is used by Catullus himself in this way elsewhere: in no. 64, 154-7, Ariadne calls her faithless lover Theseus the son of a lioness or of a sea-monster. Weinreich therefore concludes that the nameless addressee in no. 60 is not a male friend but Lesbia. The reasoning is persuasive; one may readily believe that Catullus had suffered more at her hands than from any other person. So the identity of the addressee has probably been cleared up. The circumstances, however, remain doubtful. What is meant by the *novissimus casus,* the "ultimate distress" of line 4? What exactly was the *vox,* the "plea," of the same line? Was Catullus literally a "suppliant"? What did he want of Lesbia, assuming that he was speaking to her? How could she have alleviated his distress? To these questions we can imagine many answers, but Catullus again guards his privacy.

No. 76 is clearer, much less esoteric. At first glance it seems to have much in common with no. 8, beginning as it does with a passage of self-address. But in no. 8 the superior self is urging the inferior self to be firm, to face the fact of loss and to stop chasing after the reluctant Lesbia, whereas in no. 76, 1-10 the superior self reassures, encourages and exonerates the inferior self. He has been kind, he has kept faith, he has maintained the *pietas,* "true loyalty," which a lover ought to show vis-à-vis the beloved. The memory of this *pietas* will be a source of satisfaction to him for the rest of his days. Some interpreters think that the language of lines 7-8, 19 and 26 is self-righteous. But is it? Catullus is neither smug nor hypocritical in this poem. He is anguished and bewildered. These are not the words of a pharisee but of an idealistic young man who finds himself up against the hard fact of undeserved suffering. Furthermore, it is important to recognize that Catullus is not claiming total and unblemished *pietas* in no. 76, but only *bene velle* and *fides* in his relationship with Lesbia. In other words, he is once again announcing, as he had done in nos. 8 and 87, that he has been the paragon of all lovers; but here he adds that consciousness of his *pietas* toward Lesbia will eventually provide him with some consolation for the pain he has endured.

At vv. 11-16 the superior self changes his tone and begins to speak more in the vein of no. 8, saying in effect, "Forget her; she is a faithless ingrate; by a sheer effort of the will put down the heavy burden of your unrequited love." But no sooner has he said this than he realizes the impossibility of complying with his own well-meant advice. He cannot by his own unassisted efforts master this passion. Distraught, he abandons self-address and turns to the merciful gods in prayer, v. 17 ff. He no longer asks them to change her, since she is beyond all hope of amendment. Instead, he asks them to save his life (note line 18). He wants them to cure him of the disease of passion with which he has been arbitrarily and unpredictably afflicted. He hopes that they will free him from his painful and frightening obsession. He thinks that because he has stood by his sworn word and because his life has been untainted by infidelity or deceit (v. 19) the gods are under an obligation to him.[31] It is on this note that no. 76 closes, the longest of the Lesbia poems in elegiacs (apart from no. 68).[32] As so often, the conflict is unresolved.

In no. 76 he was still tormented by desire for Lesbia. In no. 58 that desire has been quenched. This short piece is addressed to one Caelius, probably M. Caelius Rufus, who was once his rival for Lesbia's favors.[33] By this time she has rejected them both, and the old enmity has been set aside. He calls upon Caelius to witness the appalling transformation which has taken place in her. He begins by evoking her as he once saw her, idealized her and loved her. In lines 1-2 the threefold repetition of her name, twice with *illa*, "that incomparable," sounds like a lamentation, expressing a great sadness for the passing of what she had been. In line 3 he says that in those days he loved her more than himself and all his nearest and dearest. But now (*nunc*, v. 4) she is an abandoned creature, haunting street-corners and back alleys, where she *glubit* the descendants of great-hearted Remus. *Glubit* is the main verb of the one sentence of which the poem consists: unfortunately, the precise force of the word eludes us.[34] Literally it means to peel, to remove the bark. In the present context it is used metaphorically, but in what sense? It is very likely an obscenity, and might mean "take the skin off," "rub raw." Quinn suggests "strips," i.e., of clothing and money: she takes off their clothes to make love to them and receives cash for her services. In any event, she is now plumbing the depths of degradation. Catullus' tone in no. 58 is not so much contemptuous or angry as rueful and halfdisbelieving.

In no. 11 he says his final farewell to Lesbia. The poem is deliberately written in the same Sapphic metre which he had used in no. 51, which by common consent was one of the first pieces he addressed to her. As we pointed out in Chapter One, the date of no. 11 is fixed at 55-54 B.C. by the allusions in vv. 9-12 to

43

Caesar's campaigns in Gaul, Germany and Britain. The apparent praise of the great man in v. 10 has also been previously mentioned: some take it as evidence supporting the reconciliation story reported by Suetonius; others hold that the adjective *magni* is ironic, and that Catullus is still an anti-Caesarian. Neither interpretation can be proved, but the second is perhaps the more attractive.[35]

The circumstances of no. 11 are also debatable. According to a widely-accepted hypothesis, Lesbia had sent Catullus a request for reconciliation through the addressees, Furius and Aurelius. Catullus' attitude toward these intermediaries is variously interpreted. Are we to take his praise of them, in vv. 1-12, seriously and literally? Does he really regard them as true and loyal friends? In the other poems addressed to them jointly or separately, Catullus' tone seems extremely hostile. The first three stanzas of no. 11 may reasonably be taken, therefore, as sarcastic: the high-flown language of these lines mocks Furius' and Aurelius' false protestations of devotion. They are part of Lesbia's world of corruption and unfaithfulness.[36] They may even be numbered among the "descendants of great-hearted Remus" mentioned as her lovers at the end of no. 58. It must be admitted, however, that we are far from unanimity in our answers to these questions.

Whether Furius and Aurelius were false friends or true, Catullus asks them to take a brief and bitter message to "his girl" (v. 15). He leaves her to her men friends whom she "embraces three hundred at a time, draining them all limp, loving none of them truly." Catullus' language suggests that she was driven by a desire to break men and destroy them.[37] He goes on in the last stanza to compare his love for her to a flower and Clodia to a passing plow that has nicked it and killed it. A superficially similar image appears in no. 62, 39-47, where the flower symbolizes a beautiful and defenseless girl and the plow represents brutal male aggression. The image is traditional, going back to Sappho[38] (frag. 105c, Lobel-Page); but in poem no. 11 the symbolism is reversed and reapplied, as if to stress the exceptional character of the relationship between Catullus and Lesbia. Now the flower stands for Catullus' beautiful and fragile love, which has been destroyed forever by Lesbia's *culpa*: the "accident" occurred by her fault. The plow image at once excuses Lesbia and condemns her. I suggest that we have here a peculiar form of the figure of speech called oxymoron.

*

Before the time of the New Poets, Latin authors usually represented male lovers as comic figures.[39] Plautus and Terence, for instance, regard them with detached and indulgent amusement. Their agonies are predictable and evanescent. The early satirist Lucilius sets forth a similar view. Catullus and his contemporaries were the first Roman writers to take love seriously. In Catullus' case, love is the center of his existence. When he says that Lesbia is dearer to him than his eyes, dearer than self and all his own, he is not using language loosely. This is one of a number of ways in which he is at odds with the attitudes of the older generation, the *senes severiores* who embraced traditional Roman norms and ideals. Love to Catullus superseded many of the old fashioned values. It was the force which gave direction and meaning to his life. Hence it was his favorite literary topic. To this extent we may regard Catullus as an individualist and a rebel breaking with the confining pattern of accepted *mores,* and also as an innovator refashioning the Roman literary sensibility. Nevertheless, to dismiss him as an "exhibitionist," as C.S. Lewis once did in an unguarded moment,[40] would be a serious error. He did not write the Lesbia poems to shock or entertain the public. He did not even write them for her benefit. He wrote them primarily for himself, as a means of sorting out and understanding his own experience.[41]

His love certainly had a strong physical component. He does not deny that he loved Lesbia as ordinary men love their women. This aspect of the affair is clearly evident in the *basia* poems, nos. 5 and 7. But it was not solely a transaction of the flesh. The love he hoped for was to be exclusive, mutual, perpetual and inviolable. Neither partner was to subjugate or dominate the other. It was to be comparable to a deep friendship marked by *bene velle* and *consensio,* a companionship of kindred spirits. He gave *fides* and *pietas* and expected to receive both in return. He considered himself bound by a virtual *foedus,* violation of which would be a form of perjury. He even went so far as to say that he felt for Lesbia the kind of responsible and protective affection which fathers feel, or are expected to feel, for

sons and sons-in-law. Since Lesbia's marriage to
Metullus was only *de convenance,* the *sanctae foedus amicitiae*
might, in Catullus' eyes, take precedence even over the
obligations of *iustum matrimonium,* legal marriage. Why
they never married after Metellus' death is an insoluble
problem. It cannot have been because Catullus disliked
the institution of marriage. His wedding songs show
that this was far from being the case. It is a fair
inference, however, that Lesbia valued her new-found
freedom too much to tie herself down to any one man.

Lesbia had many attractive qualities. She was
formosa, venusta, uniquely beautiful. She had wit and a
vivid personality which put all other women in the
shade. But she did not conceive of love in the same
terms as Catullus. She could not share his idealism.
To her love was a recreation, with frequent changing of
partners. She was not to be trusted, was incapable of
fidelity. She violated their relationship by *culpa* and
iniuria. There was no lasting *bene velle* or *consensio* between them. In the end it became blatantly evident that
they were in no sense kindred spirits. For Lesbia,
Catullus was only one among many lovers.

The Lesbia poems are usually read as a record of
progressive disillusionment. In the beginning, all was
sunshine: *fulsere soles,* as he says in no. 9 (vv. 3 and
8). The first night together at the house of Allius
was pure ecstasy (no. 68). But soon there were quar-
rels, followed at first by joyous and unexpected recon-
ciliations. Gradually the poet began to realize that
she was not just occasionally unfaithful but promiscuous
on a massive scale. He saw his life as a directionless
otium marked by *cura* and *dolor,* anxiety and pain. Disen-
chantment receives far more extended emphasis than joy.
The majority of the short poems are prompted by pain of
some sort and end with the difficulties unresolved. He
reproaches her far more often than he praises her. They
are usually in an adversary relationship. Still, disillusionment did not in itself bring liberation. Even
when *bene velle* had disappeared and had been transformed
into its opposite, *amor* remained as desire. Unable to
shake free from jealous lust he cried out his unforgettable *odi et amo.* In the end even desire faded, wrath
began to take over. She became the object of scathing
invectives.[42] He discovered that even her brother was
numbered among her lovers. He depicts her sitting in a
taberna like a prostitute surrounded by innumerable men,
or frequenting street-corners and back alleys with the
sons of great-hearted Remus. Loathing and hate gain an

ascendency that is all but complete. He sees her as a monster of cruelty and sensuality draining countless lovers limp, but devoid of all affection and human regard.

In the short poems Catullus does not mythicize love as a wound inflicted by Cupid's arrows. He presents it in realistic terms. It comes to him through the eyes and ears, as it did to Sappho. It is a physical and psychological disorder, a disease of body and mind, a sickness or a madness. Like most illnesses, it strikes suddenly and unpredictably. It causes pain and alarm, it brings him to the verge of death. There is no human cure for such passion as his. The will struggles against it in vain. Since his sufferings are great and undeserved, he is truly *miser*, "pitiable"; since he cannot resist, he is a pathetic figure in the fullest sense of the word. In his helplessness he is driven to pray that he may be healed. Healing eventually came, as the latest poems show; but the course and nature of the cure are not described. When it was all over, he must have felt liberation and release. All the same, something valuable had been lost in the process, and in the last stanza of no. 11 he looks back with a kind of nostalgia to the beautiful flower of love which she, by her *culpa*, had killed.

Catullus takes a high view of himself as a lover. He insists repeatedly upon the uniqueness of his love. There had never been a love to compare with his in the past, and there would never be another to rival it in the future. It is necessary, of course, to discount these protestations. His love may well have been exceptional in intensity and in fidelity, but it was not unique in nature or outcome. Many men and women have been through experiences comparable to his, have known the ecstasy and pain of passion, have tried to keep faith, have been heartlessly betrayed in the end. Almost everybody can at least imagine living through such an experience. It is a permanent possibility in human life, a recurrent actuality. Classical literature is said to be universal, paradigmatic. The Lesbia poems present a paradigm of the passionate, unhappy love affair. To the modern reader they are more classical than Catullus intended, more classical than he ever dreamed they might be.

CHAPTER FOUR

Satire, Invective, Comedy

Catullus is best known to the general reader as a writer of love lyrics and as the luckless victim of Lesbia's cruelty. It may therefore come as something of a surprise to discover that by far the largest group of his short poems are the invectives. By Wheeler's[1] count there are a total of about forty of these, making up nearly forty percent of the polymetra and elegiac epigrams. Catullus is therefore a poet of hate as well as a poet of love, and the list of his enemies is a good deal longer than that of his friends.[2]

In addition to Wheeler's forty true invectives we find some half dozen milder satiric pieces directed against social faults and foibles. There is an element of attack in these, but Catullus' emotions are peripherally engaged, and comic irony outweighs wrath and indignation. The targets of his criticism are not really vicious; they are only foolish and unmannerly. They offend against Catullus' special biases in regard to public conduct. He agrees with the rest of the New Poets that a man is to behave at all times as a *lepidus, venustus, urbanus* and *facetus*[3] ought to act, or, to put it negatively, that he is never to be *ineptus*. Cicero defines this term in his *de Oratore:*

> A man who fails to realize what the cir-
> cumstances call for, or talks too much or
> shows off, or ignores the dignity or con-
> venience of the company, or is in any way
> clumsy or tiresome, is called *inept*. (II, 4, 17)

The targets of the milder invectives are *inepti* who are unaware of their own ineptitude. Catullus' basic strategy is to turn a searchlight on their unconscious faults and to reveal their ignorance of themselves to the wider public.

No. 12, against Marrucinus, provides an instructive example. This highborn young man had the unwelcome habit of stealing, at dinner parties, the guests' personal table napkins. Marrucinus meant this as a kind of practical joke, thought it "witty" (v. 4); but to Catullus it is gauche, unamusing and inept (vv. 4-5).

His brother Pollio, a man of true wit and discernment, is mortified by Marrucinus' behavior. Catullus demands his own napkin back, under pain of further invectives; this napkin has sentimental value, being a keepsake sent to him from Spain by Veranius and Fabullus. What is objected to here, therefore, is not so much the larceny as the silly ineptitude of the offender.

In two other epigrams against thievery the tone is much less mild. The Thallus of no. 25 does not have the social standing of Marrucinus. Furthermore, he has snatched not only Catullus' napkin but also his cloak and Bithynian writing-tablets, which he now shows off as family heirlooms: this foolish pretense is "inept" of him (v. 8). Catullus also jeers at him for his effeminacy, which is a convenient irrelevance, and threatens that, unless the stolen articles are returned, he will punish the thief not with mere invectives but with a literal scourging. In another epigram, no. 33, the bath-thief Vibennius and his unfortunate son are not *inepti* but actual professionals, and the invective against them is not a revelation of hidden faults, for both are notorious. This poem is little more than a versified imprecation; Catullus does not bother to ironize.

With the Suffenus of no. 22 we return to the upper reaches of society and the milder tone again prevails. Suffenus is the old-fashioned poet who had received a glancing blow in no. 14, 19. Here, since he has not injured Catullus personally, he is not threatened with retaliation in any way, as Thallus and Vibennius are. He is not socially inept; indeed Catullus makes a point of stressing his wit and sophistication. Half a dozen adjectives convey this. But Suffenus has a blind spot. He admires his own bad verse, which he produces in quantity and publishes in sumptuous editions. In this area the urban sophisticate shows the taste of a *caprimulgus aut fossor* (v. 10), a clownish peasant. The closing generalization, "we are all blind to our own failings," has the effect of pardoning Suffenus' blissful conceit; Catullus deflects the irony from him to people in general. No. 22 is unique among the satiric pieces for its Horatian mellowness and lack of rancor. It is also unusual in that it implicates the reader. Elsewhere, *we* are not questioned or criticized; our complacent superiority is unshaken.

The Spaniard Egnatius (whom Weinreich insists on calling "Don Ignazio") displays his social inadequacy in no. 39. He has a pathological weakness (*morbus*) which

Catullus finds neither elegant nor urbane (v. 8): he smiles all the time, in order to show off his dazzling white teeth. Don Ignazio is inept, v. 16. He does not realize that there are occasions when a smile is inappropriate. But why blame him for that? One can scarcely expect urbane behavior from a man born so far from Rome (vv. 10-17). As for his dazzling white teeth, Catullus knows the secret behind this and lets the reader in on it: Don Ignazio follows the old Spanish custom of using his own urine for a mouthwash. It seems Catullus is not angry with his victim here; he has not been hurt by him and need threaten no retaliation. The fact that Egnatius became one of Lesbia's many lovers (as emerges in no. 37) is not so much as mentioned. Maybe that happened later. Here he is simply exposed as a ridiculously inept provicial. The humor of Catullus' final sentence may strike some readers as boyish and heavy-handed.[4]

Arrius (no. 84) is guilty of linguistic ineptitude. He is a low-born arriviste who tries to conceal his humble antecedents by taking pains with his pronunciation. Nobody is fooled, for he goes much too far. Anxious about the lower-class error of omitting the h-sound, he over-aspirates at the beginnings of words, and this makes him sound even worse. The funniest part is that the poor fellow is foolishly pleased with his eccentric speech and quite blind to his own absurdity (vv. 3-4). Catullus has an urbane laugh at his expense.

*

The epigrams which we have been examining presuppose a Catullus who prizes tact, wit and urbanity in social relations, and who by the same token resents any failure in sensitivity or awareness in those with whom he comes in contact. He takes pleasure in exposing social blindness and ineptitude in various forms, some rather important, others unimportant in themselves but perhaps symptomatic of a more fundamental deficiency elsewhere. Yet in his defense of tact, good manners and perceptivity, Catullus' emotions are not deeply engaged. He is able to stand aside from the people and actions he criticizes, thus approaching the stance of the detached ironist. However, in the more vehement of his poems of attack (which are certainly the majority) he makes no effort to maintain objectivity. The point of departure in these poems is much more than the loss of a prized table napkin or cloak. The poet feels that he has been deeply injured in some way. Injury provokes wrath and the instinct to hit back with the readiest and most effective weapon, namely invective verse; his personal involvement is clearly evident. Becuase he was especially vulnerable where Lesbia's infidelities were concerned, a rather large number of his harsher invectives are directed against his numerous rivals for her affections.[5]

Ravidus, attacked in no. 40, was one of those who "desired to love his beloved" (vv. 7-8), probably Lesbia, though some have thought of Juventius. It is hard to believe that Catullus considered him a dangerous rival. He treats him not so much with resentment as with studied contempt. This tone is immediately established by the diminutive epithet *miselle*, "pathetic creature," "miserable creep," and by the slurred pronunciation of Ravidus' name: the three syllables are diminished to two by the metre. An element of indirection is supplied by the four rhetorical questions which make up most of the poem. Since it is manifest folly for the the defenseless Ravidus to provoke a poet who has the power to render him eternally infamous, Catullus pretends to ask Ravidus in all seriousness for information about the state of his mental health.[6] Has he suddenly been smitten with some form of insanity? Has he offended some god? (For according to the old proverb, whom the gods would destroy they first make mad.) Or is he afflicted with self-destructive yearnings for notoriety, no matter what the cost? The poet promises him that these yearnings will be abundantly gratified in time to come (vv. 7-8). And indeed the promise was fulfilled: Ravidus has been memorialized to this very day. The only thing we know about him is that he cast eyes on Lesbia and earned Catullus' wrathful disdain.

This vigorous invective is unusual among Catullus' poems of attack in that it makes its point without recourse to obscenity.[7] The series of poems directed against a former friend named Gellius are a different matter.[8] These hyperbolically uninhibited epigrams charge the victim not only with violating the bond of friendship by becoming Lesbia's lover (no. 91) but also with committing a number of hideous villainies with others: he is repeatedly accused of incest with his mother and his sister and his uncle's wife (nos. 74, 88, 89, 90) and of fellation with his boyfriend Victor (no. 80). No. 116 is probably the earliest; in this one

Catullus, looking back to the past, recalls how he had
tried to placate Gellius' hostility (the reason for
which is not given) by sending him a translation from
Callimachus. Now he senses that the gesture was in
vain, and he issues a declaration of war.[9] No. 91, the
one which identifies Gellius as Lesbia's lover, is perhaps the most appalling in the group: in this epigram
he is accused of stealing her love just in order to in-
jure a friend, i.e., out of unmitigated malice:

> tantum tibi gaudium in omni
> culpast, in quacumque est aliquid sceleris, (9-10)

> guilt brings you joy only
> if the sin is mortal,[10]

which, it is fair to say, puts Gellius close to the
moral level of Milton's Satan. The Gellius epigrams
project boundless hatred and disgust. Catullus declares
that not all the oceans in the world could wash such a
villain clean (no. 88, 5-6).

The invectives against Ravidus and Gellius attack
the rivals but spare Lesbia. Perhaps they were written
in part to make them seem disgusting in her eyes as well
as ridiculous in the eyes of the general public. There
are two later epigrams against his rivals in love, however, in which she feels the lash of the poet's scorn
and hatred along with her lovers: these are nos. 37
and 79.

We begin with no. 37. Lesbia in her degradation
and depravity now frequents a *salax taberna* (v. 1) near
the temple of Castor and Pollux in the Forum, and dis-
ports herself there in the company of the habitués
(*contubernales*). The *contubernales* are her lovers, now
numbered in the hundreds (v. 7). A *taberna* is a tavern
or a cabaret, frequently also a bordello. Are we to
take the word literally here? Or is *taberna* a contemptuous metaphor for a private house? If so, and it seems
likely, whose house is meant? Some suggest the house of
her brother P. Clodius; others the house of Allius,
which figures in no. 68; still others Clodia's own
house. We can only guess at the answer, but Cicero's
insinuation in his oration *pro Caelio* (49) that "she
opened her house to all men's desire" makes the third
suggestion an attractive possibility.

Catullus threatens retaliation against her lovers
in vigorously metaphorical terms. The verb *irrumare* (v.
8), the literal sense of which need not detain us

here,[11] is often used of a violent and humiliating
assault. In this context it refers to an attack in
scurrilous verse, of which the present poem is intended
as a sample. Lines 9-10, "I will scribble the front
wall of your *taberna* with obscenities," mean essentially
the same thing: Catullus' invectives will make clear
to the general public the character of the house as a
hangout for a band of half-witted *sessores*, "squatters,"
who consider all the women on earth their special property (v. 3-5), including Lesbia (v. 14-15). Among
their number Catullus picks out "Don Ignazio" for
special mention, and the poem closes with another reference to his repulsive mouthwash.

The first half of no. 37 is sarcastic, wrathful,
violent, and studded with choice obscenities. The moment Lesbia is mentioned for the first time, however, the
tone changes; the bitterness is crossed by nostalgic regret. Catullus calls her the "girl who has fled from
his breast," v. 11, the girl "loved more than any other
ever will be loved," v. 12. This sorrowful self-quota-
tion from no. 8, 5 suspends the savage attack momentar-
ily but darkens the present situation by contrasting it
with what once was. Baehrens[12] thought no. 37 was written not only in order to attack Lesbia's lovers but also
to remind Lesbia herself of the past and of his incomparable love for her, now all but vanished.

I have saved until last the most lurid of the invectives against his rivals for Lesbia's love. No. 79
is without much doubt an attack on her politician brother P. Clodius Pulcer. Catullus insinuates that brother and sister are not only incestuous[13] (an accusation
repeatedly made in Cicero's writings) but that Clodius
practices oral sex with her and just about everybody in
Rome knows it. These staggering charges are preferred
with a certain amount of witty indirection. If Clodia
is Lesbia, Lesbius (v. 1) must be Clodius. There is
also a pun on his *cognomen* Pulcer; it is because he is
such a "pretty boy" that his sister likes him so much.
The family pride of the patrician Claudii is also
glanced at: Lesbia prefers her brother to Catullus not
only because he is *pulcer*, but also because he is so much
better-born. Catullus pretends to accept both arguments
but ironically offers to sell himself and his whole family into slavery if the notorious Lesbius can find even
three acquaintances willing to greet him in public with
the (customary) kiss of friendship. This brilliantly
ruthless epigram must have been written at a time when
all affection for Lesbia had vanished and all nostalgia
was gone. Only hatred and disgust are left. As

Ferrero[14] says, even the love-name Lesbia is dragged in
the mud by being extended to Clodius.

*

It was probably after his definitive break with
Lesbia and perhaps after his return from Bithynia that
he embarked upon a fugitive love affair with the boy
Juventius. Some interpreters have tried to dismiss
Juventius as a fictional character and the poems addressed to him as literary exercises in the Greek manner, but this sounds like special pleading.[15] Inscrip-
tions show that families of this name lived in the vicinity of Verona; hence, it has been plausibly conjectured that the boy had been sent to Rome to complete his
education, and that he had been entrusted to Catullus'
guardianship while in the capital. If this is so, his
parents had made a rather unwise choice in a protector.
Two love poems are addressed to him, nos. 48 and 99.
No. 99, which may the earlier, describes in comic hyperbole how Juventius made Catullus suffer for having stolen a kiss. The other, no. 48, is a *basia* poem stressing
the themes of multiplicity and insatiability; it closely
resembles the *basia* poems addressed to Lesbia, nos. 5 and
7, especially the latter.

The love affair with Juventius was marred by the
interference of two rivals, Furius and Aurelius, who
will be remembered as Lesbia's emissaries in no. 11, the
farewell ode. These two men, probably both poets, had
originally been friends of Catullus.[16] It must have
been on the basis of friendship that in no. 15 he temporarily entrusted the boy--not without serious mis-
givings--to Aurelius' care. The misgivings proved well
founded, for Aurelius tried to steal Juventius from him;
but it was Furius who finally succeeded in seducing him
and alienating his affections. To Juventius Catullus
addresses a couple of sorrowful remonstrances, nos. 24
and 81. No. 24 reproaches the boy for giving himself
to the penniless Furius; no. 81 upbraids him for living
in Furius' house[17]--yet he half excuses him, vv. 5-6,
on the ground that he really does not know what he is
doing. Furius and Aurelius receive rougher treatment
and are attacked in a series of rather tiresome invectives, nos. 21, 23, and 26. In no. 21 Aurelius is accused of openly attempting to seduce the child; but

Aurelius' is a "father of starvations" (v. 1) and his
poverty makes him an inappropriate lover. Furius, too,
had financial problems, and no. 23 is a mocking refusal
of his request for a loan; although Juventius is not
named or alluded to here, it is possible that the underlying implication is similar to that of no. 21, *viz.*
that Furius cannot afford to be a lover. No. 26 is a-
nother hit at Furius' financial difficulties: we learn
that his little villa is mortgaged for 15,200 sesterces
(no great sum).[18]

Of all the invectives against Furius and Aurelius
by far the most interesting is no. 16.[19] This extraordinary poem is best interpreted as an attack on their
hypocrisy. These two perverts (vs. 2) have had the
nerve to accuse Catullus of their own vices. They have
concluded from the wantonness of the poet's verses about
basia (surely not nos. 5 and 7 to Lesbia, but no. 48 to
Juventius) that he is "just a trifle unchaste" (*parum
pudicum,* v. 4) and "not exactly a man" (*male marem,* v. 13).
Catullus replies that they are confusing art and life.
The true poet may write light verse that is a little
spicy and yet himself be *castus*, free of the fault of
wantonness (vv. 5-6). In fact, he says (going on to
exaggerate for polemical purposes) light verse cannot
have wit and charm[20] unless it is somewhat racy and im-
proper. It has to be able to excite an itch, not in the
young--who are after all easily excited--but in *his
pilosis* (v. 10), hairy creatures who without such stimu-
lation would be impotent (v. 11). Ferrero[21] holds that
pilosi refers to men like Furius and Aurelius who make an
outward show of austerity and affect puritanical attitudes but actually are dissolute *pathici et cinaedi* (v. 2):
in other words, the same kind of hairy hypocrites un-
masked by Juvenal in his Second Satire. If Ferrero's
interpretation is correct, Furius and Aurelius would be
the direct opposites of Catullus, who may seem corrupt
but is in reality *pius* and *castus*. It would be wrong to
take poem no. 16 too seriously; vv. 5-9 are not so much
a statement of Catullus' critical principles as a polemical overstatement in what is after all only an invective poem.

*

Catullus was not attracted to a political career.

There is no evidence that he ever held or sought public office. His poetry too is largely apolitical. He does not advocate a program for political, social and economic reform; he does not even express opinions on the burning issues of his time. He was not a serious thinker in this area; probably he did not understand the realities of politics very well. But although he was neither an activist nor an ideologue, he was not without interest in politicians. A dozen or so of his invectives are attacks upon public officials, not only persons of minor importance but even the chief men in the state, including Pompey and Julius Caesar.

He finds fault with politicians on personal rather than political or ideological grounds.22 Some interpreters have gone so far as to say that his criticisms are motivated mainly by youthful high spirits and a delight in contradiction and nay-saying, but this is much too loose. Catullus usually attacks statesmen from an ethical point of view. More than anything else, their infringements upon the *mos maiorum*, the traditional Roman moral code, arouse his indignation; and since he has no other recourse, his anger prompts him to castigate the offenders in satiric verse. He inflicts punishment in bitter and stinging invectives which make the victim contemptible.

Indignation of some sort must have prompted his violent assault on the aged orator Cominius in no. 108, even though we cannot say exactly how he incurred Catullus' displeasure; the emphasis falls not on his crimes, which are assumed to be well known, but on the punishment he deserves. Catullus' ferocious language expresses not merely his own detestation of the man but that of the people at large, whose spokesman he makes himself: *si...populi arbitrio...intereat* (vv. 1-2) means "if the people at large were to decide the right way for you to die." The poet goes on to list the punishments which by common consent should be visited upon the old scoundrel. First his offending tongue, dangerous to all decent men, should be torn out and thrown to the vultures; then the rest of him should be cut up and divided among the ravens, the dogs and the wolves. Cominius must not be allowed to get away with his crimes, his *impuri mores* (v. 2). If he cannot be literally dismembered, at least he can be punished by violent and insulting language. Nothing is said about the inner motives which might explain his faults or mitigate his guilt. Compassion is absent, forgiveness out of the question, and there is no attempt to be "fair." Hatred of wickedness in an old man who ought to know better is

57

the motive force here; vengeance and just retaliation are the ends in view.

The extreme violence of no. 108 is atypical. No. 49 to Cicero is much more subdued and indirect. In fact, on the face of it, no. 49 is not an invective at all but a compliment, and some interpreters still read it this way:[23] on this showing the poem would be perfectly straightforward, a sincerely meant letter of thanksgiving for some unspecified service and an expression of boundless admiration for Cicero's talent as an advocate. The praise is so lavish and the self-abasement of vv. 5-6 is so extreme as to suggest that Catullus is ironizing. Certainly he did not believe he was *pessimus omnium poeta*, "the worst poet on earth"; the prayer to the Muse at the end of poem no. 1 is sufficient proof to the contrary. Catullus had too much self-esteem ever to be abject.[24] It seems almost as if Cicero has made an unfavorable remark about Catullus' writing, *e.g.* "he's the worst poet on earth", and that Catullus now thanks him for the comment with deliberately exaggerated humility and deliberately exaggerated praise, in a parody of the style of the great orator.[25] The accumulation of superlatives is very Ciceronian; *Romuli nepotum* (v. 1) for *Romanorum* is unnecessarily elevated; the two names *Marce Tulli* (v. 2) and the use of the third person *Catullus* (v. 4) in place of the first are also suspiciously solemn. It is hard to avoid the conclusion that this poem pokes fun at Cicero's overblown style and well-known vanity. Some have seen sarcasm in the *omnium* of the last line, which might be understood with *optimus*, "best on earth," but might also be taken with *patronus*, "any man's advocate," with the implication that Cicero was not very scrupulous in his choice of clients. No. 49 is beyond much doubt an attempt at indirect and ironical mockery.

Catullus wrote only one poem against Cicero and was content that that poem should seem somewhat ambiguous. Against Caesar and the Caesarians he wrote a fairly large number of poems, and there can be no doubt about his attitude toward them: it is baldly hostile.[26] No. 52, against Nonius and Vatinius, is a good example of his anti-Caesarian vehemence. These two men, thanks to the great man's backing, are beginning to rise through the *cursus honorum*. Nonius already holds curule office. Catullus calls him a *struma*, a "scrofulous tumor" on the body politic. This unsavory affliction is a tuberculous swelling of the lymphatic glands of the neck, armpits and groin, accompanied by enlargement and cheesy degeneration. As for Vatinius,[27] he is so sure of being elected to the consulship that he is already swearing (false) oaths by that anticipated office. The worst elements are coming into power and beginning to rule the state. Catullus feels such deep disgust and despair that he wishes he could die (vv. 1 and 4).[28]

The one man most often attacked in Catullus' epigrams is the lustful prodigal Mamurra. We have already met him in Chapter One. He was an equestrian from Formiae in south Latium who had acquired boundless wealth as Caesar's chief of engineers in Gaul. He was extremely efficient in his military specialty and probably had built the well-known bridge over the river Rhine. His extravagance was notorious. He was the first man to build a marble residence in Rome. He was a great womanizer and hence is frequently called *Mentula*, "John Thomas,"[29] by Catullus. Nos. 114 and 115 make fun of his enormous but unprofitable estate at Firmum on the Adriatic. In no. 105 his literary ambitions are mocked; Catullus sees as grotesque his attempt to scale the mountain of the chaste Muses, who expel him ignominiously with (rustic) pitchforks. No. 94 hits out at him for his far-flung love life, which is also alluded to in 115, 7-8. In two epigrams he gets at Mamurra indirectly through some rather heavy-handed sarcasms directed against his provincial girl friend Ameana,[30] perhaps a Veronese. Ameana appears in no. 41 as a worn-out wench with an unfortunate nose (*turpiculo naso*, v. 3). Because spendthrift Mamurra--the "Formian bankrupt" of v. 4-- gave her a tumble and paid too much for it, Ameana now has an exaggerated idea of her own market-value; she has demanded of Catullus a cool ten thousand sesterces. He pretends to believe that she has gone off her head. Why doesn't she look into the mirror for once? Poem no. 43 is an ironical salutation to the same Ameana, followed by a list of her bad points. These are underscored by the figure of litotes, which not only emphasizes her inadequacies but at the same time indicates the qualities required in a truly beautiful woman. Ameana is the negation of beauty. Catullus scornfully dismisses the idea, prevalent in the province, that Ameana was so good-looking that she could actually be compared to his lost Lesbia. (We recall that in no. 86 she was presented as the standard of true beauty.) He ends by drawing a general conclusion about the times he is living in: people are so stupid, so imperceptive. But no doubt the provincials had political reasons for praising Ameana.

A man is known by the kind of girl he goes with;

in fact, nothing is more revealing. Mamurra goes with
Ameana and Mamurra is Caesar's friend. By attacking the
triumvir's favorite, Catullus was getting at the great
man himself. But he did not limit himself to indirect
criticism. In poem no. 29 he assails Caesar personally
and throws in Pompey for good measure. Mamurra is also
assaulted. He is probably not the major target, but he
is very roughly handled. He is condemned for his prodi-
gality and limitless greed. Catullus says that having
wasted his own patrimony he now fattens on the spoils of
Gaul and Britain. He uses his wealth to buy women and
will go the round of all the bedrooms as Venus' darling
white dove, or a second Adonis. He is a *diffututa mentula*,
a haggard lecher, devouring cash by the millions; he has
squandered the loot of Pontus (acquired by Pompey in the
Mithridatic war) and of Spain (won by Caesar in 61
B.C.). Why does this unbearable profligacy go un-
checked? Catullus implies that the responsibility rests
with Pompey and Caesar, especially the latter. Caesar
as *unicus imperator*, "our one and only leader" (v. 11),
licenses Mamurra's depradations, and he does so because
he and Mamurra are two of a kind: Caesar himself is
impudicus et vorax et aleo (vv. 2, 11). These words are not
to be taken too restrictively or too literally: *impudicus*
means that he is "lost to shame," *vorax* that he is "insatiable," *aleo* that he is "a taker of great chances"
at home and abroad. Idolized by his followers as a
second Romulus (v. 5) he is actually a *cinaedus*, a shameless pervert, but with the accent rather on shameless-
ness than on sexual vice.[31] It is as if Caesar (and
Pompey along with him) fights his wars and wins his
triumphs for the express purpose (*eone nomine*, "is it on
his account?" vv. 11 and 23) of gratifying Mamurra's
vast appetite for money and sex. In short, Caesar and
Pompey coddle and pet the villainous Mamurra (v. 21) out
of a misguided generosity, a *sinistra liberalitas*, and this
seems to be the essential grievance against them in this
poem. It is certainly *sinistra liberalitas* for the tri-
umvirs to shower upon their worthless henchman the booty
which by rights belongs to the Senate and the Roman
people. Their misappropriation of the spoils of war is
contrary to *mos maiorum*, standing custom, and it is this
virtual embezzlement, more than anything else, which
proves that they are lost to shame. Caesar and Pompey
have "ruined all" (v. 24); that is, they have devastated
the whole world and overturned the Roman constitution
for the likes of a Mamurra. Unfortunately line 23 contains a textual problem which interferes with the force
of the closing couplet. *Opulentissime*, the reading of the
MSS, is said to be unmetrical, but perhaps it is not; if
we retain it, it would refer to Crassus, the third mem-

ber of the triumvirate. Some editors accept the conjecture of Schmidt, *putissimei*, archaic for *purissimi*, "the purest men in the state": this would be heavily sarcastic and the opposite of what the poet means, for the truth is that they are lost to shame. Another possibility is to accept the conjecture of Haupt, *piisimei*, "most pious." This again would be a sarcasm: Caesar and Pompey showed mutual piety as father-in-law and son-in-law by joining forces to "ruin all." The problem is as yet unsolved.

In no. 29 Caesar and Mamurra were essentially alike but stood at different levels; in no. 57 they are still two of a kind but the difference in level has disappeared and they are on a par. Catullus begins this epigram by announcing that they are a couple of shameless profligates who live in perfect harmony. He then goes on to substantiate this charge in a kind of catalogue of their vices and faults. First he mentions the *macula*, "blot" of fiscal disgrace that stains them both: the *macula* is bankruptcy at Formiae in Mamurra's case, and failure to pay his debts at Rome in Caesar's (vv. 3-5). They are twin brothers in their sickness (v. 6). They share their skills in love and literature on one study sofa (v. 7). They are both insatiable in adultery (v. 8). And they are *rivales socii puellularum* (v. 9); the richly ambiguous Latin implies that sometimes they vie with the girls for the interest of particular males, and that sometimes they share the same girls together. Line 10 re-echoes the initial charge: they are indeed a pair of shameless profligates. Although no. 57 is a scabrous and contemptuous poem it says nothing about political matters, and I do not think it is overly cynical to say that it probably bothered Caesar much less than no. 29.

No. 54 quotes no. 29, 11, again addressing Caesar as *unice imperator*, "one and only leader." Mamurra is absent from this epigram, but in his place we find a number of other favorites of Caesar: Otho, Hirrus (?), Libo, and Sufficius (or Fuficius or Fufidius). The text of these lines is severely damaged and interpretation is hazardous. Perhaps Caesar is ridiculed for surrounding himself with a coterie of oafish and rustic simpletons: Hirrus has half-washed legs, Libo sneaks out his crepitations (*peditum*, v. 3) cautiously and discreetly, Otho is a pinhead. Sufficius seems to stand above the rest and is closer to Caesar. Bickel[32] thinks *recocto*, v. 5, means "hard-boiled" and that the name should be Fufidius, a knight who was one of Caesar's important financial agents. It seems unlikely that any

of these men were low-born nobodies. Catullus limits
himself to criticizing their minor faults but hints in
si non omnia, "not to mention all the rest" (v. 4), that
he might say much more against them; then perhaps he
checks himself in the last two lines, pretending that he
is afraid he may give further offense to the *unicus
imperator,* even though his *iambi,* his "invective verses,"
are blameless and tell nothing but the truth.

We know from Suetonius[33] that nos. 57 and 29
wounded Caesar deeply and led to a demand for an apology.
It would seem that at first Catullus refused. No. 93
sounds like an initial reply: with a show of youthful
defiance the poet professes total indifference to the
great man. He has no wish to win or regain his favor.
But eventually he must have changed his mind, perhaps
giving in to parental pressure or the advice of friends,
or perhaps deciding that his epigrams really had been
unjust. According to Suetonius, after the apology or
explanation Caesar invited him to dinner on the very
same day and continued his guest friendship with
Catullus' father. What was the reason for this sudden
turn-around? Did he hope to turn the *poète maudit* into
a friend and supporter? It seems likely. We know that
Caesar practised clemency on principle--for political
motives.[34] His main objective was to win adherents from
the upper classes. By granting clemency he conferred a
benefit; therefore, if those he pardoned turned against
him later, he could plausibly charge them with ingratitude.

*

Up to this point we have been considering Catullus'
invectives under three main headings: (1) mildly ironical exposures of minor offenses; (2) vigorous attacks
upon rivals for the love of Lesbia or Juventius; and
(3) epigrams which are politically motivated or at least
politically related. It must be admitted, however, that
Catullan satire is too wide ranging to be contained even
approximately by this simple typology. There are at
least a half dozen epigrams which resist simple cate-
gorization. In all of these it seems that the element
of ridicule undergoes some alteration: either it is diminished into something close to comedy, or it shares
attention with some other attitude and interest. No.

32, to Ipsithilla; no. 44, on Sestius' frigid oration; and no. 42, against the girl who kept his writing tablets, are to a certain extent poems of attack, but the attack coexists with an element of self-mockery which seems to predominate. No. 17, on the old man of Colonia, also has a polemic component; here, however, Catullus' attitude toward his victim is basically benevolent, and the possibility of a comic resolution is not excluded. Again, no. 67, the address to the house-door, can be seen as an invective, although the poet is not so much interested in arousing his readers' indignation against Balbus' wife as in entertaining them with a particularly juicy bit of scandal. And finally no. 45, on the love affair of Acme and Septimius, is not a poem of attack at all but a rueful exposure of the romantic illusions of two young lovers. It is now time for us to attempt a closer analysis of these uncategorized poems.

No. 32 is a versified letter in which he asks Ipsithilla for an invitation to spend the siesta hour at her place. He begins with wheedling flattery and ironical politeness, but this soon gives way to the bluntest obscenity. Ipsithilla is an unknown, and her social status is somewhat uncertain. The name may be that of a real person, or it may be a pseudonym; quite possibly she is a fictitious character, the product of Catullus' imagination. On the other hand, it is conceivable that Catullus wrote this outrageous little poem for the express purpose of blackening her reputation. It is a little more likely that he is trying to *épater les bourgeois* or more exactly to annoy the *senes severiores* by making a display of his uninhibited and liberated lifestyle. It is still more likely that he is poking fun at (and at the same time boasting about) his own hyperbolical lust (vv. 8, 11).

No. 44 is a mock prayer of thanksgiving to his Tiburtan or Sabine estate, where he has been recovering from a cold. It seems that a certain Sestius (v. 10) gave marvellous dinner parties but was a very bad writer. He had invited the poet to dine and at the same time had requested a criticism of his oration against one Antius. Catullus accepted the invitation out of pure gluttony (v. 8), dutifully read the oration, and thought it a good joke on himself when a heavy cold prevented his attendance at the dinner; he humorously ascribes the cold to the "frigidity" (bad style) of Sestius' oration. This poem is of course an attack on Sestius' literary incompetence, and still more on his bad taste in requiring prospective guests to read and discuss his writings; hence it ends with a lighthearted curse on the man. But one notices that the attack on Sestius is combined with (and thus mitigated by) humorous self-criticism. It was the "sin" (v. 17) of gluttony that got Catullus into trouble in the first place. There is further self-criticism in the opening argument (vv. 1-5) about whether the poet's estate is at fashionable Tibur or in the less favored Sabine country. In these lines Catullus disarmingly admits to a certain social anxiety which does not appear elsewhere in his writings.[35]

In no. 42 Catullus apparently attempts to recover a set of miniature writing tablets which an unnamed girl has refused to return. This is one more poem in which he has not bothered to make the dramatic circumstances entirely plain. Who is the girl? Aufilena,[36] Amaeana, Ipsithilla, perhaps even Lesbia? We have no way of knowing, and it really does not matter very much. How she got her hands on the tablets we are not told, nor what (if anything) was written on them. What we are told is that the girl is untroubled by any sense of guilt (vv. 8-9, 16-17), and that she is making fun of Catullus, laughing at him (vv. 3, 9). Enraged by this impudence he calls upon all the hendecasyllables in the world to come to his aid against her. He wants them to confront the saucy miss in public, gather in a circle around her, cry insults at her until she gives the tablets back for very shame.[37] But it does not work. She is so brazen and impervious that he finds it necessary to reverse his tactics. Since justified insults are ineffective, he will try unjustified praise instead. Perhaps if she is called *pudica et proba*, "pure chaste virgin," the rotten bitch will be embarrassed enough to give the tablets back.

It is important to recognize that the above transactions are purely imaginary. They take place solely in Catullus' mind, and the girl is not actually addressed at all; she is merely apostrophized. Hence this is not an invective but another example of Catullan self-mockery. The reader is invited to smile at the poet's disproportionate anger--all this fuss over a little set of writing tablets laughingly withheld? We are also expected to enjoy his frustration at her imagined indifference to his insults and to admire the ingenuity of his final solution; though whether it worked or not is a silly question, since it only marks the end of his reverie. No. 42 was written more to entertain the reader with Catullus' resentful day dreamings than to ventilate a real indignation.

O Colonia, no. 17, is another comic fantasy, but in
a different key. Catullus is exasperated by a stupid
and lethargic Veronese husband (v. 8, unnamed) who does
not exercise adequate control over his young wife, although she is more desirable than black-ripe grapes (v.
16) and friskier than a tender young kid (v. 15). He
suggests to the citizens of Colonia (possibly Verona,
but the locale is unimportant) that it would be a *munus
maximi risus,* "a spectacle of high entertainment," v. 7,
to fling the husband off their rickety old bridge into
the deepest, blackest, most malodorous part of the quag-
mire beneath; in fact, he offers to serve as agent for
the citizens and do the flinging personally (v. 23). He
makes the mock assumption that the river god will accept
the husband as a propitiatory sacrifice[38]--the ducking
of the husband will ensure the survival of the bridge
and will actually strengthen the old structure so that
the Colognesi will be able to dance the rites of the deity Salisubsalus on it, as they have long desired to do
(vv. 5-6). At the same time Catullus holds out the hope
that the shock treatment administered to the foolish fellow may have a therapeutic effect on him, that it may
wake him up, that he may leave his indolence and stupid-
ity behind in the mud and emerge from his ducking a new
and better man, able to take proper care of his young
wife. So Catullus' *munus* would have beneficial results
all around. The citizens would enjoy a fine laugh and
get a renewed bridge, the river god would be propitiated,
the poet's exasperation would find an outlet, the husband would be purged of his faults, and the frisky young
wife would be placed under fitting control. No. 17 is
essentially comic; invective is not absent, but genial
benevolence preponderates. It ends with a resolution
which the reader accepts as a desirable state of affairs. But the efficacious sacrifice which would set
everything right is entirely hypothetical, and remains
in the realm of wish.[39]

No. 67 is a dramatic dialogue between the poet and
the street door of a house in Verona. The door is
vividly personified as a talkative old female slave,
totally indiscreet and somewhat foul-mouthed, who tells
a number of scandalous tales about the wife of Balbus,
the former owner of the house. Balbus was not her first
husband, as the people of Verona think. She had a previous husband in the neighboring town of Brixia (the
modern Brescia, some forty miles west of Verona). As
everyone in Brixia knows, her first husband was impotent.[40] Consequently, she had a whole series of lovers:
Postumius, Cornelius, and an unnamed third party, the
tall man with the red eyebrows (vv. 45-8). What is

worse, she even committed incest with her father-in-law. When the poet asks how a mere door can know so much, she explains that she has often overheard the woman whispering with her maids about her carryings-on in the past (vv. 41-42).

It is helpful for the reader to notice that the door is a comic-fantastic surrogate for Catullus himself, who knows or says he knows or thinks he knows all about the Brixian escapades of Balbus' wife. Eager to display his inside knowledge, he takes it upon himself to reveal the full story to Verona and to all the world, perhaps under the cover of pseudonyms. His purpose is probably not simply to defame this woman and the men in her life. There is no discernible motive for this; Catullus reveals no personal involvement with her at all, nor with any of her lovers (though he does seem to be on friendly terms with the door). It is much more likely that he wishes to regale us with a bit of scandalous gossip. Admittedly, this means he is not appealing to us at a very high level; to put it plainly, he is catering to our built-in *Schadenfreude*. But from the ordinary Roman point of view, the woman and her men friends are getting what is coming to them: they deserve no mercy. The benevolent dictum of John Dryden, to the effect that no man has a right upon the reputation of another human being,[41] would probably have completely astonished Catullus and his contemporary readership.

Acme and Septimius, no. 45, is a love duet in which two young people exchange hyperbolical assurances of everlasting fidelity. Catullus is the omniscient narrator who, although he was obviously not present, knows what Acme and Septimius said and did and felt, sees or hears the sneezes of Amor, evaluates their love and makes a prediction about its future course. The poem used to be interpreted quite literally as a celebration of ideal love, perfect in its mutuality (v. 20), intensity (vv. 5, 11, 16), beatitude (v. 25) and prospects for the future (vv. 19, 26). More recently, however, critics[42] have sensed a skeptical irony lurking just below the surface and sustained throughout. Although the present happiness of the couple is beyond question and although there can be little doubt about the equality of their affections, a moment of thought will convince us that the affair cannot last very long. Septimius is said to be intoxicated with Acme, and intoxication is hardly a permanent condition. Acme's marrow is consumed by a fierce and passionate flame, and that kind of fire sooner or later burns itself out. The fact is that both of them are servants of Amor or Cupid, and of Cupid alone (v. 14): he is their *dominus*, their lord. Cupid is the flighty and capricious god of desire. The last thing one can expect from naughty-boy Cupid is stability; it takes more than a few of his sneezes to guarantee a lifelong attachment. What many readers would see as a decisive indication that their protestations are not to be taken too seriously is provided by their very names. Acme and Septimius are ethnically unalike: she is Greek and he is Roman. Furthermore, they are not social equals: she is probably an ex-slave, he a citizen. Clearly she is his mistress and he is her "protector." Such a relationship, formed in youth, is extremely unlikely to prove lifelong. Yet, deluded by mutual desire, they cannot foresee the inevitable breakup and innocently look forward to an endless happiness together (vv. 3, 4, 14). Catullus knows better. It is worthwhile to remember that the reference to Syria and Britain in v. 22 dates this poem to 55 B.C. That is the same year in which Catullus wrote his bitter good-bye to Lesbia, no. 11. By that time he had no illusions about the perpetuity of love. Still, *Acme and Septimius* is not a cynical poem; Catullus is far from mocking the lovers for their illusion that passion will be perpetual. He recognizes the bliss of the passing moment and praises it. He does not seriously question its mutuality or its intensity, but the closing prediction must be ruefully ironic. *Deliciae libidinesque*, "pleasure and desire," are fleeting, and as the old proverb has it, the gods smile at lovers' oaths.

*

The poems we have been considering in this chapter have one feature in common: all of them criticize. But the criticism takes various forms. The most numerous category is that of the strong invectives, which may be regarded as a kind of undeveloped satire. I call them "undeveloped" because they do not universalize (that is, they aim solely at a particular person or group), and because they tend to attack directly, with a minimum of irony, obliquity and wit. The targets of strong invective are major vices or serious abuses, mainly attributed to political foes or rivals in love. Exaggeration and satiric distortion are not absent; invective is not altogether fair. Granted, Catullus does not tell lies, so far as we know, and to that extent he uses the power of language responsibly; but he does not give an objective, balanced and judicious picture of the adversary either. The attack is not always in just proportion to the magnitude of the offense; overreaction and "tetchiness" are sometimes in evidence. Catullus does not consider it part of his duty to offer the opposition constructive criticism, or to propose programs for political or social reform. Invective is by its very nature non-constructive. The author claims complete freedom of speech for himself and dramatically projects his anger through violent, hyperbolic, abusive and obscene language; this is in full accordance with the tradition which our author inherited from Archilochus, Hipponax, and Alcaeus; it is also consonant with earlier Roman invective. No culprit is exempt from attack, no matter how highly placed; even Caesar and Pompey are directly and openly assaulted. Catullus' invectives usually address the enemy directly, but they do so within the hearing of the wider audience, which includes all men of good will. Sometimes the poet makes an explicit claim to be the spokesman of public opinion, or at least of a large portion of it. He does not adopt an arbitrary, individualistic or eccentric view concerning the nature of right and wrong, good or bad, nor a philosophic view either. He accepts ancestral Roman opinion, embodied in *mos*, sound tradition. Despite the high emotional temperature of the invectives, feeling seldom outruns thought; Catullus has reasons for being angry. But personal hatred is also involved. The offenses he lashes out against are usually, but not always, offenses against himself; Catullus has suffered an injury. Less frequently it is the body politic that has been hurt. The primary motive for writing the invectives is to retaliate, to take vengeance. The primary emotion is wrath, or more exactly indignation, defined by Aristotle as anger at undeserved good fortune.[43] Malice coexists with the indignation. The poet takes it for granted that it is right to harm one's enemies, not to forgive them or turn the other cheek. Compassion has no place in invective, and the modern aphorism that to know all is to forgive all forecloses the very possibility of attack.[44] Secondary motives for writing might include a desire to work off anger, to win admiration for courage and skill, to parade a liberated modernism, to *épater les bourgeois*, and (not least) to give the reader pleasure, either by appealing to his sense of justice or to his malice. (I take it that the desire to cure or to effect reform is not one of his motives.) The aggressive Catullus of the strong invectives, sublimely self-confident, has no hesitation about constituting himself

arbiter of justice and defender of *mos maiorum*. As poet
of attack he stands in marked contrast to the pathetic
miser of the many poems of complaint: bold retaliation
replaces passive suffering. But the invectives and the
complaints have one feature in common: the poet enter-
tains no real doubt that right and justice are on his
side.

In another smaller group of poems the element of
criticism is considerable muted: these we have called
the milder invectives. Here generalization begins to
appear. The individual who is attacked can typify a
whole class or category of people. Irony, indirection
and wit are more prominent. The general tone is more
nearly that of developed satire. The offenses attacked
are much less serious. They are minor vices, such as
napkin stealing: foibles, inanities, affectations,
silliness. Catullus functions here as the self-
appointed judge of good taste, good sense, good manners,
and of the social graces in general. He confidently ad-
ministers rebukes when infractions are brought to his
attention. He is not always the injured party. The
standard of judgment is *urbanitas,* as defined and understood by Catullus' social peers. The tone of anger and
hate is considerably mitigated. Belittling derision
takes the place of frontal attack. The prevailing attitude is more balanced and judicious, and the possibility
of excuse is sometimes entertained.

A third category of poems verges on the comic. It
is not easy to draw a firm line between comedy and mild
invective, for ridicule is common to both. The best
criterion for distinguishing the two is the quality of
the laughter they evoke. Comic laughter is kinder and
more generous than the laughter of mild invective. It
ridicules without rejecting. It criticizes but sees
much good in the person or persons criticized. It not
only forgives but even sympathizes. Sometimes it can
actually foresee a happy ending. Some self-mockery
appears. In one instance it is suggested that the
reader may share the fault under criticism. Anger is
diminished to a smiling exasperation or mock annoyance.
The standards for judging are the predictable norms of
human nature and the wisdom of those who know the world.

CHAPTER FIVE

Bithynia and Afterwards

In 57/56 B.C. Catullus went to Bithynia in north-
west Asia Minor as a member of the staff of the anti-
Caesarian governor (more exactly, propraetor) C.
Memmius. The usual motive for going on such an expedi-
tion was to get a start in political life and at the
same time to amass wealth at the expense of the provincials. In Catullus' case there were several additional
inducements: the trip provided an opportunity to visit
the grave of his brother in the Troad, to see the Greek
cities of Ionia (no. 46,6), and perhaps to get a change
of scene after breaking with Lesbia.

It seems unlikely that he obtained the appointment
through his father's influence. Anti-Caesarian politics
probably were decisive, but literary connections may
have helped.[1] We know that at least one other member of
the entourage was a man of letters, namely Catullus'
poet friend C. Helvius Cinna. Memmius himself was an
accomplished orator and in fact one of the *Poetae Novi*;
he wrote love poems to his mistress "Perilla," whose
real name was Metella. He is well known as the principal addressee of Lucretius' great didactic poem on
Epicureanism, the *de Rerum Natura*. Frank[2] and others have
conjectured that he showed Catullus drafts of Lucretius'
first four books during their tour of duty in the east.

There are no descriptions in the surviving poems
of the voyage to Bithynia or of his day-to-day occupations in the province. His hopes of making money were
frustrated by the uncooperative attitude of the governor. It is evident from no. 46, 9-11 that he made a
number of fast friends among his contemporaries on
Memmius' staff, but there are no poems addressed to any
of them, except Cinna. Perhaps he was too busy for
light verse (there may have been some military action)
or too depressed. Nevertheless, the years in the east
did not represent a literary vacuum. It seems quite
likely that during this period he was writing part of
his miniature epic, no. 64, the *Wedding of Peleus and Thetis*.
He may also have been gathering materials for his
strange and striking poem on the Cybele cult, the *Attis*,
no. 63. The setting for this poem is Mt. Ida; hence he
may well have had some contact with the goddess' cult
when he visited his brother's grave in the Troad. The

ending of the *Attis* suggests that Catullus had felt the
attractions of Cyble worship and perhaps had even toyed
with the idea of escaping his sufferings by becoming one
of the goddess' self-mutilated priests. We shall take
this matter up in further detail later on (Chapter
Eight). For the present, we shall confine our attention
to the shorter poems which he wrote during or immediately after his trip to the East.

Probably one of the earliest[3] of these is no. 101,
the celebrated apostrophe to his dead brother. It is
helpful to notice that this poem is not an epitaph but
a lamentation uttered at the grave site. Catullus wrote
it to express his sense of irremediable loss and not in
order to impart biographical information to the reader;
that is why he says nothing about the circumstances of
his brother's death. We are not told when he died or
where he was buried (we know it was in the Troad only
from no. 65, 7 and no. 68, 91). Nor do we discover how
he met his end, whether it was by accident--shipwreck,
perhaps--or illness or some other mischance. Even more
surprisingly, there is no praise for the deceased
either, and in fact no reference to any specific trait
of his character or personality. Only the blood relationship is stressed: *frater* is thrice repeated in the
vocative case, vv. 2, 6, 10 (cf. *fraterno*, v. 9). Nevertheless, Catullus makes it unmistakably clear that he
loved his brother very much: he travelled a great distance to visit his tomb, vv. 1-2; he sheds copious tears
while there, v. 9; he offers the funeral sacrifice, vv.
203, 7-9; he bewails his loss, vv. 5-6.

The view of death expressed in this elegy is consistent with that of no. 3, the lament for Lesbia's
sparrow, and no. 5, the first *basia* poem. Death means
utter extinction. His brother is a handful of ashes now
(*cinerem*, v. 4). He cannot speak (*mutam*, v. 4) and presumably cannot hear either. The true self (*tete ipsum*,
v. 5) is gone, taken away. It is vain to address him
(*nequiquam*, v. 4). The last greeting of salutation and
of leavetaking (v. 10) is already useless; they are
parted forever. The note of rebellion which we discerned in no. 3 is much more prominent here, especially
in lines 5-6. The verb *abstulit*, "made away with you,"
and the participle *adempte*, "taken," "stolen," connote
an arbitrary dispossession which verges upon robbery.
The robber is Fortuna. She is a mysterious and unpredictable power, like a fickle woman, who for no dis-
cernable reason or purpose seems to delight in defeating
us and depriving us of our happiness. The adverb *indigne*
further reinforces the notion of unfairness. Catullus'

brother dies without deserving his death on any grounds that man can see: he is pitiable, *miser*. In sum, the poet has again been brought face to face with the final and universal limitation of death and finds that he is totally unable to understand it or accept it. Nevertheless (*tamen*, v. 7, referring to *nequiquam* v. 4) he offers the traditional gifts, wet with tears. He recognizes that the gifts are just as vain and useless as the words he has been addressing to his brother's ashes, but he goes through the motions, simply because there is nothing else to do. Unlike the elegy on the death of Quintilia (no. 96), this poem is stripped of all consolation. The sole catharsis lies in the transmutation of inexplicable loss and pain into high art.

The death of his brother struck Catullus with enormous impact. His grief is displayed not only in no. 101 but also in three memorable passages from the longer poems, *viz.* no. 65, 5-14; no. 68, 19-26; and no. 68, 91-100. Nos. 65 and 68 may well have been written before his departure for Bithynia, but because of the similarities to and differences from no. 101 the three passages in question may fittingly be considered here.

No. 65, to Hortensius, has already been analyzed in part in Chapter Two. This is the elegy in which Catullus says he is so overwhelmed by grief at his brother's death that he is unable to comply with his friend's request for an original poem; instead, he sends him a verse translation of Callimachus' *Coma Berenices* (no. 66). The passage from no. 65 which presently engages our attention, lines 5-14, differs from no. 101 mainly in that it introduces a certain amount of mythology, not of course for any religious significance which it may once have possessed, but as a literary device making for intensification. He takes over the Homeric idea, absent from no. 101, that death is a separation of the "soul," *psyche*, from the body.[4] His brother's body is buried in the Trojan earth, actually crushed beneath it; it is impossible for that body ever to rise again. His soul has passed the river frontier of Lethe which separates the quick from the dead. The crossing is expressed solely by a close-up image of his brother's waxen-pale foot planted in the swirling waters of oblivion (vv. 5-6). The participle *ereptum*, "snatched," "stolen" from his sight (v. 8), like *abstulit* and *adempte* in no. 101, brings in the note of rebellion at the unfairness of death. He goes on to apostrophize the lost brother in lines 10-11 and to lament, in a rhetorical question expressing shocked incredulity,[5] the irreducible fact that he will never see him again. Yet he will not stop loving that brother, who he says is dearer to him than life itself. Again as in no. 101 he stresses that love, to the exclusion of any description of his brother's personality or appearance and of any details about the circumstances of his death. In the nightingale simile which follows (vv. 12-14), Catullus lingers over his inconsolable grief:

> semper maesta tua carmina morte canam,
> qualia sub densis ramorum concinit umbris
> Daulias, absumpti fata gemens Ityli.

> Always I will sing sad songs because of
> your death, such songs as the Daulian maiden
> sings deep in the dense shadows of the
> boughs, lamenting her lost Itylus.

These lines bring in more Homeric mythology. They are modelled on *Odyssey* XIX, 518 ff., a simile applied to the sorrows of Penelope.[6] Catullus abbreviates the Homeric comparison and reapplies it to his subjective experience. As the "Daulian maid" (Procne or Philomel, transformed into a nightingale) withdraws "deep in the dense shadows of the boughs" and there mourns unceasingly for the lost Itylus, so the poet withdraws and sings endlessly of his lost brother. Granarolo points out that these endless songs must be internal, sung only in the depths of the heart.[7] Ordinarily the nightingale's song connotes guilt as well as sadness, guilt over the death of the child Itylus. But guilt is probably not involved in Catullus' simile. There is no discernible reason for him to feel responsible for his brother's death. In all likelihood the simile refers to sadness only. The principal function of the comparison is to elevate and enhance that sadness. The poet feels entitled to compare his grief to one of the most remarkable instances of grief known to man, that of the Daulian maid for her lost child. At the same time he reinterprets the Homeric simile to bring in the idea of wordless inward song, continuous and inconsolable. As in no. 101, he emphasizes the conviction tht death marks an eternal separation, and that art is really the only consolation available. But in no. 65 the art is not fully shared with the reader. Most of it--the sad unwritten songs like those of the nightingale--remains private and uncommunicated.

The first passage in no. 68 is mainly about the change his brother's death produced in his way of life. He contrasts his previous *studia* ("occupations," v. 26, cf. v. 19) before this watershed experience with his

74

present utter depression. While his brother was still
alive, he pursued the interests which had engrossed him
ever since the age of sixteen, when he had received the
toga of manhood. Essentially adolescent, he had played
games: *multa satis lusi*, v. 17. Here *lusi* probably has a
double meaning: he enjoyed himself and he wrote his
love poems, for he was no stranger to Venus' bittersweet
anxieties. But his brother's death ended his interest
in such frivolous pleasures. At this point he breaks
off with a vehement apostrophe,[8] reinforced by multiple
repetitions: *fraterna, frater, frater; tu, tu, tecum, tecum,
tuus*. The phrase *misero frater adempte mihi* (v. 20), echoed
in no. 101, v. 6, brings in once again the note of rebellion at the arbitrary bereavement which has drained
his life of all joy. The apostrophe contains two cryptic statements which hint tantalizingly at the precise
relationship between the two brothers. The first is in
v. 22, *tecum una tota est nostra sepulta domus*, "with you all
our family is buried." In what sense is this intended?
Domus must be rendered "family," but he cannot mean his
brother was his sole surviving relative, unless his
father had died by this time. Did the rest of his
family (father, mother perhaps, other brothers and sisters) mean next to nothing to Catullus? Was the lost
brother the only member of the family he really cared
for? Or was the brother the family's support and protection, its glory and pride and distinction, so that
all that was best in it died with him?[9] Or is Catullus
saying that he has no intention of marrying and bringing
children into the world to continue the family name?
The verse is provokingly elusive. Equally vague is
vv. 23-4, *gaudia nostra/quae tuus in uita dulcis alebat amor*.
Here *amor* has been understood as "approval" and *alebat*
as "encouraged." Perhaps when others tried to dissuade
him, the brother encouraged Catullus in his *gaudia*, his
life of poetry and love-making. This sounds like a
permissive and unconventional elder brother. But unfortunately the Latin is very general and unspecific and
needs mean no more than "your sweet love nourished my
joys." The passage is rounded off by a return to the
thought of vv. 19-20: the brother's death brought the
frivolities of his youth to an end.

The second passage in no. 68 is triggered by a reference to Troy (and the Trojan war) which reminds
Catullus that his brother lies buried by the seashore
there. Several lines of this passage are repeated with
little or no change from the earlier one: 92=20 (see
also no. 101, 6); 94-96=22-24. These are the verses
which speak of the poet's rebellion, of the loss sustained by the family, and of the end of the joys which

his brother's "sweet love" had nourished. The only new points are the reference to Troy, reflecting no. 65, 7, and a lamentation over the fact that he was not buried back home among his kinsfolk. This is an additional misfortune, for under such circumstances his *manes* or "spirit" cannot receive regular cult offerings from his surviving relatives, as Roman custom prescribes.[10] Poetically the most interesting line is v. 93, which seems to mean at least two things at once: "alas, the light of my poor brother's life is snatched away" (in antithesis to vs. 92); and "alas, the light of my life and happiness is snatched away" (in parallel to vs. 92). Functionally ambiguous, the single line expresses a double and reciprocal loss.

We pass from the poems on his brother to no. 46, written just before he left Bithynia. It is impossible to date this poem in relation to no. 101. If Catullus visited the grave site at the start of his tour of duty, no. 101 is earlier; if he visited the grave after the tour was over, no. 46 is earlier. Fortunately the relative dates of the two poems do not influence the interpretation of either one.

No. 46 is Catullus' only spring poem. Spring poems are sometimes joyous, sometimes surprisingly sad. The most famous poem of the twentieth century begins with the line "April is the cruelest month." It is "cruelest" because the self-renewal of nature mocks our inability to renew ourselves; nature recovers her youth, but we are only one year older, one year closer to the grave. On the other hand, conventional/romantic spring songs are joyous. One rejoices at the happy prospect of communing with nature, or one's fancy lightly turns to thoughts of love. No. 46 is predominantly joyful, not sad; it is one of the relatively few poems of Catullus that can be called happy. However, it is neither conventional nor romantic. Catullus does not rejoice over love, which he does not mention, and which to him is hardly a joyous experience in any case. Nor does he exult in the beauties of nature and his closeness to them. To the contrary, he can hardly wait to put the fertile plowlands of sweltering Nicaea behind him (v. 5). He wants to get back to civilization; he looks forward to visiting the glorious Greek cities of Ionia (v. 6). Catullus, like most classical authors, is more interested in cities and human society than in the solitary contemplation of nature; he writes about people, not landscapes.[11]

What he rejoices over in no. 46 is not nature or

love but the recovery of freedom after the long constraints of winter. He does not use the word "freedom" explicitly, but the idea is implied in the verbs *volemus*, "let us take flight," v. 6 and *vagari*, "wander," v. 7. *Volemus* anticipates rapid and unimpeded movement; *vagari* denotes frequent change of place with no fixed goal in view and no deadlines to meet. Goals and deadlines are anxiety producers; the absence of either or both is liberating, exhilarating. Catullus' happy feet, v. 8, tingle with eagerness to rove, wander, roam as the spirit moves him.

It is worth mentioning that there are no complaints in this poem. Catullus says nothing about the annoyance of serving in a distasteful job under an uncongenial chief. In fact it looks as though the stay in Bithynia was not entirely unpleasant. This is suggested by the self-address in vv. 4-6. In several other poems, self-address dramatizes an examination of conscience, leading to self-condemnation or self-acquittal. This is not the case here. In this context, an eager, forward-looking self addresses a lingering, backward-looking self.[12] The lingering self is preoccupied with the joys of companionship and has not observed that spring, the time for departure, is already at hand: one notices the emphatic repetition of *iam*, "already," in vv. 1, 2, 7, 8. So the eager self exhorts the lingering self to be up and going: *linquantur*, "leave behind," v. 4; *volemus*, v. 6 (the plural perhaps designating the two selves, as in no. 8, 5). Lines 7-8 indicate a favorable response to the exhortation, but the close of the poem finds Catullus bidding a fond farewell to the *dulces comitum coetus*, his "circle of sweet friends" who are now separating and going their several ways back to Italy. The poem ends not on a note of joy but of muted regret that the group is breaking up for good.

No. 4 tells a story about the *phaselus* or light sailing vessel shaped like a beanpod which we have already met in Chapter One. This craft was built at Amastris in Bithynia on the south shore of the Black Sea, and it transported its unidentified *erus*, "master," v. 19, from Asia Minor through the Hellespont, Aegaean and Adriatic to a *limpidus lacus*, "placid lake," v. 24, of uncertain location. Now it is spending its old age in peaceful retirement, having dedicated itself to the patron gods of navigation, Castor and Pollux (vv. 25-27). Interpreters commonly assume that the poem is autobiographical: Catullus is the speaker and the *erus*, the voyage is his return from Bithynia to Italy,[13] and the *lacus* is the Lago di Garda, where he had an estate on the lakeshore (at Sirmio; *cf.* no. 31, 1). In some way or other he managed to get the vessel up the Po and Mincius and over to the lake. Admittedly this interpretation cannot be proved and involves a number of minor difficulties, but it is not unreasonable, and to reject it reduces the poem to pointlessness.

In its basic strategy no. 4 rather resembles no. 67. There Catullus was represented as conversing with a talking door. Here he reports to a number of *hospites*, perhaps a group of literary friends gathered at Sirmio, the ship's own account of its life experiences. The ship is amusingly characterized as a talkative old slave, rather pedantic, distinctly whimsical, and much given to boasting. It praises its own versatility and unexcelled speed, dwells on the dangers it successfully surmounted, dilates upon its distinguished lineage and eminent relatives, exults in its sublime self-confidence, and stresses the fact that it never got into difficulties at sea. Of course it is not the ship that is doing the boasting; it is really Catullus, the ship's master, who is telling his *hospites* what a wonderful *phaselus* he has, what a daring voyage he has made, how many strange and far-off places he has seen, how many dangers he has overcome, and so on. However, he recognizes that it is *ineptum,* the reverse of urbane, to brag to one's guests, so he avoids annoying them by the clever subterfuge of putting all his traveller's boasts into the mouth of the ship. In other words he gets away with his self-praise by making it indirect and comic. Just as in no. 67 the talking door was a comic surrogate for Catullus himself, so here again he ventriloquizes through an inanimate object. In both cases the personification is fully functional.

In no. 31[14] Catullus joyfully salutes Sirmio after his return voyage from Bithynia. Although the mood is diametrically opposed to that of no. 101 (the lament uttered at his brother's grave), the two poems have some interesting points of contact. In no. 101 he addressed the mute ashes which he knew could not reply; in no. 31 he addresses Sirmio, which cannot reply either--except in his imagination, by the laughter of its waves (vv. 13-14). Sirmio, by a sustained animating metaphor, is treated as if it were a person, as if it had a unique personality all its own and could share in and respond to the poet's mood. Clearly it is because he loves Sirmio that he personifies the place. But why does he love it? Perhaps in part because it is so beautiful.

Still, very little description is provided. It is a peninsula, it is an *ocellus*, "gem," and it is *venusta*, "lovely": the terms are not very informative. As in no. 101 he did not describe the brother whom he loved, so here he does not describe his beloved Sirmio. His brother did not need to be told about his own appearance and character, nor does Sirmio. Neither poem was intended to supply the reader with external information; both express the poet's attitude toward a "person."

In no. 101 he is of course in utter dejection, whereas in no. 31 he is blissfully happy (v. 4). Or more exactly, he is joyful (vv. 12-13): joy may be understood as that special kind of happiness which comes from the assurance that one possesses securely the object of one's love. His joy in returning is enhanced by the contrast with what came before: confinement in the flatlands of Bithynia (vv. 5-6, echoing no. 46, 4-5); *peregrinus labor*, "hardship in a foreign land" (v. 8-9: the nature of the hardship is not indicated, but the idea is repeated in v. 11); tension, expressed in the implied metaphor of knotted cares (v. 7); worry, expressed in the implied metaphor of a burden pressing upon the mind (v. 8); and a kind of apprehension verging on despair, so that even now he can scarcely believe (vv. 5-6) that he has safely returned. In this list of afflictions he must be alluding to more than the physical hardships of travel. (Poem no. 4 makes the journey home seem almost effortless.) He has chosen to be somewhat reticent about his tribulations. Perhaps he is alluding to his grief at his brother's grave. Conceivably he has in mind certain nightmare terrors, inspired by contact with the Cybele cult at Mt. Ida, which have left a trace at no. 63, vv. 91-3. Quite probably he is thinking of all the uncongenial aspects of his tour of duty with Memmius, during which (despite the consolations of companionship glanced at in no. 46, vv. 9-11) he may have felt he was trying to play a role he was not cut out for. Whatever the precise nature of his past anxieties, now that he is back at Sirmio he feels liberated from them and at peace with himself. At last he is back in his beloved home (*lar*, v. 9), the household where he is master (*erus*, v. 12);[15] finally he can rest in his own bed, v. 10. In line 13, *Lydiae lacus undae*, "Lydian waves of the lake," he seems to recall how earlier refugees from Asia Minor, the ancient Etruscans, had also escaped from Lydia to the west, settled in the Po valley, and there in the end found a better place to live. Both no. 31 and no. 4 conclude on a note of resolution. Catullus' problems are solved, difficulties and dangers are conquered, tensions and frustrations are success-

fully overcome. All the poems about getting away from
Bithynia and back home are happy and joyous. Even no.
46 is predominantly light-hearted.

He did not stay long at Sirmio. No. 10 finds him
back in Rome, shortly after his return from Bithynia.
This poem provides another example of the vein of self-
mockery which we have already met in nos. 32, 42, and
44. It is rather unusual in form, for it is not addressed to a particular acquaintance but to the general
reader, to whom the developing situation is explained
step by step: we notice, in addition to the opening
narrative, vv. 1-8, the asides and stage directions at
vv. 9, 16-17, and 21-23.[16] Catullus and his friend
Varus are at the house of Varus' mistress. The reference to the foreign deity Serapis in v. 26 suggests that
she was a Greek freedwoman from Egypt. Catullus sizes
her up as a *scortillum*, "a regular little floozy," but
condescendingly adds that she was "not without wit and
charm," v. 4. The conversation turns to Bithynia; they
ask the poet whether he made any money on his trip. He
gives a candid answer: Bithynia is a terrible province
to start with (vv. 9-11, cf. 19), in other words poverty
stricken; moreover, his propraetor Memmius was an *irrumator*, "an absolute bastard." (Strictly, an *irrumator* is
one who treats others with contempt, as if they were
spurci ore).[17] He "didn't give a damn" for his subordi-
nates (vv. 13-14). Catullus seems to be implying that
Memmius grabbed everything for himself. Varus and the
scortillum reply with one accord, "Surely you at least
brought back litter-bearers; they're a native product"
(and therefore cheap in Bithynia). Both Varus and the
girl have litter-bearers on their minds; it is a fair
guess that she has been asking Varus for a team of such
slaves, and he has been putting her off. By this time
Catullus has taken a shine to the girl and cannot resist
the temptation to brag a bit, even to the point of
telling a flat lie. Yes, he tells her, he bought eight
straight-backed bearers in Bithynia. But he had under-
estimated the girl; his lie backfires at once. Completely shameless (*cinaediorem*, v. 24), she makes up to
the poet as if he were an old friend and asks him to
lend her his bearers so that she can visit the temple of
Serapis in style, like a noble matron. There is no malice in her request, just sheer effrontery. She is not
trying to catch Catullus in his falsehood; she simply
wants to exploit an opportunity. Catullus is reduced to
spluttering embarrassment (comedy, as we know, typically
deals in discomfiture and the exposure of pretension).
He stammers out that the bearers really belong to his

friend Cinna, but friends have all things in common. The reader is probably expected to recognize a contradiction here: if Bithynia is such a terrible province and Memmius such an absolute beast, how could Cinna have picked up eight straight-backed bearers and Catullus not? He ends by venting his embarrassment on the innocent *scortillum*: "You're really too tiresome and annoying--won't let a fellow be a little careless with his words." The poem is a comic trifle, no more; but it is interesting to notice how utterly detached the Catullus who narrates is from the Catullus who figures in the narrative, and how he makes us feel that he richly deserved the embarrassment which he brought upon himself. At the same time, the brief invective of vv. 9-13 carries no comic implication. These lines unveil the truth (*id quod erat*, v. 9) about Memmius' relations with Catullus and the rest of his staff: he would not allow his entourage to enrich themselves at the expense of the provincials. And Catullus regards this as no laughing matter but a ground for indignation.

When he came back from Bithynia, his dear friends Veranius and Fabullus were still serving in Macedonia under L. Calpurnius Piso,[18] as we learn from no. 28. This versified letter indicates that Veranius and Fabullus had the same grievances against their chief that Catullus had against Memmius. The poem begins with Catullus asking whether all goes well or ill with them these days and whether or not they have had their fill of "that degenerate" Piso. He then goes on to speak in vigorously obscene terms of the disappointments he endured under the absolute beast Memmius in Bithynia. He sighs over the folly of chasing high-born friends and ends by calling down curses on both Memmius and Piso, who are a disgrace to Rome. This curse is devoid of serious ethical content, expresses nothing more than exasperation and frustration. No. 28 is an invective poem, unseasoned by comedy. Catullus is trying to console and avenge his friends here. At the same time he is also consoling and avenging himself for the capricious mistreatment which he received at the hands of Memmius, and which still rankles.

No. 47, in somewhat similar vein to no. 28, again sides with Veranius and Fabullus against Piso, but this time without bringing in Catullus' own experience in Bithynia. Instead, he contrasts the lot of his two friends with the undeserved good fortune of Porcius and Socration, whom he labels as "Piso's two left hands, the scab and covetousness of the world." Porcius may be one of the Catones; Socration, "little Socrates," is possibly a pseudonym for the poet and Epicurean philosopher Philodemus, who from what is said of him in other sources hardly deserves the abuse Catullus heaps upon him here.[19] But Catullus' love is perhaps blind, and devotion to his *sodales* may well have lured him into hyperbolic attitudes. In three indignant questions he excoriates his friends' rivals: the thievish Porcius and Socration have grown so rich under Piso that they are giving lavish dinners at Rome (or perhaps, if they are still in their province, at Thessalonica), whereas good Veranius and Fabullus are reduced to cadging dinner invitations on the street corners. Such is the sense of justice of that *verpa Priapus,* that "obscene lecher," Piso.

Catullus' Bithynian poems are of course interesting for what they tell us about his travels, about his attitude toward his brother, about his relations with his *sodales,* and about the provincial governors under whom they served. But they are also significant for what they do not state explicitly but merely take for granted. His vexation with the governors is certainly not based upon social idealism or a sense that the provincials are being unfairly treated. He takes the ordinary unreflective Roman's attitude toward the exploitation of subject peoples. Far from being an anti-imperialist, he assumes that the empire exists for the economic advantage of its overlords; and it never occurs to him to question the propriety of oppressive tactics, whether on humanitarian or ideological grounds. The only regret that he expresses in the Bithynian poems is that Memmius and Piso, for unrevealed reasons, had frustrated his own and his friends' schemes for self-enrichment. That regret he expresses in unbridled and exasperated invective. In short, he never bothers to justify empire, whether to himself or to others. In his view of Rome's relation to the conquered populations he is unenlightened and self-centered, like the vast majority of his contemporaries.

CHAPTER SIX
The Marriage Theme

Up to this point we have been concentrating our attention on Catullus' shorter poems, the so-called *polymetra* (nos. 1-60) and the elegiac epigrams (nos. 69-116). One of the most striking features of these poems is their rich diversity. They vary in metre, style, mood, subject matter, and level of elaboration. Some are carefully organized, others seem rather casual and unstudied. Sometimes the poet is the spokesman of public opinion or the upholder of traditional ways. More often he writes for a special and private sub-group which dissents from or rebels against majority views. Still more often he addresses an individual, or even himself, paying little or no attention to the needs and convenience of his readership. Yet in spite of these wide variations it is possible to discern certain constants in the shorter poems. The features common to all or most of them are these: (1) the poet aspires to distilled concentration of expression; (2) his subject matter is drawn not from mythology but from personal experience; and (3) his central character is the first person singular, considered as a man of feeling, who gives expression to his personal moods, attitudes, states of mind, processes of thought and emotion.

In the present chapter and those following, we shall turn from the lyrics (as they may be loosely termed) to Catullus' longer and more ambitious works. These include the two wedding songs, nos. 61 and 62; the Attis poem, no. 63; the miniature epic, no. 64; the translation of Callimachus' *Coma Berenices*, no. 66; the long elegy, no. 68; and the hymn to Diana, no. 34.[1] These longer poems are at least as dense and concentrated as the shorter ones, but in most of them the lyric element recedes sharply. The first person singular, referring to Catullus himself, is virtually abandoned, although no. 68 is an outstanding exception in this regard. The attitudes expressed are less private and personal, more likely to be traditional and communal. Mythology takes the place of personal experience, but usually serves as a kind of metaphor for it. All of these poems are carefully organized and highly finished; they are ambitious works, written at the highest level of elaboration. Internal evidence makes it clear that Catullus intended them to be taken very seriously indeed, and it seems probable that he based his claim to literary eminence largely, though not exclusively, upon these longer compositions.

We begin our discussion of this aspect of our author's work with a study of three poems dealing with the theme of marriage. These are the two wedding songs, nos. 61 and 62, and the translation of Callimachus' *Coma Berenices*. To these we shall add the epithalamium of Peleus and Thetis which is introduced into no. 64 at lines 323-381. Of these it will be appropriate to examine first the simplest and most compact, no. 62.[2]

This hexameter poem may be termed a "pseudo-epithalamium" in the sense that it was not written with a view to performance at any particular wedding ceremony. But it is not a mere "literary exercise," as it has so often been called. It gives vivid expression to the traditional upper-class Roman idea of matrimony. Formally, no. 62 is an amoebaean singing-contest[3] between two hemichoruses, one of youths and the other of maidens. In this respect it is fundamentally Hellenistic. But a good deal of the imagery, especially the sweet and melancholy flower comparisons with their sentimental anti-male bias, appears to be derived from the epithalamia of Sappho. On the other hand, the trenchant replies of the male hemichorus are anti-Sapphic, patriarchal and Roman. Likewise the image of training vines on trees (vv. 49-55) is based on a custom which, although not unknown in the east, is preeminently Roman or Italian. Roman too is the emphasis in lines 27-30 and climactically in lines 59-65 upon law, justice, tradition and male authority. The absence of the bride from the wedding feast is an additional Roman feature. No. 62 is therefore a complex blending of Greek and Roman elements; it is impossible to regard the poem as a straightforward translation of a Hellenistic original.[4] In essence, it is Sappho Alexandrianized, Romanized and turned inside-out.[5]

Although it is written in dactylic hexameters, no. 62 is supposed to be sung (note *canent*, v. 9) and hence must be regarded as a form of lyric. However, the first person singular is absent. Its place is taken by the first person plural. Obviously the poem is not a monody but a choral lyric. Monody expresses the feelings and attitudes of an individual, whereas choral lyric expresses the point of view of a group, a collectivity.[6] These social attitudes may of course coincide with the attitudes of the author. In the present instance, Catullus undoubtedly has enough human feeling to empathize with the apprehensions and resentments of the maidens, but he sees to it that the youths outargue them. The youths are plainly supposed to be in the right, and the poet agrees with them. He adopts a strict, old-fashioned view of matrimony. This is the reverse of what one might have expected. In his adulterous affair with Lesbia had he not put his love for her before the presumed sanctity of her marriage with Metellus? But in no. 62, he exalts the institution of matrimony and says little about love, limiting himself to one rather cool reference to marital affection in the first half of line 58. Actually there was not much room for sentiment in Roman marriage. According to the traditional view, the purpose of *iustum matrimonium* was not to unite two lovers but to perpetuate the husband's family line. The Roman bride did not choose the man she was to marry. He was chosen for her by her parents, especially her father. Naturally her wishes could be taken into consideration, but the actual contract was arranged and agreed upon by the heads of the two families or sometimes by the bride's father and the bridegroom (as in vv. 27-29). By this contract she passed from her father's control to that of her husband. Although she had little voice in the matter, she was expected to live in harmony and affection with her new spouse. Apparently it was believed that a woman should be able to feel affection for almost anyone of her own station (notice the reference in v. 57 to *par conubium*, "a fitting and proper match"). All that was required was an act of the will on her part, a firm decision to live up to the responsibilities expressed or implied in the contract. The will was the best guarantee of stability. After all, feelings change, and it is impossible to predict how long they will endure. Nothing lasting can be built on them, but the will can and should stand fast. Such is the chilly, hard-headed and highly traditional view of marriage which Catullus upholds and advocates in the present wedding song.

We turn now from these general observations to the specifics of literary technique. An excellent starting point would be to notice that essentially the poem displays two hemichoruses in conflict. Because of the prominence given to the element of conflict we are entitled to regard no. 62 as a *dramatic* choral lyric. Like all dramas it has a plot; in this case a very simple one that reaches a typically comic conclusion when the youths' views on marriage prevail. The maidens are reduced to silence (they fail to respond after v. 58b), and their silence presumably gives consent; they are brought to an acceptance of natural norms. Their

85

"humour" or eccentric attitude is exorcized, and a new harmony is created.[7] Another dramatic feature may be seen in the poet's approach to the hemichoruses. He treats them as collective characters. The young men are eager and confident, identify with the bridegroom; the maidens are negative and fearful, ally themselves with the timid bride. In addition, the young men exhibit a certain *sprezzatura*: they have not bothered to learn their songs (vv. 15-17), but they sing superbly anyhow. Actually, of course, they could not possibly have learnt their parts in advance; according to the rules of the amoebaean contest, they must always speak second, in reply to the maidens. They are supposed to wait and see what the maidens will say and then are to frame an impromptu answer, reversing their opponents' words, parodying their syntactic patterns, reinterpreting their imagery and rebutting them to the best of their ability. The youths therefore have much the harder task techni- cally, for they are obliged to extemporize within very stringent limits. But they have much the easier case, because in defending marriage they are defending an institution which is in accordance with reason, nature, law and immemorial tradition.

How are we to interpret the maidens' resistance to the whole idea of marriage (expressed in vv. 20-25, 32 and a number of lost lines, and 39-48)? Certainly they are not to be regarded as a group of female Prufrocks shrinking from experience out of sheer neurotic hyper- sensitivity. The youths suggest (vv. 36-37) that their complaints may be feigned and are only a ladylike dis- simulation of their real sentiments. Is this the truth? Or is their reluctance a form of flirtation? Do they want to be wooed, persuaded, cajoled into acceptance? In that case their negativity might be in accordance with human nature, or at least girl nature, and not a "humour" or a neurosis. More fundamentally, though, it would seem that the maidens have good reason to show a certain hesitancy. We must not forget the harshness of ancient marrige customs.[8] Traditionally, the bride was required to leave her own family completely, to become in effect the daughter of her husband, to enter a new home with new Lares and Penates, with new *manes* to wor- ship, a new hearth fire to tend, and a new domestic cult to maintain. She was expected to accept complete re- sponsibility for her husband's household as its *domina* or mistress with the power of the keys, and to supervise the *familia* of slaves, sometimes very numerous and hard to control. In addition, we must recall that this trau- matic experience often took place at a very early age. Some brides were not much more than twelve years old.

Hence the maidens' vicarious shrinking from marriage and their identification with the timid bride are natural and predictable, not seriously blameworthy. We can readily understand their childlike attachment to safety and security, their resistance to change and their fear of the unknown. This is the reaction one might expect from a young girl brought up in seclusion, Mediterranean style, and faced with the rigors of Roman marriage.

But even if their attitude is predictable, it is nevertheless carried too far, to the point of seeming sentimental and regressive. The complaint addressed to Hesperus in vv. 20-25 implies that marriage brings cruel pain. It is like being burned with fire (*ignis* v. 20; *ardenti*, v. 23). It means loss and destruction. No affection or love is involved but only a rude humiliation and abasement. A bride's surrender is like the fall of a city: it entails a breaking down of walls, brings about an end of freedom, enslavement in fact, and the permanent loss of friends and home. In brief, marriage amounts to the experience of being completely uprooted and displaced.

Even though the maidens' comparison conveys a valid emotion it is plainly overwrought and their analogy limps. They must be led to a better understanding by the youths. (According to Roman ideas, it is fitting that women should be instructed by men and brought to wisdom by them.) The youths affirm in rebuttal that marriage takes place in a context of ordered social relationships (vv. 26-31). It is not random violence and desecration. It is a contractual agreement between two families, entered upon in accordance with long-standing tradition. It is not a breaking of old ties but a pact or covenant establishing new ones. In fact the boys go so far as to maintain that the hour of marriage is the gods' best gift to the human race.

Likewise at v. 39 ff. the maidens' flower comparison is undeniably beautiful but nonetheless inadequate. They say that a virgin is like a flowering plant in a "garden enclosed." As the enclosure keeps cattle and rude peasants out of the garden, so a young girl is carefully guarded in the seclusion of her father's house, never venturing outside. Her parents and her nanny and the rest of the servants take care of her, as the sun and rain and breezes and fertile earth (all four elements are included) take care of the flowering plant; the enclosing wall recalls the mother's enfolding arms (in vv. 21-22) and even more the wall of the besieged

city (in v. 24). This part of the simile expresses an
adolescent desire to be beautiful, though useless; also
(in vv. 42, 44, 47) a desire to be accepted by one's
peers and, if possible, to queen it over them. That a
carefully nurtured flower should be plucked for casual
enjoyment and after that simply left to fade and die
seems cruelly unjust, altogether unacceptable.

The youths' reply (v. 49 ff.) is tart. A bride is
not a flower but more like a vine which needs to be
raised up, supported and generally taken care of. She
will not be callously mistreated. She will be produc-
tive, not just decorative. Whereas the maidens' comparison had stressed purity and beauty, the youths emphasize fruitfulness. To the maidens, marriage is a
kind of death; to the youths it is fulfillment. The
bride will fulfill herself in motherhood, as the vine
fulfills its nature in producing grapes. And as a
parting shot (v. 58) the youths remind the maidens that
their parents do not wish to be saddled forever with the
expense of maintaining them. Marriage at the right time
is good for all.

This reduces the maidens to silence and presumably
to acquiescence. Or do they break off the amoebaean
contest simply because the bride has arrived for the
deductio? At all events, the last stanza is spoken by
the young men alone, and not to the hemichorus of maidens but to the girl who is about to be married. It
sounds like a kind of charge to the bride. In the
charge we notice a very Roman emphasis on right, justice, authority, tradition and peace. The *virgo* is
called upon to accept the law of man which (as the previous comparisons make plain) is in accordance with the
law of nature. Individualism is firmly rejected here,
and nothing resembling Romantic Love[9] is even remotely
envisaged. Yet there is no hard-heartedness, either;
only a robust realism. In fact, in the reference to the
girls' being outvoted in the family council (vv. 62-65)
there is even a kind of dour humor (perhaps).

*

The longer wedding song, no. 61,[10] is composed in
lyric strophes of four glyconics followed by a pherecratic: this is a light, quick rhythm.[11] It is not a

"pseudoepithalamium." As we learn from lines 16-25 and
82-86, it is written with a specific wedding in mind,
that of the patrician Manlius Torquatus and his high-
born but technically plebeian bride, Junia Aurunculeia.
But the couple, though described in general terms, are
given no individual characterisitics and appear in the
poem simply as the ideal bridegroom and bride. He is
wealthy, distinguished and handsome; she is beautiful as
Venus when she came before her "Phrygian judge" (Paris)
and delicate as the flowering myrtle of Asia (the best
variety). It is generally agreed that the piece was not
intended to be sung on the actual occasion of the wedding but was a kind of literary present sent by the
author to his friend the bridegroom for his private pe-
rusal. In form, no. 61 is neither choric nor dramatic.
There is no *agon* or debate between hemichoruses, no conflict, no case against the institution of marriage. The
sole speaker is the poet himself. He is represented as
taking part in each stage of the festivities, speaking
to the (imaginary) choruses and acting as master of ceremonies. He moves about, directs and comments upon the
events of the evening. Every strophe is addressed to
someone who has an active role to play in the rite: the
god Hymen, the chorus of maidens, the chorus of youths,
the bridegroom's favorite slave, the bridegroom himself,
the bride, the *praetextatus* or young lad who takes the
bride's arm during the procession, the *pronubae* or ma-
trons of honor, and finally, the bridal pair. The poet
invokes, urges, instructs, apostrophizes, guides, en-
joins, commands, prays; but his voice is unindivi-
dualized and virtually choric. All his directions are
traditional and fully expected, and he expresses no
purely personal opinions; occasionally he slips into the
first person plural (vv. 139, 225; cf. *nostra*, v. 94),
identifying with the larger company present. This procedure appears in some of the hymns of Callimachus, but
Wheeler[12] gives good reasons for concluding that it goes
back to Sappho. Actually pre-Sapphic and indeed pre-
historic is the traditional refrain *Hymen Hymenaee* irre-
gularly placed at the ends of fifteen of the forty-
seven strophes.[13] There are also several sub-refrains:
quis huic deo/compararier ausit (thrice); *concubine nuces da*
(twice); *sed abit dies* (four times); *viden ut faces/splendidas
quatiunt comas* (twice); *prodeas nova nupta* (five times). In
form and technique, it seems that Catullus is mostly
following Greek precedent, yet the actual details of the
wedding ceremony are in the main Roman, and the marriage
ideals which the poem supports are Roman as well.

The epithalamium opens with a long hymn to Hymen,
vv. 1-75 (interrupted, however, by a brief aside to the

chorus of maidens in vv. 36-45). This god, who is ordinarily considered the presiding deity of all wedding
ceremonies, is conceived rather differently by Catullus.
He is primarily the divine personification of the
wedding song itself, and only by a kind of synecdoche
is he god of the wedding celebration in its entirety.
Since the epithalamium is a specialized subdivision of
lyric or hymnic poetry, he is called son of the Muse
Urania, lives on Mt. Helicon with his mother, and frequents the caverns and springs which ancient religious
sentiment associated with poetic inspiration.[14] Curiously, he wears the dress of a Roman bride, including
the characteristic flame-colored veil and a wreath of
sweet-smelling marjoram; he has reddish-yellow slippers
on his snow-white feet. Wedding songs are mostly about
brides, and therefore, by the peculiar logic of mythology, Hymen is dressed up to look like his own principal
subject. (The bridegroom is essential but comparatively
uninteresting, and in any event wears no distinctive
attire). Hymen also sings in a high silvery voice,
dances, and swings a lighted pine torch, traditionally
carried in the wedding procession.[15] In these respects
he resembles not the bride but the youthful wedding
guests, the members of the chorus.

Standing before the bride's house, Catullus calls
upon Hymen to wake, dress, come from Helicon, and attend
the wedding of Manlius and Junia. May he come *laetus* (v.
8), singing and dancing, because the happiness of the
marriage depends upon his grace and favor. And that he
may come the more willingly, Catullus proceeds to sing
his praises in vv. 46-75. In these lines, Hymen is conceived less as the personified wedding song, more as the
god of the marriage rite. As such he is the fulfiller
of honorable love, the deity who insures the continuity
of families and gives the state new citizens to guard
its frontiers. He is repeatedly saluted as matchless
and preeminent among all gods: *Quis huic deo compararier
ausit* ? This may seem hyperbolical praise for such a
peculiar little sprite, but when the actual moment of
marriage arrives, who can be more important than he?

After the hymn to Hymen is completed, the bride is
invited to come forth from her father's house and take
her place in the procession to her new home. It is
taken for granted that she is very much in love with
Manlius (vv. 31-35), but at the same time she is also
extremely young,[16] and that is one reason why she is
bashful, timid and in tears (vv. 79-81). In order to
quiet her anxieties and cheer her up, the poet praises
her beauty. Earlier (vv. 17-25) he had compared her to

the goddess Venus and to Venus' favorite plant, the
delicate myrtle; now he declares (vv. 82-86) that no
fairer woman has ever gazed upon the rising sun, and in
another plant simile goes on to equate her with a "hya-
cinth"[17] which stands tall and proud in the garden of
some rich lord (vv. 87-89). At v. 97 ff., still trying
to allay her fears, overcome her shy reluctance and coax
her out of doors, he promises that Manlius will be completely faithful and devoted to her. He will cling to
her as the vine clasps the tree. This reverses the vine
simile of no. 62, 49-58: the vine here represents the
bridegroom and the tree the bride; the notion of fruitfulness disappears. The figure now carries the implication of natural and rooted stability, of lifelong
union. And to clinch his appeal the poet refers openly
to the joys of physical love which the bridegroom is
shortly to enjoy with his bride. No. 61 brings up this
topic more than once and applies it to both partners,
the bride as well as the bridegroom. We recall that in
no. 62 love was hardly mentioned.

Reassured by Catullus' words the bride plucks up
courage and finally appears at v. 115. The chorus of
youths raise their torches in acknowledgement of her
arrival and the procession gets under way. The poet
next turns his attention to the bridegroom. If Junia
was timid and in need of encouragement, Manlius is if
anything too happy and triumphant. The joys that are
in store for him are so intense that he is in danger
of incurring the envy of the gods. The poet therefore,
following the ancient Roman custom, sings the abusive
and ribald "Fescennine verses" of lines 119-143. He
tells Manlius[18] that he will have to give up homosexual
relations with his favorite slave. To the modern
reader these charges may seem highly scurrilous; to the
Romans they were both amusing and prudent. They are of
course entirely baseless and have a merely apotropaic
function; that is, they are intended to diminish
Manlius' felicity a bit and avert the divine resentment
at his surpassing good fortune. Wheeler reminds us
that the traditional abuse of a victorious general in
the triumph-songs sung by his troops had a similar purpose.

In vv. 144-173 we return to the bride. Although
she is spared any Fescennine teasing, she is given a
bit of candid marital advice in vv. 144-146. Catullus
tells her that if she wishes to keep her man from stray-
ing, she must remember never to deny him her embraces.
Having delivered himself of this seriocomic warning, he
resumes a more encouraging tone. He reminds her that

she is soon to become the sole mistress of a great and wealthy house which will be hers until extreme old age. It is clearly assumed that the union of this young couple will be life-long.

Finally at v. 159 the procession arrives at its destination. Junia steps carefully over her new husband's threshold. He waits within, on fire with love for her, as she for him. The *praetextatus* relinquishes her arm, the *pronubae* put her in bed. Catullus pictures her face as alternately pale as a "maiden flower" (*parthenice*, v. 187, probably the white camomile) and red as a poppy. These color changes are a visible and external sign of inward emotional turmoil: fear, shame and desire contend within her heart.[19] Manlius' handsome appearance is alluded to, almost as an afterthought, in vv. 189-192; elsewhere the emphasis falls on his distinguished lineage, his wealth, and his eager but honorable love. Catullus brings the poem to its emotional climax by expressing the hope that the love of the bridal pair will soon bring new life into the world and thus renew the ancient stock of the Manlii Torquati. He imagines their first son--ideally the first of many-- lying in his mother's lap, smiling and holding out his arms to his father. He prays that the child may resemble Torquatus in feature and may inherit the virtuous character of his mother, a Telemachus to Junia's Penelope. With this aspiration the doors of the marriage chamber are discreetly closed by the chorus of maidens and the poem comes to an end.

Which of the two epithalamia is poetically superior? Each has had its champions. The distinguished French Catullus scholar Jean Granarolo has called no. 62 the most successful of Catullus' longer poems.[20] On the other hand the 19th century poet Walter Savage Landor writes of no. 61, "Never was there, and never will there be probably, a nuptial song of equal beauty."[21] Wheeler also preferred no. 61. It is not easy to decide between these two opinions. Virginia Tufte reports[22] that the Renaissance epithalamists imitate the conventions of no. 61 more frequently than those of any other wedding song, but that they do not very often imitate the poem as a whole; the general structure of no. 62 is much frequently followed. This may only indicate that the technique of no. 62 is easier, and in any case Renaissance taste does not necessarily coincide with our own. No. 61 is by far the more comprehensive and detailed poem; it seems to develop a good deal more spontaneously and unpredictably than no. 62. No. 62 is attractive because of its compact unity and systematic antitheses, but it moves in a straight line of development through amoebaean conflict to a foreseen end. Many readers will find no. 62 oppressively didactic; no. 61 proposes a distinctly more genial view of the marriage relation.

*

The third epithalamium forms part of the mythological epyllion, no. 64. It is sung at the wedding feast of the mortal hero Peleus and the sea-goddess Thetis. The song therefore has a specific occasion and is not a pseudo-epithalamium like no. 62. However, the occasion is not historical, as in no. 61, but entirely mythical and imaginary. The poet is no longer a participant, and the guests are exclusively divine, the bridegroom Peleus being the only mortal present. Since the bride Thetis has not yet arrived (v. 329), the song is addressed to Peleus alone (notice the vocatives in vv. 323-4; also *Pelei*, "to Peleus", v. 382). It is sung not by a choric first person singular, as in no. 61, nor by hemichoruses of youths and maidens, as in no. 62, but by the aged Parcae, three palsied beldames who spin woolen threads while they sing. The Parcae are birth-goddesses.[23] They foreordain and determine the course of all human lives; hence their song expresses not merely the good wishes and high hopes which appear in ordinary wedding songs, but that which inevitably must come to pass. It is an oracle (v. 321 and 326), a grim prophecy, a revelation (*pandunt*, v. 325) of futurity, an ambiguous wedding gift of the Parcae to the mortal bridegroom who is privileged to hear it. But it is also an epithalamium and as such exhibits several of the motifs we have already noticed in nos. 61 and 62, especially in the opening and closing stanzas (vv. 323-337 and 372-381).

The Parcae begin by praising Peleus for his good looks (*decus*, 323) and for his heroic achievements that match them. These achievements are unspecified but they must have high social value, for he is called the pillar and bulwark of the country which he rules. Because of them he has won the admiration and esteem of Jupiter, god of kings, and a goddess' hand in marriage. Soon the evening star will unite him with Thetis: making love to her will be a mind-bending experience (*flexanimo*, v. 330). The love the bridal couple will share is going to be absolutely unique, a true union of hearts, an ideal *foedus*. We are inescapably reminded of

that ideal *foedus* which Catullus had once hoped he might
share with Lesbia (no. 109, vs. 6).

The Parcae now turn from the bride and bridegroom
to the son who will shortly be born to them, the hero
Achilles. According to a well-known prophecy, Thetis'
son was destined to be greater than his father. However, he is not destined to be better than Peleus and
he will certainly not be happier. Achilles will be
above all the victorious warrior, so swift of foot that
he will outstrip even the fleet hind (vv. 340-341).
Contrary to what Homer says, he will know no fear (v.
338). He will be exempt from that universal human emotion because of the divine component in his personality,
which will give him total superiority to all his adversaries.

He will display his talents as a warrior on the
bloodsoaked fields of Troy (v. 343ff). There he will
be fighting far from home, not in defense of his own
country, like Peleus. The Trojans never did him any
harm. He will be supporting the cause of Agamemnon,
the "third heir of perjured Pelops," for no discernible
motive other than self-glorification. His heroic
achievements begin to seem not so heroic after all.
They will be purely physical exploits, mere killing, and
no god will lend him assistance. What the Parcae give
him in the epithets "excellent" and "renowned" (v. 348)
they immediately take away in the subsequent image of
weeping mothers beating their breasts at the funerals
of their sons, slain by Achilles. Catullus' sympathy
rests not with the "glorious" killer but with these
women who have lost their beloved children (*gnatorum,* v.
349, is an emotion-laden word), and who lament them the
more inconsolably because they will never have others
to take their place: that is the point of specifying
that their breasts, *pectora,* are flabby, *putrida,* v. 351.

In the epic simile at vv. 353-355 the pathetic
reactions of the bereaved mothers are contrasted with
the impersonal efficiency of the killer at work.
Achilles mows down the helpless Trojans with no more
emotion than a reaper mowing thick grain in the yellow
fields at harvest time. It is no contest. The emphasis
falls partly on the vast numbers of the slain, but more
on the hero's inhuman detachment from their deaths. He
is just not involved. The man who cannot know fear cannot know pity, for the two emotions are necessarily
interdependent. Nor can he know true courage. Certainly this epic comparison does Achilles little honor.

The Parcae go on to predict that he will block the channel of Scamander with the bodies of the slain, so that the river will run warm with gore (357ff.). These hyperboles, coming after the hyperbolic reaper simile, reinforce the impression of Achilles as a wholesale killer shedding blood on a fantastic scale. Moreover since Scamander is divine, the staining of his waters is a sinful desecration, a sacrilege. According to Homer, the river turned on him in anger and almost destroyed him. The Parcae suppress that episode, but presumably the educated reader is supposed to recall the rest of the story.

The climactic witness to his greatness will be the sacrifice of the maiden Polyxena at his tomb. According to the legend, Achilles had fallen in love with her shortly before his death; after Troy fell, his ghost demanded her life as his rightful share of the spoils of victory (*praeda*, 362). His son Neoptolemus slew her at the burial mound. Catullus underscores the bloody violence of this deed (v. 370) but even more the perversion of religion which it entails: Polyxena is treated as if she were no better than an animal victim (v. 369), whereas Achilles is honored as if he were a god. Yet the Parcae apparently admire this brutal and unjust action. The more they extol Achilles' greatness, the more we are made to feel that it would be better if he had never been born, for his heroism consists entirely in creating pathetic and helpless victims. All the same, the barbaric violence of his career, repulsive as it is, is only a foretaste of the further degeneration of mankind which is still to come (cf. the final paragraph of the epyllion, especially vv. 397-408). Catullus could have presented an entirely different and much more appealing picture of Achilles if he had so desired. He could have displayed Achilles resisting the injustice of Agamemnon, Achilles avenging his friend Patroclus at the cost of his own life, Achilles fated to a brilliant but brief existence, and the like; but he deliberately omits the favorable aspects of the hero's personality, presenting him instead as an inhuman killer, a victim-maker, whose useless glory is founded on the misery of others, people who do not count because they are only "the enemy."[24]

In the last two stanzas, the Parcae turn from Achilles' bloody exploits to the bride and bridegroom. In tones of sublime indifference they call upon Peleus and Thetis to join in the love they have longed for and to enter into their happy covenant of union. The prophetic song makes it clear that happiness is brief and fugitive, the perfect moment exceptional and evanescent. Since the moment cannot last, Peleus and Thetis are to enjoy it while they may. But the bliss of their love will only give rise to violence and lamentation. The divine epithalamium of poem no. 64 shows little of the joy and none of the optimism of nos. 61 and 62. As happens so often in classical literature, prophecy brings in the tragic note.

*

To the poems we have been considering so far it is appropriate to add no. 66, Catullus' translation or adaptation of Callimachus' elegy *The Lock of Berenice*, which is probably the version of "Battiades" sent to Hortensius along with no. 65. Although not an epithalamium, this elegy is very definitely concerned with marriage. It tells how Berenice, Queen of Egypt, vowed a lock of her hair to all the gods for the safe return of her newly-wedded husband Ptolemy III from his military campaign in Syria, 246/5 B.C. Her prayer was answered, and after Ptolemy came home Berenice duly offered the lock in a temple at Alexandria. When the lock suddenly and mysteriously disappeared, the court astronomer Conon announced that he had discovered it translated to the sky as a brilliant new constellation, near Virgo, the Bear, Leo and Boötes (Conon's star-cluster is still known as Coma Berenices). Callimachus amplifies and extends Conon's flattery. He declares that Aphrodite Zephyritis[25] commanded the West Wind to bring the lock to her, divinized it and set it among the stars of heaven. The poet personifies the lock as a loyal handmaiden of the Queen and puts the whole elegy into her mouth. He represents her as telling the story of her own translation and proclaiming to her former mistress her undying love and devotion.

Why did Catullus go to the trouble of translating this airy Callimachean court poem? What qualities in it attracted him? Perhaps he was drawn by Callimachus' concentrated brevity, his Alexandrian learning and finesse. He may have hoped to acquire some of the secrets of his poetic technique, and he may have wished to suggest to his fellow-poets at Rome ways in which the best features of Alexandrianism might be brought over into Latin verse. But much more probably it was Callimachus' treatment of the love motif that appealed to him: here

I refer not so much to the love of the Lock for Berenice (vv. 39-76) as the love of Berenice for her husband Ptolemy (vv. 15-38).

There can be no question that the naive little Lock loves Berenice very dearly, but she expresses her emotional attachment in a series of straight-faced comic hyperboles. From the height of heaven she swears that she left the queen's head unwillingly, yielding only to the invincible power of steel; steel mastered even the mighty peak of Athos when Xerxes dug his canal through it, so how could a mere lock of hair resist such a force?[26] Even the glory of living in proximity to the Olympian gods cannot console the Lock for her separation from the head of her beloved Berenice. In fact, if we accept Mynors' text of the closing lines, she actually prays that the stars of her constellation may fall from the sky so that she may return to Alexandria, be reunited with her former lady and satisfy her innate thirst for hair oil. The Lock's love lament is obviously mock pathos, that is to say, pathos playfully exaggerated. It is a comic form of court flattery. But Catullus is too Roman to have much interest in this sort of game. Contemporary Rome had no court, and in any case Catullus was far from possessing the temperament of a courtier; his own invective poems are the best proof of this.

Much more Catullan is the Lock's praise of Berenice's wifely love for Ptolemy. Vv. 25-26 allude to the "courage" with which she had won him: at the age of fifteen she had ordered the assassination of Demetrius, her suitor and Ptolemy's rival for her hand, to punish him for his love affair with her mother. Her grief when she had to part from her young husband the day after their marriage is described in vv. 19-25. Bridelike, Berenice pretended to weep for Ptolemy as a "brother," but actually she was mourning her empty bed; the passage about the false tears of brides who in reality enjoy married love (vv. 21-22) reminds us of the hexameter wedding-song (no. 62, 36-7), and the scene as a whole rather resembles the parting of Protesilaus and Laodamia, no. 68, 79-130, which we shall examine in a later chapter. When Ptolemy leaves for war Berenice weeps, anxiety gnaws at the marrow of her bones, her mind reels, she is bereft of her senses (vv. 23-25); these pathological symptoms are very like those of the Sappho ode, no. 51. Particularly reminiscent of Catullus' epithalamia is the picture of ideal marriage implicit in vv. 79-88.[27] Full-blooded passion is by no means excluded from this picture, but the main emphasis

falls on the sacredness of the tie which binds bridegroom and bride; chastity and faithfulness are the indispensable basis of marital harmony and concord. This
high-minded conception is in all likelihood what appealed most to Catullus in the *Lock of Berenice*, and led
him to translate it with exact and appreciative care.
Hence even though his version of Callimachus' elegy is
not an epithalamium and not an original composition, it
is both legitimate and illuminating to bracket it with
poems 61 and 62 and the song of the Parcae in no. 64.
No. 66 reinforces the poet's idealization of marriage
in the wedding-poems.

*

Catullus praises and glorifies marriage to a
greater extent than any other Latin poet; he has even
been called the greatest epithalamist of the western
world. Yet he is also a self-confessed adulterer. How
are we to explain this discrepancy, resolve the blantant
contradiction? As I see it, there are at least five
ways of dealing with the problem. (1) Perhaps the contradiction ought not to be resolved; it may be that the
poet was simply inconsistent, in one mood attacking in
others what in another mood he permitted himself, and
deliberately steering clear of the life-long commitment
which he sometimes praised. Or (2) perhaps he was simply a hypocrite and wrote the epithalamia as mere literary exercises, following the lead of other New Poets
such as Calvus and Ticidas, and upholding traditional
social conventions because it was customary to take that
approach in choral lyric. More constructively, (3) it
is conceivable that he came to regret his adultery,
changed his mind about it, repented; perhaps he began
as an amoralist and then, on the basis of his experience
with Lesbia, learned to value and appreciate the traditional Roman teaching regarding marriage; in which case
there would be a change and progression in his point of
view, and the wedding songs would represent his matured
opinions on matrimony and adultery. Or (4) it is possible that he regarded his love for Lesbia as privileged,
exceptional; he would not commend adultery on principle
or advocate it for one and all, but her marriage to
Metellus was only a *marriage de convenance*, in fact a marriage in name only, and as such no valid bar to the
claims of true love. Finally (5) it is possible that
he never changed his mind, that he had idealized mar-

riage from the beginning and secretly desired it for himself; that after Metellus' death he asked Lesbia to marry him but that she turned him down, valuing her liberty too much ever to tie herself down with one man.

Any one of these hypotheses may conceivably be correct, but all remain purely speculative. There is no solid, conclusive evidence for or against any of them. Actually the text of the poems supplies no ready solution to the paradox. We can only acknowledge that the contradiction exists and that it is not likely to be dissipated. The judicious reader will accept the fact without vain repining and will be grateful not only for the searingly brilliant poems about his adulterous love for Lesbia but also for the radiant wedding songs which seem to belong to a different world.[28]

CHAPTER SEVEN

The Long Elegy, No. 68

We have already had occasion to discuss (early in
Chapter Five) two passages on the death of Catullus'
brother contained in the long elegy, no. 68. It is now
time to consider this brilliant and difficult poem in
its entirety.

No. 68 appears in the MSS. as a single composition.
Nevertheless Mynors, along with the majority of modern
editors, prints it with a break following line 40 and
another following line 148. The reason for this is that
the style of the central section differs markedly from
that of the prologue and epilogue. Lines 1-40 and 149-
60 constitute an informal versified letter. The recipient is addressed in the second person and the thought
moves from point to point in a logical albeit rather
prosaic progression. But in lines 41-148 the corre-
spondent is referred to in the third person; the tone
is elevated, the structure intricate; the thought de-
velops not in accordance with strict logic but by association of ideas, or one might almost say by surprises.

Despite the lack of stylistic homogeneity many
interpreters have held that the three parts of no. 68
are closely interconnected and in fact form a single
unified whole. They show an undeniable thematic coher-
ence: thoughts of friendship, of hospitality, of gift-
giving and of love pervade all three divisions. The
recurrent key terms, *munus, domus, officium* and *hospes* serve
to bind the sections together.[1] Furthermore, there is
a striking structural similarity between 1-40 and 41-148
in that an extended reference to the brother's death
occurs at the center of each. For these reasons and
others to be mentioned later I shall assume that no. 68,
although divided into three distinct segments, is nevertheless one poem, a unified and consistent whole.

One consideration seems, at first glance, to cast
doubt on this conclusion. There is a certain difficulty
about the name of the recipient. According to Mynors'
text, the first forty lines are addressed to one Manius[2]
(vv. 11, 30), whereas the rest of the poem is concerned
with a friend named Allius[3] (vv. 41, 50, 66, 150). However, a convincing resolution of this (apparent) discrepancy is readily available. Manius is a Roman *praenomen*

101

or first name; Allius is a *nomen gentilicium* or family
name. The full name of Catullus' friend was Manius
Allius. He is called by his first name in the informal
opening letter and by his family name elsewhere.[4]

This friend, presumably in Rome, has written a
"tear-blotched missive" (v. 2) to Catullus, who is now
in Verona. He complains that he has met with a grave
calamity. He is *fortuna casuque oppressus acerbo*, "overwhelmed by ill fortune and bitter disaster" (v. 1). He
is like a man who has suffered shipwreck (v. 3). Venus
allows him no sleep (v. 5). He is forsaken in an unshared bed (v. 6). He feels that he is at death's door
(v. 4). If we take these complaints seriously, then
lines 1-9 must refer to the death of Manius' wife or
some comparable bereavement. But if the language of
these verses is deliberately hyperbolical, then Manius'
tear-blotched complaints could refer to something no
more calamitous than a temporary separation from his
wife (who might be absent on a trip or perhaps slightly
indisposed) or a tiff with his current girl friend.
Line 155 in the third section of the poem provides the
solution to our problem:

sitis felices et tu simul et tua uita

May you be happy, both you and your beloved.

This verse shows that Manius Allius has not lost his
lady permanently and that he may reasonably look forward
to sharing a happy future with her. The tear-blotched
complaints of vv. 1-8 are therefore facetiously exaggerated, and Manius' "poor little letter" to Catullus was
written in a tone of mock lamentation.

Manius asks Catullus to console him in his distress
by sending him two things:[5] *munera...et Musarum...et Veneris*,
"gifts which the Muses and Venus give" (v. 10). This
phrase has been variously interpreted. It might mean
"gifts of poetry and the delights of love,"[6] in which
case the friend would be asking Catullus not only to
send poetry but also to provide him with a mistress.
This crass explanation sorts ill with v. 155, quoted
above. Much to be preferred therefore is the translation "gifts of learned poetry and gifts of (light) love
verse."[7] The friend is asking for new poems, as distinguished from the old (Alexandrian?) which fail to
console (vv. 7-8). No doubt he has in mind poems written by Catullus himself: both original "neoteric" works
based on Hellenistic models and light-hearted verse
about the poet's current(and casual) love affairs.

102

Catullus refuses both of Manius' requests. He does so reluctantly, because he recognizes a special obligation to his friend, in view of his many past kindnesses.[8] However, the fact is that Catullus, too, has been overwhelmed by the waves of misfortune. But whereas Manius' troubles are only minor vexations that are whimsically overstated, Catullus' sufferings are devastatingly serious. He has just lost his brother. He concedes that there was a time in his life when he indulged in recreational love affairs and wrote light verse about his experiences. But now the springtime of his adolescence is past and his happiness is over. The stark reality of bereavement has brought all his youthful frolicking to an end. Manius must not expect *dona beata*, "gifts which only a happy man can give" (v. 14), from one who is now truly *miser*, sunk in utter dejection. The poet simply cannot supply the *munera Veneris*, the light love poems which his friend has requested. Nor can he supply the *munera Musarum*, the "gifts of learned poetry," either. The reason for this is that he does not have adequate source material available; he is now in Verona with a single box of books, having left the rest of his library behind in Rome. Therefore he can send Manius neither light love-verse nor learned poetry. However, Manius is a friend, a very close friend, a guest friend, and Catullus feels that he is especially indebted to him. He must not send him away empty-handed. He forwards to him, in gratitude for his past kindnesses, the best poem he can manage (*quod potui*, v. 149): not light hearted verses, yet verses about love; not learned poetry, but the nearest approximation to it that he can provide under the circumstances. And the poem he sends is of course precisely the poem enclosed by the epistolary portions of the present elegy; that is, no. 68, verses 41-148.

The formal poem, 41-148, refers repeatedly to a woman whom Catullus calls *domina* or *era*, "mistress," *candida diva*, "radiant goddess," and *lux mea*, "the light of my life." It is all but universally conceded[9] that this woman can be none other than Lesbia. But does Lesbia appear at all in the opening epistle? In order to answer this question we must attempt an interpretation of the highly controversial passage vv. 27-30. I quote the lines as printed by Mynors:

> quare, quod scribis Veronae turpe Catullo
> esse, quod hic quisquis de meliore nota
> frigida deserto tepefactet membra cubili,
> id, Mani, non est turpe, magis miserum est.

therefore when you write that it is a shame
for Catullus to be at Verona because here all
the upper-class warm their chilly limbs in
an empty bed, that, Manius, is not cause for
shame; rather, it is a reason to pity me.

The difficulty is the maddeningly imprecise adverb of
place *hic*, in line 28. Does it refer to Rome? On that
assumption, Manius had written that it was a shame for
Catullus to stay in Verona while at Rome all the best
people were warming themselves in the bed he had left
empty, *viz*. Lesbia's bed. The trouble with this explanation is that it represents Manius, who was
Catullus' close and dear friend, as speaking to the poet
in crudely jocular terms about massive infidelity on
Lesbia's part.[10] Hence many scholars (Mynors included)
have held that *hic* refers to Verona. According to this
view, Manius had written that it was a shame for
Catullus to stay in Verona, for Verona is a dull community where young men of the upper class try to keep
their limbs warm in an unshared bed, i.e., must spend
their nights alone. Against this interpretation it is
sometimes objected that there is no evidence to show
that Verona was considered a puritanical or straight-
laced town; but surely it offered fewer opportunities
than Rome, and that was all Manius meant by his little
joke.[11] It is preferable to conclude therefore that *hic*
indeed refers to Verona, and that Lesbia, although she
figures prominently in the formal poem, is not alluded
to in the prefatory epistle.

*

We pass now to an analysis of the formal elegy.
As is well known, this part of the poem exhibits an
elaborate pyramidal structure: we rise through a series
of themes (friendship, Lesbia, Protesilaus and Laodamia,
Troy) to a climactic midpoint, the passage on the
brother's death; we then descend through the same
themes, now in reverse order, to the conclusion. The
pyramid may be diagrammed as follows:[12]

A. *Foedus* of Catullus and Allius: 41-50 (10 vv.)
  B. Torment of Catullus' love: 51-56 (6 vv.):
    C. Two similes, 6 & 4 vv.; *diva* arriving
       (6 vv.): 57-72 (16 vv.)

        D.   Laodamia and Protesilaus: 73-86
           (14 vv.)
          E.   Helen and Troy: 87-90 (4 vv.)
            F.   Brother's death in the
                Troad: 91-100 (10 vv.)
          E^1. Paris and Helen: 101-104 (4 vv.)
        D^1. Laodamia and Protesilaus: 105-118
           (14 vv.)
      C^1. Two similes, 6 & 4 vv.; *diva* arriving
        (6 vv.): 119-134 (16 vv.)
    B^1. Torment of Catullus' love: 135-140 (6 vv.)
  A^1. *Foedus* of Catullus and Lesbia: 141-148 (10 vv.,
  assuming a lacuna of 2 vv.)

In order to make the structure clear to the reader we
shall follow the above diagram section by section as we
analyze the poem.

    A, 41-50. Catullus begins the formal elegy by
informing the Muses of his intention to immortalize the
name of Allius out of gratitude for the kindness he has
shown him. The Muses are brought in partly in order to
establish an elevated tone after the versified prose of
vv. 1-40, and partly in allusion to the fact that his
friend had asked him to provide *munera Musarum*, "the gifts
which the Muses give," v. 10. It is worth noticing that
Catullus' conception of the Muses is somewhat unusual.
In other authors they are a metaphor for the experience
of inspiration or a personification of the literary tradition. Here they seem to stand for technical skill,
acquired expertise, mastery of the traditional literary
methods. Catullus imparts his thoughts to the Muses;
they put them into appropriate form and transmit them to
his readers. It is the form which guarantees that the
poetry will be read by many and remembered for a long
time.

    B, 51-56. Because he has written of it in previous
poems, the Muses already know of the baffled and frustrated love for Lesbia that caused Catullus so much pain
before Allius intervened in his behalf and provided him
with a place to meet her. Two hyperbolical similes
speak of the ardor of his passion: it was like the
ever-active volcano Aetna, the greatest of all known
volcanoes, and it was like the waters of Thermopylae,
the most famous of all hot springs. He then modulates
from the hot waters of the spring to a statement about
his ever-flowing tears. These are tears of pain, an
external manifestation of the *cura*, "torment", one feels
when one is overwhelmed by *duplex Amathusia*, the treacher-

ous goddess of love.

C, 57-72. This section introduces two more similes, that of the mountain stream (vv. 57-62) and that
of the storm at sea (vv. 63-66). The first of these begins as if it were an amplification of what immediately
precedes, namely the image of Catullus' incessant tears
in vv. 55-56. But if we follow Mynors' text, reading
ac at the beginning of v. 63, then the opening *qualis* of
v. 57 is correlative with the *tale* of v. 66, and the
simile refers (surprisingly) not to Catullus' tears but
to Allius' assistance.[13] That assistance, which alleviated his burning pain and delivered him from his sufferings, was like a drink of cold water to a weary traveller trudging along a highway during the dog days.
Most of the topographical details in vv. 57-60 have no
discernible relevance to Catullus' situation, but it is
interesting to note that in these lines we have moved
from an image of hot water welling up (in the Thermopylae simile, v. 54) to an image of cool water flowing
down (in the simile of the mountain stream). The simile of the storm at sea which follows next has the same
function as that of the refreshing stream. It reiter-
ates and intensifies the idea of saving help which is
sent in a time of critical need. Allius' assistance was
like a favorable wind granted by Castor and Pollux to
storm-tossed sailors in answer to their prayers.

In vv. 53-66 we have had four similes in a row. At
line 67 we finally turn from simile to narrative as
Catullus recalls the moment, now long past, when Lesbia,
beautiful and graceful as a *candida diva,* a "radiant goddess," first crossed the threshold of Allius' house. At
that important moment in Catullus' life, when their love
was about to be consummated for the first time, Lesbia
does an unexpected thing. Instead of stepping carefully
over the sill (as a Roman bride would do; cf. no. 61,
159 ff.) she plants her slippered foot upon it and
pauses there. Baker[14] sees this as a gesture of defiance, a deliberate and wanton act which is both an indication of her willful character and an evil omen for
the future of the love affair. Alternatively, Poeschl[15]
interprets the scene as simply a dramatization of
Catullus' eager anticipation; he holds the situation, so
to speak, by taking two whole lines to describe the decisive step. Perhaps this is better, for nowhere else
in the poem is Lesbia deliberately defiant. In the
section which follows Catullus speaks not of any voluntary provocation on her part but of the overmastering
passion which led her to the house of Allius.

D, 73-86. Here Catullus starts up another simile. This one is drawn not from nature but from mythology. Having called Lesbia his *domina*[16] and *diva*, his "lady" and his "goddess," he now proceeds to compare her with a celebrated heroine. Her arrival at Allius' house makes him think of Laodamia arriving *flagrans amore*, "on fire with love" (v. 73), at the house of her promised bridegroom, the Thessalian Protesilaus. He adds that Protesilaus' house was "begun in vain," v. 75; in other words, the hero did not live to finish building it. The reason for his death was that a necessary sacrifice had been omitted, and that omission provoked the anger of the gods. As a result, Protesilaus and Laodamia were prematurely separated. Protesilaus sailed to Troy with the Greek host and was the first warrior to be killed there. Catullus assumes that his readers are familiar with the story, but unfortunately his sources have not survived, and so several important details remain tantalizingly obscure. In particular, we would like to know what kind of sacrifice was omitted and who omitted it and for what reason. But to these questions no secure answers can be given. So far as we can decipher the simile with the defective evidence at our disposal, the main point of comparison seems to be intensity of passion: Lesbia like Laodamia was so deeply in love with her man that she came to him of her own accord. How the omitted rites and the tragic disaster which resulted therefrom apply (if at all) to Catullus and Lesbia remains uncertain.[17]

E, 87-90. Catullus sets the stage for the death of Protesilaus by describing how the Argive heroes gathered in the Troad after the "rape" of Helen. Thinking of the many casualties which were to ensue, he cries out against Troy as the "common grave of Europe and Asia" and "the untimely funeral pyre of brave men and all their valor."

F, 91-100. At this point it begins to appear (surprisingly) that the Laodamia simile applies to Catullus as well as Lesbia; in fact, it is almost more relevant to him than to her.[18] The death of Protesilaus at Troy which ended Laodamia's happiness reminds the poet of his lost brother. That brother died in the same place, robbing him of all his joy. Catullus hates Troy as Laodamia must have hated it. To him as to her Troy is the sinister setting for the untimely death, far from home, of a deeply loved, unique and irreplaceable human being. The details of the lament for his brother, which marks the midpoint and climax of the formal elegy, we have already analyzed in Chapter Five above; they require no further comment here.

E^1, 101-104. In this section we have passed the midpoint and begin to repeat the themes of the first half in reverse order. E^1 takes us back to the Trojan war, referring once again to the gathering of the heroes and the rape of Helen. Catullus' affair with Lesbia resembles the love of Paris and Helen in being adulterous, but the correspondence is not explicitly noted and is probably irrelevant.

D^1, 105-118. After the Trojan inset EFE^1, D^1 marks a return to the Laodamia simile which had got under way in D. Turning to the heroine in direct address the poet exclaims, "That disastrous event"--he means the outbreak of the Trojan War--"robbed you of your mate"--this refers to Protesilaus' death, not merely his departure from Troy--"who was dearer to you than life and soul."[19] Catullus goes on to emphasize the intensity of her love in a bold and highly compressed image (vv. 107-8). It begins easily enough: Laodamia could not live without Protesilaus, for "the floodwaters of love engulfed (her) in a mighty whirlpool." The eddying flood which overwhelmed her and carried her off is an obvious figure of the passion which had seized her much earlier, at or before the time when she came to his house. In the continuation of the image, however, there is a sudden and confusing shift in the time-reference: the floodwaters that engulfed Laodamia "swept her into a deep abyss." It is widely agreed that the abyss connotes unhappiness and distress;[20] the poet is saying that the overwhelming whirlpool of love which had carried her away *before* she came to Protesilaus' house also plunged her into a vast abyss of despair *after* he had left for Troy and *after* she received word that he had been slain.

At this point Catullus begins the first of three sub-similes within the overarching Laodamia comparison: that abyss of misfortune, misery and pain was as deep as the *barathrum* or underground conduit dug by Hercules near Pheneus in Arcadia in order to drain the marshy land in the vicinity. This simile offends the taste of some modern readers; one scholar[21] goes so far as to call it "grotesque." It is true that drainage systems do not strike us as a particularly elevated or "poetic" topic. Granarolo and Quinn[22] understand the passage as a deliberate satire on Alexandrian pedantry, but literary polemic seems out of place in the present context. Perhaps Catullus is trying to gratify Allius' taste for mythological complexities. At all events, the basic thrust of the passage is clear enough: the Hercules narrative is included in order to magnify the *barathrum*. The poet wishes us to picture the most enormous *barathrum* imaginable, the one that is supposed to have been constructed by the greatest of all heroes: as deep as that *barathrum* was the despair of the bereaved Laodamia.

But by the time Catullus emerges from the Hercules simile at v. 117 we discover to our astonishment that he has decided to alter the bearing of his image. Now the *barathrum* no longer refers to Laodamia's despair; instead it applies to the depth of her love, that love which "taught her though untamed to bear the yoke" (v. 118), i.e., compelled her to give herself to Protesilaus before their marriage had been formally solemnized. So in the end the *barathrum* means essentially the same thing as the *aestus* and *vertex* of vv. 107-8 and all three images relate to the vehemence of Laodamia's passion.

C^1, 119-134, closely reproduces the structure of the corresponding section C, lines 57-72. Again we have two similes, the first six lines long and the second four lines, followed by another six-line description of Lesbia's arrival at the house of Allius. The two similes emphasize first the devotion and then the desire which Laodamia felt for Protesilaus during the brief time they spent together. In tender affection her love exceeded that of an aged grandfather for his late-born heir, the son of an only daughter; in joyful and shameless ardor it exceeded the eager passion of a she-dove, who cannot "kiss" her mate often enough. Thus Laodamia's love for Protesilaus is a combination of the same two elements that Catullus elsewhere sees in his love for Lesbia. Those two elements are tender affection or *bene velle* (recall no. 75, 3 and 72, 8), imaged in no. 72, 4 by the love of a father for his sons and sons-in-law; and insatiable passion, exemplified in the *basia* poems, nos. 5 and 7. Once again we see that the Laodamia simile, which ostensibly applies to Lesbia, has an even greater applicability to Catullus himself.

Finally at line 131 we emerge from the enormous Laodamia comparison. Catullus returns to the point he had left at line 72, the arrival of Lesbia at Allius' house. He says that when Lesbia crossed that threshold and came to his embrace, her passion equalled or almost equalled[23] that of Laodamia. At that time she was attended, in the poet's imagination, by the god Cupid, dressed in a saffron tunic and hovering about her head. The presence of this imaginary Cupid seems to make Lesbia into a second Venus.[24] Some have seen the

saffron tunic as a deliberate allusion to Hymenaeus,
who in no. 61, 8-10 appears clad in reddish-yellow slippers and the flame-colored veil of a Roman bride; the
saffron tunic would therefore hint that the meeting at
Allius' house was, in Catullus' mind at least, a virtual
marriage.[25] But this interpretation places upon the
adjective *crocina*, "saffron," a weight of meaning which
it probably cannot bear. It should be remembered that
for our author Hymenaeus is not a god of marriage *tout
court* but principally a divine personification of the
marriage song, and we can be certain that no choral epithalamium was sung that night at Allius' house. It may
be safely concluded that the saffron tunic is a picturesque detail with no particular figurative significance.
Lines 133-134 mean that Lesbia seemed to Catullus to be
as beautiful as Venus and the sight of her filled him
with irresistible desire.

B^1, 135-140. Here we move ahead in time from the
first assignation of Catullus and Lesbia to the dis-
couraging present. The ecstasy of that *mira nox* (v.
145), the "wondrous night" at the house of Allius, is
now long past, and the poet is obliged to admit that
Lesbia's current behavior at Rome is far different from
that of a faithful and devoted Laodamia. Lesbia is not
satisfied with a man like Catullus and there is no reason to expect that she should be;[26] she has to cheat
once in a while, requires plurality. Looking to the
future, the poet says he will put up with her infidelity
because (or provided that?) she is discreet and her
lapses are only occasional. He will not react like a
jealous fool lacking in *savoir faire*. Naturally he is
annoyed by her independence, but he will try not to show
it. He will model his response on that of the goddess
Juno: Juno is angered by Jupiter's numerous escapades,
but she chokes back her resentment in order to avoid a
final showdown. If Juno restrains her wrath even though
she is a goddess, even though Jupiter's infidelities are
many, and even though he is her wedded husband; shall
Catullus, who is only a mere mortal, upbraid Lesbia,
whose offenses are few (he hopes), and to whom, after
all, he is not legally married?

A^1, 141-148. In point of fact (he continues, in
the final section) she was married to someone else when
they first met, and when she gave herself to him at
Allius' house she was cheating Metellus. He admits that
he has no binding claim upon her at all. In lines 147-8
he says he will be satisfied if she considers him her
favorite lover. He hopes she will prefer him to the
others and will count the days she spends with him

as her red-letter days. More than this he has no right
to expect. As he had said earlier, she is *era*, "the mistress" (v. 136), and he is only her servant. In no
other passage does Catullus take so meek and submissive
a view of Lesbia's misconduct as he does here. Can it
be that out of gratitude to Allius he is summoning up a
more than usual forbearance? This is possible. It is
more likely that he is as yet unaware of the full extent
of her depravity. At this stage, things are beginning
to go badly between them, but Catullus still very much
wants the affair to continue. Although he is definitely
disillusioned he still has not plumbed the depths of
loathing and despair. Quinn[27] would date no. 68 to a
period well before the trip to Bithynia.

*

The formal elegy ends at v. 148 and Catullus returns in the last dozen lines of the poem to the epistolary style of vv. 1-40. Allius, who was referred to
only in the third person in the formal elegy, is again
addressed in the second person. Catullus tells him that
the present poem is a gift given in return for his many
kindnesses. It is not exactly the gift Allius asked
for, but it is the best the poet can provide under the
circumstances, and he hopes that it will confer immortality upon his friend's name. He also prophesies that
the gods will shower all manner of gifts upon him here
and now, in his own lifetime; gifts such as Themis, goddess of Justice, conferred upon the men of the Golden
Age. It is implied that Allius is the antithesis of the
hard-hearted egocentrics of contemporary Rome about whom
Catullus so often complains in the shorter poems.
Allius is a survivor of a better world, a leftover from
an unfallen society of perfect innocence and kindness.

The poem ends with a series of benedictions.
Catullus wishes happiness for Allius and his lady, and
for someone else whose identity is hidden by the textual
corruption in lines 156-157. Above all others he
blesses Lesbia. He calls her the light of his life and
says he loves her more than he loves himself; as long
as she lives, life is sweet for him. This is a surprising conclusion. It contradicts the central and
climactic statements both of the epistolary introduction
and of the formal elegy; twice he had said (vv. 23 and

95) that his brother's death took away all his joy. He
had also said (v. 93) that it deprived his life of all
light. Now he takes back these statements. Lesbia's
flawed and half-lost love is light enough for him. It
makes life sweet. It enables him to transcend even the
loss of his irreplaceable brother.[28]

*

No. 68 is a boldly experimental poem, verging on
the bizarre. Among Catullus' most daring and most
questionable innovations is his handling of simile. In
the formal elegy, sixty-two lines out of one hundred
and eight are taken up by comparisons. The Laodamia
simile alone comprises forty-eight verses and is surely
the longest in Latin literature; it even incorporates
three sub-similes. The disproportion is obvious.
Catullus has reversed the ordinary practise of the epic
poets. In epic, narrative and speech predominate; similes are widely spaced, as a rule, and are kept comparatively brief. In the formal elegy, simile takes precedence over narrative, which is rather sketchy and has
to be eked out by the reader's imagination.

The vast Laodamia comparison is exceptional in
another way: it is constructed in the "modern," i.e.,
neoteric, manner. In an ordinary epic simile as seen in
Homer or Virgil it is the narrative which is mythological, whereas the simile is as a rule non-mythological.
Its subject matter is derived from ordinary day-to-day
experience, and it is written in the present tense, the
tense of recurrent and customary action. In the
Laodamia simile, all this is reversed. The narrative
of Catullus' meeting with Lesbia is non-mythological,
and the simile speaks of a celebrated heroine; necessarily, therefore, the passage is written in the past
tense rather than the present. It refers to an experience which was unique and extraordinary, as the meeting
of Catullus and Lesbia was extraordinary: they spent a
mira nox together (v. 145), a wondrous night. Some have
doubted the authenticity of the reading *mira* on the
ground that it sounds too modern and "romantic," but
such criticism is beside the point. The poet means that
the night spent at Allius' house was unmatched for its
joy and sweetness. The Laodamia simile expresses the
same basic idea.

112

This simile also is unusual in its ambiguity. Does it apply to Lesbia or to Catullus or to both of them? Beyond any doubt it applies to both. Explicitly, it refers to Lesbia, both as she really was (beautiful and passionate) and as Catullus wishes she were (totally devoted and totally faithful). Implicitly it refers to Catullus, who was robbed of his brother at Troy as Laodamia was robbed of Protesilaus at the same place; moreover, her love, like his, combined *bene velle* with passion. He identifies with her to such an extent that he calls out to her in the vocative (v. 105) and writes eight lines of the comparison in the second person singular. But whether the resultant gain in complexity and rich suggestiveness compensates for the loss of firmness and lucidity is an open question.

With respect to the artistic merits of no. 68 the critics are far from unanimity. To Georg Luck[29] it is "one of the most beautiful poems ever written in Latin." On the other hand, Tenney Frank[30] wrote that "the subject matter needs a psychopath rather than a literary critic for its successful interpretation." Both exaggerate. Although Luck is obviously closer to the truth than Frank, no. 68 is not an unqualified success. If we believe with Booth[31] that great literature is characterized by "complexity with clarity," then the long elegy clearly falls short of the highest excellence. The complexity is there in full measure; but no other poem of Catullus pays so heavy a price in obscurity.

*

Whether or not no. 68 succeeds as a poem, there can be no doubt of its historic importance. It is the earliest surviving example of "subjective" love elegy.[32] So far as available evidence indicates, here for the first time an elegiac poet has dealt with his own love experience in a fully developed meditative poem. The surviving love poetry of the Alexandrian Greeks is not like this. It is limited to (1) epigrams, mainly in elegiac verse, in which the author deals briefly with his own love encounters; and (2) narrative elegy in which the author tells love stories taken from mythology. No. 68 combines the subjectivity of Hellenistic epigram with the mythology of Hellenistic elegy. Catullus relates particular events in his own life to

the experiences of heroes and heroines of the remote
past. The story of Laodamia's doomed passion becomes a
paradigm for his own love for Lesbia and for his lost
brother. This blending of myth with autobiography, or
what purports to be autobiography, foreshadows Augustan
love elegy. The technique is common in Propertius and
in Ovid's *Amores*, and it is not unknown to Tibullus.

No. 68 also anticipates the Augustans in striking
the note of elegiac frustration, especially in lines
135-148. Catullus recognizes and accepts the infidelities of Lesbia. He cannot do otherwise, for she is his
superior, his *era* or *domina*, and he is her servant; the
relationship is presented as a *servitium amoris*. The basic
idea of love as an enslavement is nothing new; it goes
back to Plato and Euripides. One Alexandrian poem seems
to give it more precise definition, introducing the male
partner as an enslaver and the female as the enslaved.[33]
Catullus' innovation lay in reversing the terms of this
equation. It took courage and originality[34] on his part
to make the transformation, but once made it became a
staple of Augustan elegy and from there passed on to the
literature of medieval and modern Europe.

An intensification of the idea that the woman is
domina and the lover her servant is to envisage her as a
goddess[35] in beauty or power, dispensing bliss or suffering to her lover/worshipper. This form of exaltation
of the beloved is not original with Catullus, but it is
very prominent in no. 68, and it is in large measure
from this source that it comes to pervade Augustan elegy
and to enjoy a long subsequent history.

There is therefore good reason to agree with
Wheeler[36] when he writes that in no. 68 Catullus is "a
real pioneer...laying the foundations and in many ways
clearly indicating the lines which (the Augustan elegists) were to follow." Wilkinson[37] puts the case even
more strongly: "His passion for Lesbia was so overmastering that the lyric poet in him made elegy, hereto-
fore mainly objective, as subjective as lyric monody:
his strong passions broke through the conventions.
After nos. 68 and 76 there is nothing surprising in the
development of Latin love elegy." But to go beyond
Wilkinson and call Catullus the actual founder of the
new genre would be a mistake. Although no. 68 widens
the scope of elegiac poetry, it remains a unique and
extraordinary poem, and nothing quite like it was ever
written again. The idea of enclosing a personal love
poem within a versified letter, the linking of apparently free development by association of ideas with a

114

strict and elaborate pyramidal structure, the insertion
of a dirge into a personal love poem: this combination
of unusual elements, together with the profusion of
lengthy and sometimes ambiguous similes, was to find no
imitators in the Augustan age.   In the last analysis,
no. 68 is an isolated experiment, daring but only partially successful.   Luck and Butler/Barber[38] are right
in warning us not to exaggerate the influence of no. 68
on subsequent writers.   It is correct to say that
Catullus anticipates some of the directions elegy was to
take in the following generations.   But we need a literary link between no. 68 and a work such as the
Monobiblos of Propertius.   The most likely connection[39]
is provided by Cornelius Gallus.   Gallus' poems to his
mistress Cytheris have not come down to us, but subsequent Roman writers regarded him and not Catullus as the
founder of Augustan love elegy.   From that traditional
judgment we need not dissent.

CHAPTER EIGHT

Catullus and the Gods

Classical poetry appears to have originated in liturgical song, hymns, oracles and the like; and it remained true to its origins throughout its long history. From beginning to end, it is closely connected with religion, even when (as in the case of Lucretius' great poem *de Rerum Natura*) it is written in professed opposition to the cults of the city-state. To this broad generalization the writings of Catullus are certainly no exception. Although some of his shorter pieces (invectives, love lyrics, and poems to friends) seem to be "secularized" in the sense that the subject matter is non-mythological and the gods are not mentioned, Catullus' work as a whole has distinctly religious coloration; and three of his poems, nos. 76, 63 and 34, concentrate on the gods in a particularly explicit and emphatic way. In this chapter I propose to analyze the theology of these three poems in some detail.

We have already discussed no. 76 in connection with the Lesbia affair (Chapter Three). This is the poem of self-address in which he speaks of his love as a painful sickness and prays to be delivered from it. Here Catullus adopts a moderately hopeful view of the gods. He does not doubt that they are on the side of virtue and justice. He believes that they define virtue and justice as a traditional Roman would define them. In particular, they uphold the sanctity of good faith (*sancta fides*, v. 3) and the fulfillment of obligations and promises (*pietas*, v. 26, cf. v. 2). Furthermore, they are of one mind with respect to these virtues; no dissension or difference of opinion divides them. Finally, it is not in accordance with their will that the innocent should suffer; Catullus who has lived *puriter*, free from all treachery, perjury and deceit (v. 19), suffers *dis invitis*, "against the will of the gods," (v. 12). What then is the source of the suffering of the just? Since it strikes against the gods' will, they must be less than omnipotent. The *longus amor* (v. 13) which brings anguish to the blameless Catullus cannot come from them.[1] Nor does it come from any special weakness and susceptibility in the sufferer, or from other human beings. Its sources are in fact mysterious and its onslaught arbitrary and unpredictable. That is one reason why Catullus, following a long literary tradition, compares it to a disease.[2] Man is unaccountably vulnerable to, subject to, this painful, dangerous and disfiguring malady. Even the benevolent gods cannot prevent it from striking us. But when it has struck the innocent, they feel pity. Catullus does not doubt that pity. In v. 17 when he writes

> o di, si vestrumst misereri,

si, "if," introduces a real condition. It means not "if it is yours to feel pity, and it probably isn't" nor "if, as they say, it is yours to feel pity, but I am not wholly convinced of it," but "if it is yours to feel pity, as it certainly must be." As Fordyce suggests, *si* in this context is practically equivalent to "since" or "because," as also in lines 1 and 19. Pity for the man who is suffering unjustly is an essential attribute of the gods, and those whom they pity they help. In his extremity the poet prays that the gods may heal him and restore his peace. Or rather he demands it as his right:

> o di, reddite mi hoc pro pietate mea.

> O gods, grant me this in return for my *pietas*.

In this line we see something of the *quid pro quo* attitude characteristic of traditional Roman religion. Since Catullus has kept his part of the contract, the gods are duty-bound to make a just return. The converse of this, namely that they punish those who are false to their oaths, appears in no. 30, 11-12 and in 64, 188-201, but is absent here.

*

No. 63, the so-called *Attis*, is in many ways the opposite of no. 76. No. 76 envisages the gods, considered collectively and anonymously (*di*, vv. 12, 17, 26), as basically just and benevolent, though limited in power. No. 63 presents one of them, the Great Mother Cybele,[3] worshipped on Mt. Ida, as wholly evil. As we have already suggested (in Chapter Five), it is possible that this poem was first conceived during the visit to his brother's grave in the Troad.[4] But he must have heard the music of the goddess long before his journey east. Cybele had a temple on the Palatine very close to Lesbia's house, and it was no doubt there, in the heart of Rome, that Catullus first became acquainted with the Mother's cults and rites and first saw her strange, emasculated dancing-priests.

Cybele was the divine Mistress of wild Nature, worshipped especially upon mountains and attended by lions and other formidable beasts. In addition, she was a goddess of fertility and as such capable of conferring immortal life upon her devotees. Ecstatic states were a prominent feature of her cult, the sacred dance a powerful support to ecstasy, and sexual mutilation[5] a mark of her priesthood. She was officially brought from Asia Minor to Rome during the Second Punic War; a remote ancestress of Lesbia, the Vestal Virgin Claudia Quinta, had miraculously freed the goddess' barge when it got stuck on a sand-bar in the Tiber. (She towed it out with her girdle.) In time, the emotionalism and violence of the cult proved offensive to the sensibilities of the Roman Senate, and during Catullus' lifetime she was strictly confined to her temple on the Palatine, except for an annual festival, the Megalesia, and occasional processions in the streets. Romans were forbidden to become initiates and her priesthood was limited to orientals. The attitude of Roman ruling circles toward the Mother was, therefore, decidedly ambiguous; though her divinity was not denied nor her rites abolished she was mistrusted and feared and was given only a grudging welcome in the capital.

No. 63 is a narrative poem of moderate compass and as such it is commonly referred to as an epyllion or miniature epic. However, the term is likely to mislead the unwary and should be avoided in this connection. No. 63 is not at all like epic. The plot is not derived from myth or legend; the events narrated did not take place in the remote mythical past. The central character, Attis, is a man of the (Hellenistic) present. He is in no sense of the word a hero; he is far too passive to qualify for that exalted status. We must think of him rather as a victim of the goddess' cruelty, one not to be admired but pitied. Attis in short is *miser*, vv. 51 and 61, another Catullan pathos-figure.

Also distinctly non-epic is the versification. Instead of the massive hexameter, Catullus here employs the exotic galliambic. Galliambic means "iambics" of the Galli, i.e., iambics of the priests or devotees of Cybele. This is, therefore, a sacral metre, a liturgical metre; and there is a certain fundamental irony in the author's choice of this verse-form for a poem which, far from glorifying Cybele, rather unmasks the horror of her cult. The basic pattern of the galliambic is

$$\smallsmile\smallsmile \;-\; \smallsmile \;-\; \smallsmile \;-\; -\;\Big|\;\smallsmile\smallsmile \;-\; \smallsmile\smallsmile\;\smallsmile\smallsmile\; \mathbf{X}$$

There is disagreement about how the closing phrases should be treated,[6] but this much is abundantly clear: with its many short syllables and swift syncopated movement, the galliambic line creates a rhythm that is strangely oriental and utterly un-Roman. Read aloud in the Latin it at first delights, then hypnotizes, then gradually repels; in the end the reader longs to be set free from its tyrannical beat. No. 63 offers a spectacular example of how metre can support the theme of a poem and actually become part of its meaning.

The central figure is a young Greek who has undergone a radical conversion to Cybele worship, as a result of which he has exiled himself from his homeland and has crossed perilous seas to the foot of Mt. Ida in the Troad with a company of like-minded friends. At the start of the poem he has already taken the sacred name of Attis, the resurrection god who is Cybele's divine consort; he already possesses the sacred instruments of music; he already knows how to dance the sacred dance; he already is in the grip of the sacred madness; and he already possesses the archaic flint knife which will be the instrument of his complete capitulation to the goddess' power. He perpetrates upon himself the awful rite of self-castration, and then, accompanied by his fellows, dances to the summit of Mt. Ida in wild ecstasy. Catullus supplies double motivation for this violent act; at the human level, Attis is driven by a "hatred of Venus exceeding great" (v. 17: the reason for this hatred is not given[7]); at the divine level, he is goaded by a raving madness (v. 4, 31, 38, 44, 57). In the light of vv. 91-3 and 78-80 it can hardly be doubted that this madness is a divine visitation sent by Cybele upon one whom she has arbitrarily chosen to be her own for the rest of his life.

To the rites of the city-states one was admitted by birth and citizenship. But the religion of the Great Mother was a mystery-cult: the only way to enter it was by initiation. Attis' final initiation is by self-castration with the archaic flint knife, followed by a mad dance to the peak of the sacred mountain (in many ways comparable to the Dionysiac *oreibasia*).[8] Catullus calls the tambourine or bongo drum which accompanies this dance the *initia* of Cybele (v. 9), i.e., the musical instrument by which the initiation is completed. The ineffable revelation of what Cybele means is communicated not in words but through the kinesthetic experience of the dance. As is well known, the choral dance is also a way of losing consciousness of oneself as a separate and distinct individual.[9] By yielding to the sacral rhythm, the followers of Cybele forget their personal identities, rid themselves of the pain of isolated heterogeneity. They submerge their self-awareness in the collective personality of the enraptured chorus, and the chorus in turn escapes into deindividualized oneness with the goddess. The music takes over and they seem to share in her divine life forever.[10] That, at any rate, is the kind of ecstasy that the initiates must have hoped for.

But the preliminary price exacted by the goddess in exchange for this frail hope is high indeed. Catullus emphasizes the physical cost by repeatedly referring to Attis (from line 8 onward) in the feminine gender.[11] This is partly in allusion to the fact that after their emasculation the priests of Cybele wore women's clothing and ornaments for the rest of their lives.[12] Yet it is obvious that castration does not turn a male into a female. No matter how he may dress, after the act Attis is at most a *notha mulier*, a "counterfeit woman," v. 27. That must be part of the meaning of the shift in gender, but it is not the whole of it. In Catullus' imagination Attis is not only a counterfeit woman but also metaphorically female. In a context such as this, femininity connotes incompleteness. Attis has suffered a radical loss; he is now broken and bereft, a mere fragment of his former self (note *mei pars*, "only a piece of what I was," v. 69). The physical cost of initiation is partial suicide.

To return to the narrative: after his ghastly self-mutilation with the sharp flint knife, Attis goes white and cold with loss of blood and surgical shock. Fasting[13] and still bleeding, he addresses the Gallae in joyful song. He is clearly mad. He urges them to dance with him to the summit of Ida. He glories in the fact that Cybele is their *domina* and *era* and they are her slaves. Worse than that, he even rejoices that they are *pecora*, wandering "cattle" of the goddess. He congratulates them upon their self-imposed exile from their homeland and praises them for bravely enduring the hardships of the long voyage from Greece. He is glad that they have escaped the tyranny of Venus by emasculation. He calls upon them to delight the Mother's heart in the mazy movements of their dance. In a great climax of emotion marked by excited anaphora (*ubi* is repeated six times in five lines) he eagerly and confidently looks forward to joining a non-existent throng of ecstatic worshippers on the mountain peak. This strange and disquieting song dramatizes and unmasks Cybelean madness, the victims of which perversely exult in degradation and loss of freedom. For the deluded Attis we are expected to feel not only a kind of fascinated disgust but also, since his insanity is not after all of his own choosing, compassion as well. At the same time we fear the goddess who can so radically twist and distort the mind of man.

After they have arrived at the summit of Ida the ordeal is over. Exhausted by their extravagant outpouring of physical and emotional energy they drop down and sleep a sleep that is like a coma. The following morning Attis awakens with his sanity temporarily restored. The sun rises and the god of sleep departs to rejoin his consort Pasithea. Both details are meaningful and call for comment. The sunrise (vv. 39-41) serves as a dramatic symbol of *anagnorisis*, the moment of tragic realization.[14] As sunrise brings light to a darkened world, so the awakening of Attis to sanity brings illumination to his mind. With awful clarity he sees the full extent of his loss (v. 46); by his own irreversible act he has died to his own humanity, has renounced his former selfhood and identity forever.

The departure of Somnus, the god of sleep, vv. 42-43, is no less significant that the pitiless sunrise which accompanies it. In classical love poetry dawn is ordinarily a time of sadness, because it is at dawn that lovers part. Ovid's aubade, *Amores* I, xiii, containing the well-known phrase *lente, currite Noctis equi* (v. 40), is a good example of this motif.[15] Catullus goes out of his way to reverse the normal situation. Somnus works at night, so for him and Pasithea sunrise is the time for happy and loving reunions. In line 42 Somnus hurries eagerly back to her; in line 43 she welcomes him with fluttering heart. The poet reminds us that Venus is not always hateful, even though Attis found her so (v. 17). The meeting of the divine lovers in reciprocal joy is brought in solely for the sake of the contrast with Attis' waking to remorseful awareness of all that he has lost.

The distracted young devotee runs down the mountain to the seashore and gazes out over the appalling waste of waters with tears in his eyes. Once again the setting is significant. The uncrossable sea is a token of the irreversibility of Attis' surrender to the goddess. This sea is henceforth a barrier separating him from

his past, a great gulf fixed between two antithetical
ways of life--life on Cybele's holy mountain and that
life in the Greek city-state which he had radically
repudated when he traversed the "deep waters" (v. 1)
separating Europe from Asia.

Attis' soliloquy by the seaside marks the high
point of the poem. This lamentation is in many ways the
antithesis[16] of the joyous song to the Gallae in vv. 12-
26. That strange song had presented Attis as the mad,
deluded leader (v. 15) of Cybele's *thiasos*, confidently
exhorting his followers to dance in the goddess' honor,
blindly exulting in his own subjugation and brutaliza-
tion. As leader, he had issued orders, given directions; imperatives abound.[17] In the lament by the seaside, on the other hand, he is no longer a leader but
the pathetic victim of the goddess' cruelty and his own
fanaticism. No longer does he glory in his degradation
and loss of freedom; no longer does he give commands.
The lament is written not in the second person plural
but in the first person singular. There are no fewer
than fifteen occurrences of the emphatic *ego* in this
speech. Also the characteristically Catullan adjective
miser appears (vv. 51, 61; cf. 49), evoking pity for sufferings which are largely undeserved. The soliloquy
may, therefore, be regarded as a kind of lyrical inset
in the narrative. Catullus is fundamentally a lyric
poet. At the climax of the Attis poem, i.e., at the
moment of maximum emotional intensity, he instinctively
turns to the genre in which he excels, namely lyric, and
to the typically lyrical theme of *amechania*, helplessness.[18] For all of Attis' lamentations are in vain. It
is useless for him to apostrophize his native land,
which cannot hear; useless to conjure up his lost past;
useless to pile up rhetorical questions; useless to
commiserate with his own poor suffering heart.

The soliloquy is addressed partly to his lost home
(vv. 50-60), partly to himself (vv. 61-73). One notices that Cybele is not invoked and that Attis nowhere
begs the goddess for pity or release. It is as if he
knows in advance that she will grant neither, that he is
enjoying only a temporary respite (v. 57) from the madness she has visited upon him, that she is utterly without love or mercy. The Great Mother of the Gods is not
very motherly. Other poets such as Virgil or Lucretius
emphasize Cybele's maternal protectiveness.[19] But to
Catullus the *Magna Mater* is a *schreckliche Mutter;* in this
poem the proudest of her titles, *mater*, is used only
once, and there without emphasis (v. 9). At v. 50 Attis
realizes, too late, that it was not Cybele but the city-

123

state that was his true mother all along. Even though
his decision to follow Cybele had been largely involun-
tary, he reproaches himself for being a runaway. He ran
out on the city-state that had given him life. He did
not honor his obligation to his native land, he broke
all the bonds. Henceforth he is destitute of citizenship, of family, friends and possessions, of sanity and
will and all else that goes to make up a human identity.
He will be subject to the goddess and a member of her
mindless *thiasos* all the days of his life.

Not only has Attis lost the sanity of his mind; he
has also destroyed the strong, disciplined, athletic
body he one had. Euripides in the *Bacchae* establishes a
contrast between wrestling, which is regarded as western, masculine, competitive and egocentric; and dancing,
which is eastern, feminine, cooperative and self-
forgetful.[20] A similar contrast is latent in Attis'
soliloquy. Once he was not a mad dancer but a champion
wrestler (v. 64). He was admired and lionized by all.
His house was hung with garlands in honor of his athletic victories (v. 66). But now he is a counterfeit woman living in a female-dominated world. It is interesting to note that Catullus presents the public society
of the city-state as exclusively and ideally masculine;
in contrast, the world of the Asiatic goddess is a dis-
torted matriarchy in which the cruel Cybele exercises
despotic sway over her helpless eunuch-slaves.

Cybele's response to Attis' vain complaint is to
send one of her lions after her reluctant worshipper.
The lion is a sort of extension of Cybele's power and
an expression of its nature; the savage cruelty of the
powerful beast corresponds with the savage cruelty of
the unmotherly mother who will tolerate no disobedience
or insubordination on the part of her servants. If
Cybele has such power over the mighty lion, Attis and
the rest of the poor "cattle" with him have no chance
ever to escape her domination. Attis is immediately
driven back into his madness, back into the wild forests
of Ida forever (vv. 89-90), or rather, until the end of
his days; v. 90, the last line of the narrative, makes
it clear that Attis, whether he sought it or not, never
obtained the gift of everlasting life, which according
to other documents is the great blessing Cybele confers
on her faithful worshippers. The Dionysian pines and
ivy, evergreen amid the snow, which betoken immortality
in other contexts[21] hold out only a false and delusive
promise in this poem. According to Catullus, Cybele
takes everything, gives nothing in return. His picture

of her cult is entirely negative. Anything which might speak in her favor is ignored or denied, and conversely whatever is opposed to her is affirmed and exalted. No. 63 is an oblique celebration of the value system of the Greco-Roman city-state.

Catullus ends his poem by making what seems to be a personal application (vv. 91-93). As if waking from a nightmare or stepping back in horror from the brink of an abyss he prays that the goddess may drive others mad but spare him. Expanded somewhat these apparently self-centered lines mean, "I know that you are a divinity and a powerful one, and that as such you must have your human devotees and servants. I, therefore, do not pray that you may lose your power: that is impossible. Rather, I acknowledge your divinity and only ask that you will not choose me or any member of my family to be yours forever."

Some scholars deny that the first person singular in this closing prayer refers to Catullus at all. They hold that no. 63 is a translation of a (lost) Hellenistic original, and that the last three lines are merely a formula of leave-taking such as is found at the end of many Greek hymns; they express the sentiments of a typical worshipper.[22] But this interpretation is unpersuasive. The final verses of no. 63 hardly express the sentiments of a worshipper, typical or otherwise, and the poem as a whole is in no sense of the word a hymn. Furthermore, the theory of a Greek model is unprovable. It has been losing ground in recent years; nowadays it is a minority opinion. There is no real reason to doubt that in lines 91-93 Catullus is expressing his own reaction to the story of Attis.

Others see the poem as an original composition which symbolizes Catullus' involvement with Lesbia.[23] According to this hypothesis, Catullus, like Attis, was once a happy and uncomplicated youth, but he has been seized by the madness of passionate love which has enslaved him. He is dominated by a "female demon" who takes away his manhood[24] and destroys him, yet keeps him alive to demonstrate her power, so that (in one version of the theory) the future holds out only "a succession of orgies, joyless fits of insane excitement and unsatisfied desire, separated by periods of deathlike unconsciousness and hopeless remorse."[25] Despite its Freudian glamour, this interpretation has little to recommend it. It is hard to imagine anyone becoming a slave to Lesbia out of a "hatred of Venus exceeding

great" (v. 17), which, it will be remembered, was Attis'
chief motive for becoming a Gallus. His *furor* was associated not with love but with an aversion to it. Moreover, Catullus would scarcely have added the final
prayer of vv. 91-93 if he had meant Cybele to stand for
Lesbia, for he had already caught the madness from her,
and it would have been too late to tell her to keep her
furor from his door. It is true that Catullus empathizes
with Attis as *miser*, as a pathos figure; but the last
three lines of the poem make it clear that Attis is
distinct from the first person singular, cannot be identified with Catullus. The psychosymbolic interpretation
of no. 63 is, therefore, untenable.[26]

A more likely possibility is that Cybele is meant
literally. We may speculate that Catullus at one time
entertained the mad hope of finding deliverance from the
tyranny of Venus and an escape from the corruptions of
Greco-Roman civilization by ecstasy and a kind of partial suicide. He may have toyed with the idea that he
could kill a part of himself and then live in peace as
a fragment of what he had once been.[27] Perhaps on second thoughts he recognized the perilous folly of such
dreams and came to the realization that there was no
other world for him than that of Greco-Roman civilization, no other way of life which would not be even more
unacceptable. If he once thought of himself as a possible second Attis, poem no. 63 may be read as a successful attempt to exorcize the pull of Cybele, to overcome
the sinister attraction of her cult, and to achieve
catharsis.

*

Between no. 63 and the brief hymn to Diana, no. 34,
the difference is enormous. No. 63 presents a goddess
of the mystery cults in wholly negative terms. No. 34
celebrates a goddess of the cult of the city-state and
envisages her as responsible and benevolent.

Since no. 34 is a hymn, it belongs to a subvariety
of choral lyric and is written in the first person
plural. As in the wedding songs, Catullus will keep in
the background, subordinating his personality to the
requirements of a public occasion. His task will be to
put into the mouth of his chorus words which express

the sentiments, attitudes, anxieties and aspirations of the larger social group, the collectivity of which he forms a part and with which he feels sympathy. He will say what is expected, will embrace tradition and uphold the ancient ways. He will add nothing that is purely personal, private or idiosyncratic.

No. 34 is supposed to be sung by a chorus of boys and girls, *puellae et pueri integri,* v. 2, who function as spokesmen for the entire people of Romulus. The poet chooses them for the task because they represent Rome's future, and the hymn will conclude with a prayer that this future may be prosperous. Another reason for choosing a child chorus is that young girls and boys are the particular objects of Diana's solicitude. They are *Dianae in fide,* under her protection; she has taken them into her care as a patron takes responsibility for his clients. Still another reason is that these children are as yet *integri,* and in view of their undoubted purity, Diana who is herself *integra* may be expected to give their requests a favorable hearing.

In accordance with the classical principle of decorum,[28] the language of the chorus is accommodated to the presumed occasion and the literary genre. Since the genre is elevated and the occasion solemn, Catullus' young people are somewhat idealized. They do not speak of the topics real children would spontaneously talk about but of what the situation calls for: Diana's power and Rome's need. They do not use the language real children would use in daily life, but a mean between that and adult speech. Thus the vocabulary of the hymn is simple, sober and restrained, the style relatively unadorned, the word order perspicuous, the syntax uncomplicated. That much is childlike. On the other hand, Catullus permits them a trace of archaism, a touch of elevated diction and some echoes of Roman liturgical language; that is what the genre and occasion demand. Their speech is dramatically appropriate yet satisfies the requirements of the hymnic style.

Having identified themselves to their audience, the chorus proceed to invoke the goddess (in stanzas two through five). They begin by rehearsing Diana's ancestry and birth. She was born on Delos beside the sacred olive tree, daughter of Jupiter and Latona; her pedigree is glorious and therefore her power is great. The genealogy is a form of praise, and the praise is intended to conciliate the goddess' favor, so that in the end she may be willing to grant the chorus' requests. This approach is, of course, part of the accepted rhetoric of prayer.

Continuing in the traditional hymnic pattern, Catullus turns from the lineage of the goddess to her special powers and prerogatives, or more accurately to the four spheres of her activity. First, he praises her as *domina* of unspoilt nature, the divine power ruling over mountains, greenwood, remote forests and roaring rivers. By a kind of metonym, the listing of the places of her activity evokes the activities themselves: Diana is mistress of wild beasts, goddess of huntsmen and herdsmen. Second, he praises her as a birth goddess under the name of Juno Lucina. Next, he identifies her with Trivia, powerful in the underworld, and Luna, mighty in heaven, who measures out the months and promotes the fertility of the land. Her power, therefore, pervades every level of the three-deck universe and is nothing short of cosmic. Finally, all her names are summed up in the traditional escape clause, "be worshipped under whatever name pleases you" (vv. 21-22): this is a pious precaution against giving offense by omission.

Only after Diana has been named with all her names and propitiated by a listing of all her offices does the chorus venture to name their sanction and utter the petition for which all that precedes has been preparation:

> Romulique,
> antique ut solita es, bona
> sospites ope gentem (vv. 22-24)

> and preserve the people of
> Romulus by your kindly protection as
> you were wont to do in days of old.

By "sanction" is meant the reminder of past kindnesses granted by the deity to her worshippers.[29] Since Diana has helped them in the past, she will be inclined to do so again. The chorus, one notes, make no mention of past offerings or services rendered to the goddess (sacrifices, etc.).[30] In view of the pervasively contractual character of Roman religion, this omission is rather surprising. However we interpret it, the fact remains that the chorus plead no merit on the part of the Roman people but throw themselves upon Diana's generosity. To obtain a favorable hearing they rely partly on their tribute of praise, but even more on

their special relation to the goddess. Since they are
in fide, she as a good patroness is virtually duty-bound
to grant what is asked for. The chorus are full of
naive confidence and trust. They have no real doubt
that she will hear and grant their request.

The prayer proper, tendered by the shy jussive subjunctive *sospites,* "preserve the people of Romulus,"
seems disappointingly unspecific, and *bona ope,* "by your
kindly protection," is equally vague. Exactly how is
Diana expected to protect and preserve them? The answer
must be, in every way that she can; and in the light of
the aretalogy in stanzas three through five, we know
that she can give good hunting, healthy herds, many live
births and plenteous harvests. It is worth noticing
that her gifts are all life-sustaining and non-politi-
cal; there is no mention of victory in battle or im-
perial aggrandizement, as might have been the case if
other deities had been invoked by a different choir.
All the same, the operative verb of supplication remains
hazy and indefinite. The petition does not seem to be
elicited by any clear and present need.

Hymn implies cult. Was no. 34 intended to be per-
formed on a specific religious occasion? Was it written
for the annual festival of Diana on the Aventine, for
example, or that of Diana Nemorensis at Aricia, or some
solemn ceremony at Verona? The text contains no references to cult practices. The chorus does not move in
procession to a temple or altar; there is no allusion
to dancing or to a musical accompaniment; no sacrifice
is offered; Diana is not summoned from any particular
shrine where she is supposed to dwell to a place where
her rites are being celebrated (as is normal practice
in Greek "cletic" hymns). Many have concluded that no.
34 is simply a literary creation, written as if for a
cult occasion, but with all specifics deliberately
omitted.[31] But the truth is that we know nothing about
how or why this poem came to be written. The most we
can say about it is that it manifests a serious concern
for the future welfare of Rome.

Although the hymn to Diana has no demonstrable connection with Catullus' lived experience, it is consistent with certain major themes and preoccupations which
we have met elsewhere in his writings; for example, his
respect for ancestral tradition and his devotion to
fides. Perhaps it is best seen as a complement to no.
63, of which it is the direct antithesis. Every reader
must be struck by the contrast between the cool, sedate,
western cult of Diana, as Catullus protrays it, and the

129

wild violence of Cybele's mysteries. There is a corresponding contrast between the quiet tinkling of the
glyconics of no. 34 and the strange, swift beat of the
galliambics. Diana as a goddess of the city-state re-
sponds to the needs of a collectivity. She is not concerned with ecstasy, madness, everlasting life, deliverance from the tyranny of Venus, absorption into the divine and similar impossible aspirations, which concern
only the individual. She is reasonable and her worship
is rather colorless. It lacks excitement, electricity;
her hymn is reassuring but dull. The reader is not
drawn to her as he is to the mystic Bacchus of no. 64
who seeks Ariadne, on fire with love for her, and joins
her to himself in marriage. Nor is he repelled by her
as he is by Cybele, the unmotherly *Magna Mater* who treats
Attis as a slave or an animal. Diana is neither a lover
nor a tyrant. Her relation to her chorus of boys and
girls is governed by the ethical, almost legal, concept
of *fides,* protection, which is the watchful help of a
goddess who guards the innocent and avenges any injury
done them. In short, Diana accepts responsibility for
their welfare.

                              *

        It is sometimes said that no. 34 is Catullus' only
hymn. This is not strictly the case. The first seven-
ty-five lines of no. 61, the longer wedding song, constitute a hymn to Hymenaeus. Even though these stanzas
are not detachable from the larger whole of which they
form a part, they invite comparison with no. 34. As
might be expected, the two hymns show a number of structural resemblances. But because of the difference in
scale and occasion there are important dissimilarities
as well.

        All hymns are by definition songs in praise of a
deity, and the praise normally leads up to some kind of
request, i.e., a prayer. Catullus' two hymns obviously
have that much in common. In no. 34 the prayer is
limited to the rather vague and indefinite *bona sospites
ope,* vv. 23-24, "preserve and prosper the people of
Romulus." No. 61 addresses manifold and specific requests to Hymenaeus, but the most important one is that
he grace the wedding with his "happy" (*laetus,* v. 8) presence. It also happens that both hymns are written in

the same light, shortlined meter, the glyconic-phere-cractic stanza,[32] although the stanza is one line longer in no. 61 than in no. 34. Both refer to the pedigree of the god concerned: Diana is daughter of Jupiter and Latona (vv. 5-6), and Hymenaeus is the son of the Muse Urania (v. 2). Both poems detail the powers, functions and offices of the divine addressees. Diana, as we have seen, rules over the uncorrupted countryside; she is Lucina, Trivia and Luna, the goddess who fills the farmer's barn with the fruits of the good earth. Hymenaeus' functions are repeatedly alluded to, yet though ostensibly varied, they are essentially one: to join young men and women in legitimate marriage. Last-ly, both poems contain what we have called a sanction, a reason why the prayer should be granted: in no. 34 it should be granted mainly because of the patron-client relationship between the chorus and Diana, and in no. 61 because the love of Junia and Manlius is a good and honorable love. Most of these similarities are trace-able to the traditional structure of the Greco-Roman hymn.

Although it is much the shorter of the two, the Diana hymn has one feature which is absent from no. 61: the singers begin by identifying themselves to their audience as *puellae et pueri integri*. At the same time they also specify their relation to the goddess: they are *Dianae in fide,* under her protection and patronage. In the wedding song the dramatic situation is different. There is probably no chorus here. As was pointed out in Chapter Six, it is likely that Catullus is singing throughout, taking charge of the festivities and func-tioning as a master of ceremonies; but he never bothers to present himself to the reader, never attempts to claim any special relationship to Hymenaeus.

As the longer poem, no. 61 has room for several motifs which are not found in no. 34. For one thing, no. 34 tells us nothing about Diana's normal place of residence, whereas no. 61 is remarkably precise in this respect: Hymenaeus lives on Helicon in the Aonian ca-vern near the waters of Aganippe (vv. 1-2, 26-30). Again, no. 34 provides no description of Diana's physi-cal appearance, whereas no. 61 opens with a rather de-tailed picture of Hymenaeus dressed in the accoutre-ments of a Roman bride. Furthermore, in no. 34 the chorus do not ask Diana to come to them, but only to preserve and prosper (*sospitare)*; presumably she can do this by remote control. In no. 61 Hymenaeus is asked to wake, to dress, to leave Mt. Helicon, to come

(repeatedly); to sing, dance, and swing the wedding
torch; and to call the bride to her new home. In other
words, no. 61 is distinctly a "cletic" or summoning
hymn, and no. 34 is not. Another difference is that no.
34 has no refrain, whereas the hymn to Hymenaeus has
two, including the traditional *o Hymenaee Hymen/o Hymen
Hymenaee*. Finally, the Diana hymn does not specify the
time or place or occasion of the choral song, while no.
61 repeatedly stresses that this is the evening when
Junia is taking the marriage veil for Manlius. It follows, therefore, that no. 61 was written for a specific
family occasion. The Diana hymn, since it ends with a
prayer for the general welfare, seems to be intended as
a public poem, but the festival is not identified.

Despite their differences, nos. 34 and 61 have an
undeniable generic resemblance. Many specific details,
prescribed by literary convention, are shared by both.
It is only when we look away from these details and consider the general effect produced by each poem that the
radical difference between them emerges. No. 34 is formal, regular, restrained, brief, monochrome and static.
No. 61 is joyful, uninhibited, exuberantly rich and
varied, full of color, movement and life. To the modern
reader, no. 61 is incomparably the more attractive and
vivid composition. Weddings are just more interesting
than children's prayers to an austere Diana.

*

Catullus is a poet, not a theologian. He has no
systematic ideas about the gods, or about anything else,
for that matter. Nevertheless, he speaks of the gods
often, sometimes as objects of cult, sometimes as the
familiar figures of mythology, sometimes as an anonymous
aggregation who may be addressed in personal prayer. In
non-mythological contexts, his conception of them is
generally coherent. It is also surprisingly traditional. A non-conformist or rebel in certain other
areas, Catullus is not far removed from old-fashioned
Roman opinion in matters of religion. (In this particular, he is poles apart from his distinguished contemporary, the Epicurean Lucretius). It is true that he
is uninterested in liturgical niceties and generally un-
concerned with the contractual aspect of the old sacri-
ficial system. The principle of *do ut des*, "I give in
order to receive," is not prominent in his prayers and

hymns. He is in no sense superstitious. He certainly doubted the efficacy of the *inferiae* which he offered at his brother's grave (no. 101). Yet he shows none of the resigned pessimism concerning the gods and divine providence which we meet in many of the early Greek poets, Archilochus, Alcaeus and Semonides of Amorgus, for example. For Catullus, the gods of the city-state not only have a real and effective existence; they are benevolent as well, and are concerned for the well-being of their worshippers, individually and collectively. It must be granted that they are not all-powerful. Fate and ill fortune exact their toll in the world, and the gods are either unwilling or unable to prevent the suffering of the innocent. However, they do not ignore such suffering. In the end they are merciful and even just, in the limited sense that they support and defend the traditional Roman virtues of *pietas* and *fides,* heed the supplications of those who maintain loyalty in personal relations, and punish betrayers. For Catullus personally these gods are a source of hope, not of anxiety or despair.[33]

Roman, too, is Catullus' mistrust of the deities of the mystery cults, or at least of the mystic Cybele. Although he did not for a moment doubt or deny the reality of her power (and thoroughly understood the nature of her rites), he conceives her as a power making for evil in the world. He presents her devotee, Attis, as a pathetic victim of divinely sent madness. As we have already said, Cybele is a goddess who demands everything and gives nothing good in return. Her worshippers are deprived not only of dignity and liberty but of their very humanity. Nowhere is Catullus' attachment to the life of the Greco-Roman city-state so strongly marked as in the Attis poem.

So much concerning the religion of Catullus may be concluded from the five poems we have considered in this chapter. However, these poems do not exhaust his views of the divine. His most elaborate treatment of the gods is to be seen in the miniature epic, no. 64. We shall turn in the next chapter to this extraordinary poem, the crown of his life work.

CHAPTER NINE

The Miniature Epic, no. 64

No. 64 is Catullus' longest poem, perhaps his latest, certainly his most ambitious. It is an epyllion[1] or short mythological epic. The epyllion was one of the more important literary innovations of the Hellenistic age. The genre was taken up and naturalized at Rome by the New Poets as part of their reaction against historical epic in the Ennian manner. We have already had occasion to mention in Chapter Two Cinna's epyllion, the *Zmyrna,* which is praised in no. 95. From other sources we know of an *Io* by Calvus, a *Glaucus* by Cornificius, and a few others. Of these works only a handful of tantalizing fragments survive. Catullus' 64th poem is the earliest Latin epyllion which has come down to us entire. In this masterwork the poet incorporates much of what is most characteristic in his previous writings. As Putnam[2] says, it contains "reflections of almost every major subject which interested him." It expresses the essence of his experience in life and literature, the sum of his discoveries. Hence the old hypothesis that no. 64 is a mere translation or paraphrase of a lost Alexandrian original is extremely improbable and has for the most part been laid to rest.

The epyllion usually deals with a love theme and often includes a contrasting "digression." Catullus' poem adheres to this formula. The framework narrative tells of the happy wedding of the Argonaut Peleus and the sea-goddess Thetis. This encloses a contrasting digression of approximately equal length on the disastrous love affair of two mortals, Theseus and Ariadne. I shall try to explain the relationship of these two narratives later on.

Instead of plunging *in medias res,* Catullus begins at the beginning. He gives a brief account of how the ship Argo was constructed from the pines that grew on Mt. Pelion. This is a reminiscence of no. 4, 10-12, where the poet's *phaselus* was also traced back to a stand of timber on a mountain top. But there are differences between the two passages. The *phaselus,* for all its excellences, was but one craft among many, whereas the Argo was the first ocean-going vessel, an unprecedented *monstrum* and a marvel to all beholders. Therefore the building of the Argo is described in high epic style;

no. 4, 10-12 on the other hand is a mock-heroic inset in an informal and conversational poem.

In addition, the opening paragraph offers a characterization of the Argonauts in general and goes on to tell us something about the hero Peleus in particular. The Argonauts were men of valor, outstanding among the Argive youth, bold pioneers who had the courage to sail to far-off Colchis. It was because of their heroic excellence that they were honored by the assistance of Athena, for it was she, the goddess of handicraft herself, who built the marvelous Argo for them. During the outward voyage they received another tribute to their surpassing worth when with mortal eyes they were privileged to gaze upon the divine beauty of the unclad Nereids as they rose from the gray waters. It was then that Peleus, the pillar and bulwark of Thessaly, fell in love with Thetis. Thetis accepted him, and Jupiter himself sanctioned their marriage. At this point, Catullus breaks with the convention of epic objectivity in a quasi-lyric outburst modelled upon the closing paragraphs of the Homeric Hymns.[3] He cries out his praise of the whole race of heroes. He says he will often invoke these "excellent sons of excellent mothers." Born in an evil generation, he rejoices to escape, at least in fancy, into the glorious heroic age. The enraptured questions of vv. 25-30 sustain the lyric mood. Peleus' surpassing good fortune in being allowed to marry a goddess is almost too good to be true; Catullus can scarcely believe such a thing ever happened. Yet it did, for ancient tradition affirms it, and tradition does not lie.

In line 31 we leap forward in time from the first meeting of Peleus and Thetis to their wedding at Peleus' palace in Pharsalus. It is just before the meeting of bride and bridegroom. We have here a heightening and intensification of that magic hour which Catullus had glorified in poems 61 and 62. From all Thessaly the guests arrive with wedding presents, their faces shining with happiness. No one is envious or disaffected; all rejoice that the king is honored, for when he is honored, his subjects are honored as well. Indeed, the whole human race is exalted by Thetis' acceptance of Peleus. On this glorious day, field work ceases for ordinary folk, the curse of labor is lifted, and there is a temporary recovery of the bliss of the Golden Age. Within the palace, all is bright and shining. The color imagery of lines 43-48 matches the primary mood of festal joy. White predominates: this is the color of

136

happiness and the color the Olympian gods love best.
Associated with the whites of the palace interior is the
sheen of silver, gold and ivory. These are beautiful,
precious, and long-lasting materials. Gold and ivory
have sacral significance:[4] from these were fashioned
some of the holiest and most revered images of the gods,
e.g., that of Athena in the Parthenon and that of Zeus
at Olympia. Peleus welcomes Thetis and the divine wedding guests with the best that man has at his disposal.

Why does Peleus play such a prominent role in no.
64? It is difficult to be sure about the reason. One
attractive possibility is that the Peleus story is related to Catullus' own experience.[5] It has been well
said that Catullus approaches myth empathetically, not
objectively.[6] He has to be able to see himself in it
somehow; otherwise he does not need it. This is evident
in the long elegy, no. 68; it is equally evident in no.
64. Peleus' marriage to Thetis marks the perfect attain-
ment of a bliss that the poet had imperfectly experienced at the beginning of his relationship with Lesbia.
In the long elegy he exalts her as a radiant goddess and
compares her arrival at the house of Allius to an epi-
phany of Venus. But she was a goddess only in the metaphorical sense and only for the duration of the *mira nox*.
Thetis on the other hand is a true goddess and according
to Catullus' account deeply in love with Peleus. She
lived with him in perfect concord, and their union apparently lasted until Peleus' death. As we shall see
later on, the perfection of their happiness was eventually marred after the birth of their son, but apart
from this their relationship is unflawed. Thetis' con-
descension to the hero Peleus is the nearly perfect ac-
tualization of an ideal approached in some degree and
fleetingly experienced by Catullus at the house of
Allius. It is because the poet once aspired to and partially attained a felicity analogous to that of Peleus
that he chooses the marriage with Thetis as the principal
subject of the epyllion.

In the midst of all the chryselephantine splendor
within Peleus' palace, there is one object of contrasting hue, the crimson coverlet that is thrown over the
marriage bed. This coverlet is embroidered with figures
taken from heroic myth. Under the pretext of describing
this coverlet Catullus launches into his second subject,
the sad story of how Theseus carried Ariadne away from
her Cretan homeland and then abandoned her on the island
of Dia (Naxos).

He begins the story with a description of Ariadne

on the shore of the island. She has just discovered
that her lover has betrayed her. She looks out over the
uncrossable sea, grieving for all she has lost. Her
situation resembles that of Attis in no. 63.[7] Both have
been driven by passion to take an irreversible step.
Ariadne had been impelled by Venus, Attis by hatred of
Venus. Ariadne awoke from sleep to discover (too late)
that she had been abandoned. Attis awoke from sleep to
discover (too late) that he had lost all to Cybele.
Ariadne in her distraction rushes to the seashore; so
does Attis. At the shore they look out over the sea,
Attis in the direction of his far-off *patria*, Ariadne in
the direction of the far-off ship[8] of Theseus. Both are
surrounded and cut off by hostile nature. In front of
them is the vast sea, the uncrossable gulf that separates them from all they love. Behind her Ariadne has
the craggy bluffs of Dia, the dwelling place of wild
beasts and birds; behind him Attis has the Phrygian
mountain where wild creatures make their lairs. Both
are alone. Ariadne, after a night of love on the beach,[9]
has been forsaken by Theseus. Attis at the shore has
left his companions behind him on the mountain top; they
are no longer human in any case. Finally, both break
into impassioned and pathetic soliloquies by the seashore. The similarities between the two scenes are extraordinary.

However, there are also important differences. In
Ariadne's case there is nothing to compare with the symbolic sunrise in the Attis poem. Conversely, the sea
imagery of no. 64 is much richer in implication than
that of no. 63. The literal and external sea around Dia
cuts the heroine off from her past in Crete and from her
hoped-for future with Theseus. It imprisons her in an
intolerable present on a desert island (so Dia is conceived by Catullus) to die of starvation. But in addition she is lashed by a metaphorical, inward sea:[10] not
merely a sea of troubles as in no. 68a but a high sea
raised by Venus and Cupid, which is therefore a sea of
passion. Ariadne is a helpless swimmer in this metaphorical sea. Like a person tossed by vast waves she
has lost her autonomy, her power of self-determination.
The metaphor, first used at v. 62, recurs at v. 97ff. in
a heightened and intensified form. In these lines, unless the figure is mixed, she is no longer a swimmer but
a ship, a ship on fire, driven by a storm at sea. These
images establish her as a victim of the passion of love
and as a pathetic figure.

As we said above, Catullus views myth empathetically, not objectively. In the light of that principle,

we discerned an analogy linking the poet to Peleus. There is also a significant correspondence between Catullus and Ariadne. He goes out of his way to identify with her. At v. 61 he adds an *eheu* in order to sigh for her and with her. At v. 69 he adds the vocative *Theseu,* calling on Theseus by name, as she did; he is one with her in her affliction. The exclamations *a misera* in v. 71 and *heu* in v. 94 have a similar effect. He knows what she is going through. Her storm-tossed passion, her pathos, reflects his own sufferings as a victim of passion. Her rejection by Theseus is comparable to his own experience of rejection. The infidelity which destroyed her happiness resembles the infidelities that had darkened his life. Ariadne has been humiliated, mistreated, and Catullus' heart goes out to her.

Catullus not only identifies with Ariadne; he also justifies her. In his eyes she is *misera,* pitiable. She is pitiable because she suffers far beyond her deserts. It is true that she turned her back on her father, her family and her homeland. People in her society would say that she had done wrong in forsaking all other loves for one love (v. 120) and in presuming to choose her own husband. Nevertheless, it was impossible for her to do otherwise. She could not be expected to resist the maddening passion which had been visited upon her by the cruelty of Venus and Cupid (vv. 71f., and 95ff.). It was by their prompting that she fell in love with Theseus at first sight (v. 86), the moment he arrived at her father's palace. She was not drawn to him because of his inner qualities or character traits. In personality the two had nothing in common, were in fact direct opposites. She was drawn by his looks alone, his *dulcis forma* (v. 175). It was the sight of that splendid male animal that set Ariadne on fire: Venus willed that it should be so. She sowed in Ariadne's heart a seed which grew into a great thorn-bush (v. 72), signifying all the anxiety and pain (*curae, luctus*) which love inevitably brings, in Catullus' view. Ariadne is not to be condemned for falling in love, believing Theseus' false promises of marriage, and running away with him.

Once Cupid and Venus have done their work, Ariadne is totally transformed. Catullus emphasizes the extent of the transformation in the contrasting images of v. 87ff. Before Theseus' arrival she resembled the chaste unmarried girls of the wedding poems,[11] secluded and protected, safe in her mother's arms. Like them she is compared to a flower, a myrtle that is refreshed by river waters and caressed by spring breezes. After she has gazed upon him she is a woman on fire, burning. Her love is described in terms which had been used to describe Catullus' love for Lesbia. Desire penetrates to the very marrow of her bones; line 93 is reminiscent of the imagery of liquid fire in no. 51, 9-10 (the Sapphic ode). The fire metaphor connotes pain, among other things. Love, to Ariadne, is far from being unalloyed bliss, delight and fulfillment. It is joy mixed with suffering (v. 95) as it had been in Catullus' own experience (cf. no. 68, 17-18). Ariadne's love for Theseus is as distressing and intense as Catullus' love for Lesbia had been.

A large part of her pain comes from humiliation, from the experience of being rejected. This is hard for any lover to bear, but it is especially hard for a royal princess like Ariadne, the daughter of proud Minos. Her pain is still further increased by Theseus' base ingratitude. Because she loved him, she helped him to escape from the labyrinth and return home a hero. Then, believing his false oaths of fidelity, she had given up all she possessed to leave Crete with him. Her assistance, her sacrifices and her trust are repaid with stony-hearted betrayal. Theseus is *immemor*, v. 135. Like the Alfenus of no. 30, he is unmindful of past benefits received, promises given, obligations incurred.[12] In fact he has decided to destroy her. In exchange for the gift of life he gives her death by abandoning her on a desert island. He does this not so much because he hates her as because he hates her cruel and unjust parent. In other words, he carries her off and forsakes her in order to punish his enemy Minos. The innocent daughter pays for the sins of her father.[13]

To Catullus, Theseus is a hero, but he is not a character with whom he can empathize. He does not identify with Theseus in any way. Perhaps that is why he is not given any speeches in the poem. He is known to us not by his words but by his actions and by Ariadne's attitude toward him. Naturally she heaps reproaches on his head, and they are richly deserved. Nevertheless the poet stops short of presenting him as a "villain" motivated by sheer malevolence. The malign and diabolical villain is on the whole a post-classical phenomenon. Theseus cannot be considered diabolical. His heroism is conceded from the start: the crimson coverlet displays *heroum virtutes*, v. 51. Although the plural is somewhat peculiar, it certainly includes Theseus' exploits.[14] As hero, he is *ferox*, "bold" (vv. 73, 247). He thirsts for fame, glory and praise (v. 102, cf. 112). That is

140

perhaps the very essence of heroism. The hero's one
overriding purpose in life is to acquire prestige, to
make himself worthy of honor by performing deeds of val-
or, to obtain glory by meeting the challenge of a crisis
situation. In determining to free Athens from the burden of paying tribute in human life to an unjust king,
Theseus shows heroic devotion (v. 80 ff.). The verb
optauit in line 82 should not be overlooked. It means
"chose." He went to Crete of his own free choice, not
because any other person, human or divine, had imposed
the task on him. He is motivated not only by love of
fame but also by loyalty to Athens. However, his conception of love and loyalty is irreconcilable with
Ariadne's. Theseus is loyal to the ancient pieties, devoted to country and to his father Aegeus. His great
courage, his willingness to sacrifice himself for the
commonwealth, remind us of the Roman heroes of the early
Republic.[15] Ariadne is the reverse of this. She is
loyal in her personal relationship to Theseus. She deserts father, family, country and the altars of her gods
in order to be with the one person whom she perceives as
irreplaceable and upon whom she concentrates all her
affection and desires. Furthermore, where Theseus is
heroic, Ariadne is pathetic. Every kind of hero, good
or bad, is the antithesis of the pathos figure. The
hero acts, the pathos figure reacts; the hero is the
vigorous agent, the pathos figure is the passive victim;
the hero in some sense wins, the pathos figure, after
struggling feebly against overwhelming odds, goes down
to inevitable defeat.

Since Theseus and Ariadne are direct opposites we
should not be surprised to discover that the deities
associated with each of them are opposites also; for the
god who influences and sways any individual is the god
who is most in accord with his basic nature and selfhood. By virtue of his birth, upbringing and circumstances, Theseus is under the patronage of Pallas
Athena:[16] Athena is controlled and rational, a goddess
of warfare, a protectress of city states (especially of
Athens, the city state named after her), and a special
guardian of heroes (we recall that she built the Argo
for the Argonauts); but she is cold, inclined to cruelty, and of course, as virgin goddess, impregnably
chaste. Chastity is not one of Theseus' virtues, but
apart from this he participates in the qualities perfectly exemplified in the goddess Athena. Ariadne on
the other hand is swayed by the deities of instinct,
passion and natural human impulse, Venus and Cupid.
Moreover, we find out later on that she is loved by
Bacchus, another god identified with man's instinctual

141

side. At first her acceptance of natural impulse leads
not to happiness and liberation but the opposite: loss
of autonomy, rejection, humiliation, pain and despair.
In the end, however, she escapes unexpectedly into joy.
Theseus, apparently victorious and triumphant, is suddenly thrust into disaster.

His valor peaks at v. 105ff. In answer to Ariadne'
prayer the gods grant him victory over the Minotaur.
Catullus condenses the story of their fight into seven
lines. The end result is given in v. 110: Theseus
"laid low" (*prostravit*) the monstrous bull. How this was
accomplished is not directly narrated; instead, it is
implied in the five-line simile which immediately precedes.[17] The Minotaur is compared to a mighty oak or
pine on an exposed mountain top; Theseus is like a still
mightier force, the unconquered whirlwind. The whirlwind wrenches the tree up by its roots and throws it
flat. The imagery suggests that the adversaries were
not duelling with weapons but wrestling with bare hands
Apparently Theseus manages to lift his opponent from the
ground and goes into an "airplane spin"; this is followed by a body-slam which has fatal consequences.
Guided by Ariadne's clue he emerges from the labyrinth
unharmed and exultant. The brevity and obliquity of the
account do not detract from Theseus' glory, but it is
worth noting that his *aristeia* is bracketed by references
to the help Ariadne gave him. Catullus does not want u
to forget this.

If Theseus' victory over the Minotaur marks the
physical climax of the epyllion, the emotional climax i
provided by Ariadne's lament at the shore, vv. 132-201.
As we have already suggested, her monologue shows a num
ber of correspondences with the climactic soliloquy of
Attis in no. 63 (vv. 50-73). Both speeches are written
in the first person singular and may be regarded as
lyric insets in a third person narrative; both give
pathetic expression to a sense of overwhelming loss.
But Ariadne's lament is three times longer than the com
plaint of Attis. It is a far more varied and complex
composition. Attis' speech shows little dramatic progression. He hardly gets beyond self-accusation and the
expression of vain regrets. Ariadne does not accuse
herself; she accuses Theseus. Her mood evolves continuously; she passes from helpless lamentation to deep
despair, then in the end turns to the gods for help and
calls down angry curses on her false lover: these
curses are not vain. They bring death, not upon the
hero himself but upon his father, who suffers for the

sins of his son. Although both Attis and Ariadne are presented sympathetically, one senses that the poet projects himself far more deeply into the experiences of the heroine than into those of Cybele's victim; Attis represents to him only a terrifying possibility, but Ariadne recalls the agony of lived experience.

She begins by addressing the absent Theseus in apostrophe. The opening adverb *sicine*, [18] followed by seven lines of rhetorical questions, shows (by a technique now very familiar to us) that she can scarcely believe that he has left her. [19] She is appalled by the sudden revelation of his cruelty, ingratitude and treachery. All his promises were false and worthless; like the assurances of Alfenus in no. 30, 9-10, they have been carried off by the winds. Then at 143ff. she checks herself, tries to make excuses for him. He is not unique, he is just a man; all men are like that, opportunists and deceivers. Catullus had attempted to excuse Lesbia in similar terms in no. 70. But she soon veers back to reproach, remembers her past acts of kindness and how they have been repaid by monstrous cruelty. She calls him the child of a lioness or a sea monster (v. 154ff.). The poet had used comparable imagery in crying out against Lesbia's inhumanity (no. 60), but the present passage is even more vehement. At v. 155 in place of the neutral *genuit*, "bore," she uses the ugly metaphor *exspuit*, "spewed out." The implication is that even such subhuman mothers as Syrtis, Scylla or Charybdis must have rejected with horror and disgust what they had conceived: the birth was a spitting out, a vomiting forth, a throwing up. At v. 158ff. she again shifts and relents, declares that she would be willing to accept almost any humiliation just to be close to him. Passion abases its victims. Already enslaved to him in the figurative sense, she would serve him literally as well. Although a royal princess, she would be glad to make his bed and wash his feet. For her, even footwashing could be beautiful, an act of love (v. 162).

But there is a limit to her capacity for self-abasement. In line 188 she turns from useless self-address to prayer. She does not pray for healing and release from her love, as Catullus had done in no. 76; she calls down curses in the name of justice. She asks the Furies, those powers of vengeance who take the part of innocent victims, to punish the guilty Theseus in accordance with the law of the talion, measure for measure. She hates him for his cruelty and deception, for giving her death in exchange for the gift of life; she hates him for his injustice. Yet at the same time she

143

curses him against her will. *Cogor*, "I am compelled" (v. 197), makes this clear. The curse is wrenched from her; something within resists. That something is what is left of her love. *Ardens* and *furore* in the same line are usually understood as referring to her wrath, but it is better to take them as functionally ambiguous. They refer both to anger and to love. Ariadne is going through something very like the quintessentially Catullan experience of no. 85 (*Odi et amo*). Anger, hatred, love and a sense of outraged justice coexist within her tormented heart.

After Ariadne's soliloquy Jupiter gives solemn assent to her prayer and she is avenged. This is followed by a flashback to the time of Theseus' departure from Athens. The hero's father Aegeus (in the second extended speech of the poem, vv. 215-237) gives his son his final instructions: if he succeeds in killing the Minotaur he is to change his sails from sad violet to joyful white. In its pathos Aegeus' speech resembles that of Ariadne. He is extremely old and feeble; Theseus is his only son, dearer to him than life itself. They had been separated for many years and were only recently reunited. He grieves (vv. 223, 226) that he must now part from him again and expose him to mortal danger in Crete; yet circumstances (*fortuna*, v. 218) and Theseus' bold resolve (*feruida uirtus*, ibid.) tie his hands (vv. 216, 219). He does not expect his son to return; he mourns and pours dust on his head as if he were already dead (v. 224). Aegeus is presented as wholly sympathetic figure. Ariadne in line 159 had misjudged him, imagining in him a severity which is alien to his character. Certainly Theseus is more eager to go to Crete than Aegeus is to send him. Although Catullus is sometimes hard on the older generation, especially on rigid puritans and killjoys who are envious of the happiness of young people, he shows no animus against Aegeus. On the contrary he sympathizes with him as a lover and a sufferer, as one who suffers through his love and indeed dies because of it.[20] The old can be lovers too. One thinks of the aged grandfather in the simile of no. 68, vv. 119-124. Aegeus is a pathetic expansion of that old man.

The epic is often called the most comprehensive form of poetry on the ground that it creates a whole world. A whole world from the ancient point of view will include a divine dimension. Hence in our epyllion the gods have an important role to play. What is the relationship between men and gods, according to this

poem? In the extremity of her pain Ariadne briefly en-
tertains the idea that the world is not governed on any
rational basis whatsoever (vv. 169-170). She feels that
what she has been through is meaningless. What made it
happen, really? What purpose did it serve? Or worse,
she suspects that the universe may be ruled by *fors
insultans*, diabolical evil, an unpredictable power which
is not merely indifferent to human suffering but ac-
tively and inscrutably cruel. However she does not hold
this view for long. Almost immediately she turns to the
gods in supplication. According to the theology of this
poem she is right to do so; for the gods do exist, they
do rule the universe, they do listen to prayers. Sometimes, to be sure, they grant them to the hurt of the
person praying, as at vv. 103-104, where they accept
Ariadne's prayer that Theseus may be victorious over the
Minotaur. But they also accept prayers that wrongdoing
may be punished: Theseus is made to suffer for his perjury. At v. 204 Jupiter nods in solemn assent to
Ariadne's prayer for vengeance, and at v. 207ff. Theseus
forgets his father's instructions. What has happened?
Has Jupiter invaded Theseus' personality and forced him
to forget? The curiously contorted simile in vv. 238-
240 hints at an answer. A high and snowcapped mountain
(representing either Aegeus and his instructions or
Theseus) usually has at its summit a plume of cloud (representing Theseus' thoughts). Just as a blast of wind
may blow the cloud away, so an unnamed force analogous
to the wind made Theseus forget. All winds are under
the control of Jupiter as god of the upper air and of
weather generally;[21] likewise the unnamed force operates
according to his will. Since there is no discernible
motivation at the human level, it is a fair inference
that Jupiter alone causes Theseus to forget.[22]

Is justice then done? A very rude and approximate
kind of justice at best. Minos pays for his pride,
cruelty and injustice, as we have seen, and Theseus is
not permitted to get away with his perjury. The gods
punish the guilty Theseus by direct interference and
the guilty Minos by a more circuitous route. That much
is understandable. But they do not protect the innocent. Ariadne, the victim of Venus and Amor, who did
no voluntary wrong, suffers far beyond her deserts. The
gods, in order to get at her father, allow her to endure
agony. Likewise Aegeus, through no fault of his own,
dies because of the offenses of a son whom he loved more
than life itself. The divine justice is flawed and in-
complete. The gods cannot bring perfect good out of
evil. There is a margin for tragedy in the world.

There is a discrepancy between the ideal justice man
longs for and the rough-hewn justice which the gods
dispense. Nevertheless that discrepancy is far from
total. Wrongdoing is punished, however clumsily, and
the prayers of blameless victims are not ignored. According to Catullus, the powers that govern the universe
are not blankly indifferent to our need. Man is not a
passion inutile, malevolent *fors* is not in control; the
world is not absurd.

The story is not over. Theseus' sad end is contrasted with a sudden rebound in Ariadne's fortunes.
Her sufferings are ended by the unexpected arrival of
the god Iacchus.[23] Iacchus is Dionysus or Bacchus. He
is much more than a jolly god of wine and intoxication.
Finley[24] rightly calls him a god of liberation, especially a god who frees women from all that restricts and
confines them. As a god of release he delivers Ariadne
from her imprisonment on the desert isle of Dia. He
does not come to her in answer to a prayer: she never
prays to be saved, the possibility does not even cross
her mind. Nor does he come in the interests of justice
or compassion. He comes to her, winging his way across
the sea, simply because, for no apparent reason, he is
on fire with love for her:

> te quaerens, Ariadna, tuoque incensus amore.
>   (v. 253)
> seeking you, Ariadne, and on fire with love
>   for you.

Loving her, he must have seen her somewhere, before her
flight with Theseus; seeking her, he must have lost her:
but Catullus does not go into details.[25] Once he has
found her she joins his ecstatic entourage, the *thiasos*
or holy company of Satyrs, Sileni and Maenads, and becomes his bride.[26] She is united with Iacchus as Peleus
is united with Thetis. The parallelism and contrast between these two major myths helps to fuse the two halves
of the epyllion into a thematic unity. Marriage with
divinity is the common term. As Thetis condescended to
accept Peleus, so Iacchus raised up and glorified
Ariadne.[27] Love, which brought her all her sufferings
in the first place, finally releases her from the crimson world of her pain.

In the long elegy, no. 68, Catullus uses mythology
as a mirror of his own experience. It seems probable
that the Ariadne legend also had some private and personal meaning for him. Certainly he never thought of
himself as a hero. Theseus is the antithesis of all he

146

valued most, and he must have known that the glory of a
Peleus was not available to him. But what of the passionate Ariadne, with whom he so clearly identifies?
Having shared her pain did he long to share in some sort
of final liberation and joy comparable to hers? Did he
ever hope he might be loved without reason or deserving
by a god of release and thus share the divine life forever? If so, he must have realized the hope was illu-
sory. In his time, the gods no longer show themselves
to man (v. 397ff). Attis in poem no. 63 had hoped for
a blissful union with the goddess Cybele but in the up-
shot was subjected to a life of hellish servitude.
Catullus knew he could never be a second Ariadne, but
the hopeless yearning may still have existed within him,
deep down. I suspect that lines 251-264 express that
yearning in mythical terms.[28]

The poet breaks off his description of the crimson
coverlet at v. 265. The mortal wedding guests, who are
not allowed to look upon the gods face to face, and who
therefore must not be present when the divine guests arrive, depart from the graced palace of Peleus to resume
their normal occupations in the familiar world. Their
departure is described in the longest and most elaborate
simile of the poem,[29] vv. 269-77. In these lines the
guests are compared to the waves of the sea at dawn,
which under a freshening wind grow higher and higher,
move faster and faster toward the rising sun and make
more and more sound as they go, finally reaching a point
where they are clearly seen. Likewise the crowd of
guests moves slowly at first, then gathers speed as it
advances; at first silent, they gradually begin to laugh
and speak as they move out of the dusky megaron of
Peleus' palace into the bright sunlight. The effect of
the simile is to suggest that the collective mood has
changed. A moment before they had been gazing with
eager intensity at the images of Ariadne's suffering and
exaltation which were embroidered on the coverlet (vv.
265-8): now they leave the palace and start home.
Their state of mind has shifted, the spell is broken;
they are about to resume their ordinary and unexalted
lives as field-laborers.

*

The most obvious difference between epyllion and
epic is that the one is short and the other is long.

Because of the ample scale of his genre, the epic poet
has to cope with the problem of retardation and expansion; he must know how to provide passages of relaxation
between the climaxes. In the miniature epic these problems are less pressing; it is possible to secure continuous concentration and speed. Catullus maintains in
poem no. 64 a density and richness comparable to that
which we find in the best of his shorter poems. But if
there is any passage in the epyllion in which a relaxation of intensity is permitted, lines 278-302 seem to
provide the likeliest example. This is the verse paragraph in which the gods begin to arrive at the palace.
Once again, as in his narrative of the arrival of the
Thessalian guests (v. 32ff.), the device of the epic
catalogue is utilized. The catalogue is not without a
principle of organization. The gods are listed in order
of rank, first the lesser and then the greater. Chiron
heads the list, followed by Peneus; next comes the Titan
Prometheus, and finally the Olympians.

Chiron is the wise centaur who lives on Mt. Pelion.
He was famous for his skill in hunting, music, "gymnas-
tics," and the art of prophecy. Many of the most distinguished heroes of Greek mythology were trained by
him. Jason, Castor and Pollux were among his pupils;
so too were Peleus and Achilles. He brings as a wedding
gift not the celebrated Pelian spear[30] but garlands of
wild flowers, simple emblems of festivity.

Peneus is the chief river god of Thessaly and as
such the source and sustainer of all life in the country. He is also, as it happens, a close relative of
Thetis. He has his hands full: he brings five kinds of
trees, to be planted at the entrance of Peleus' palace;
there they will provide shade for generations yet un-
born. Among his sylvan gifts are the poplar and cypress, both of which connote death and are perhaps prophetic of the brevity of Achilles' life.[31]

Prometheus' presence is heavy with significance.
It was he who had warned Jupiter not to marry Thetis,
as the high god had once intended to do: she was des-
tined to give birth to a son greater than his father.
Jupiter therefore renounced her and allowed her to marry
Peleus instead (cf. vv. 26-27).

Jupiter and the other Olympian gods arrive last.
Like Prometheus they bring no gifts; their mere presence
is gift enough. Two of the Olympians are absent, Apollo
and his twin Diana. As god of prophecy, Apollo fore-

148

knows that Achilles, the future son of Peleus and
Thetis, will kill Hector and thus seal the fate of Troy,
his favorite city. He also foreknows that he will himself take Achilles' life in retaliation. The absence
of the children of Latona, like the earlier references
to poplar and cypress, casts an ominous shadow on the
otherwise ideal happiness of the occasion.

After the gods have arrived the Parcae sing their
wedding song. Since we have already analyzed this passage in Chapter Six there is no need to linger over it
here. It is sufficient to remind the reader that the
song is double-edged in its effect: while it praises
the perfect love of Peleus and Thetis it also prophesies
the birth of a terrible son, greater than his father but
a shedder of blood, violent, cruel and inhuman. The
perfect joy of the wedding day will bring fresh evil into the world.

There is a marked element of paradox in Catullus'
portrayal of the Parcae. To the casual observer they
are three insignificant little old ladies suffering from
something like Parkinson's disease: their infirmity is
mentioned twice, vv. 305 and 307. Festively attired for
the occasion in crimson and white, they have nevertheless brought with them baskets of fleece and (as
Merrill[32] points out) refuse to stop their incessant
spinning even during the wedding feast. As they spin,
they strip the finished threads clean with their teeth,
and flocks of bitten wool cling to their withered lips.
But despite their unprepossessing appearance and curious
behavior we know that these little old ladies are really
all-powerful birth goddesses who foreordain the course
and duration of every human life. If they are old and
infirm, it is because they have been carrying on their
aeternus labor, their "everlasting occupation" (v. 310)
ever since mankind first appeared on earth. Although
the description of their clothing may seem purely orna-
mental, recent investigation[33] has shown that it is part
of a pattern of color contrast which pervades the entire
poem: white is insistently associated with happiness
and crimson with suffering. In the present passage the
combination of the two colors hints at the varying pro-
portions of joy and affliction that the Parcae assign
us at birth. It is not over-subtle to say that the
white and crimson garments together with the crimson
headbands are emblematic of their awesome divine power
over the lives of mankind.

They are engaged in the humdrum and unremarkable

activity of spinning (described in meticulous detail at vv. 311-14), but their spinning has no ordinary utilitarian purpose. The woollen threads they are forming are obviously symbolic. Since thread is a fragile commodity that has a beginning, grows steadily in length as it is spun, and comes to an end when the fleece on the distaff is exhausted, it is an apt image for the frail brevity of human life. Everyone is familiar with the developed form of the myth according to which one of the Parcae spins, another measures and a third snips the thread. Catullus, however, here follows Homer's earlier and simpler version in which all three spin and the measuring and cutting are not mentioned. Only the spinning matters in the present context.

As they spin they sing; their song is modelled in part upon primitive work songs. Such songs often have a refrain comparable to that sung by the Parcae,

currite ducentes subtegmina, currite, fusi

run, spindles, run and spin the threads (v. 327 etc.),

in which a tool or utensil is apostrophized as if it were a lazy animal or slave and verbally encouraged to hurry up and get the job finished as soon as possible.34 Work songs are sung by people engaged in boring and repetitive jobs; the idea is to turn routine into something like play. No doubt the Parcae are rather bored by their everlasting occupation of spinning our innumerable lives into existence; after all we are only "threads", more or less alike, and our minor differences are rather uninteresting. The little old ladies are mainly intent on keeping up their schedule, getting through their quota of fleece on time.

But because it is sung by goddesses the song of the Parcae differs from ordinary work songs. As was pointed out in Chapter Six, it is prophetic and inerrant; the point is stressed, vv. 321-3, 336, 383. The threads may fix the length of each life, but it is the song that determines[35] its nature; the Parcae sing our whole future into being, in all its distinctive particularity.[36] As they sing they offer evaluations that jar on the sensibilities of any enlightened human being. Of course we are not disturbed by their praise of the harmonious love shared by Peleus and Thetis, but when they go on to describe the career of Achilles, their comments begin to strike us as alarmingly inappropriate. Indifferent to the sufferings and injustices endured by the vanquished, childishly superficial in their conception of heroic *arete*, they seem malicious or senile or both. Enormous power is seen to rest in irresponsible and incompetent hands, and the three sisters, as Quinn[37] puts it, are at once sinister and absurd. Apart from the Cybele of no. 63 and the Orcus of no. 3 they represent Catullus' least attractive, most disquieting image of divinity.

After the Parcae have sung their ambiguous epithalamium, one expects to read a description of the arrival of Thetis and the entry of the happy pair into the bridal chamber. However, Catullus omits this and proceeds to draw a contrast between the world-wide *pietas* of the heroic age and the wholesale corruption of human relationships in the present. In olden times, the gods "often" visited the houses of mortal men, showed themselves to human eyes, descended to earth on festal occasions, accepted generous sacrifices, led their worshippers in sacred dances upon the mountain tops, came to their aid in time of war. Men's homes were still *castae;* the family was unstained by impurity and wickedness; *pietas* was not yet scorned; religion and justice were not yet forsaken. Hence men lived on terms of intimacy with the gods in those days. Now, however, all that is changed. We are living in an Iron Age, sodden with sin. Justice is forgotten and evil desires have taken over in the form of avarice, ambition and lust. Family life is defiled. Brother offends against brother as sibling rivalry is pushed to the point of fratricide. Children offend against parents and begin to look forward eagerly to the deaths of their fathers and mothers. Parents offend against children: the father lusting after his son's fiancée desires his death in order to be free to marry the girl himself, thus saddling his remaining children with a stepmother; the mother makes incestuous love with her offspring, daring to pollute by her sin the sanctity of the household gods. The end result has been an irrational overturning of all values and an alienation of the gods from the human race. Affronted by our universal degeneracy they no longer visit man's world or show themselves to mortal eyes.

The idea that the human race is degenerate was a commonplace in antiquity. Hesiod and Aratus, to mention no others, provide examples of the motif. Catullus follows in their footsteps, yet his version of the myth is generally felt to be unsatisfactory. Some have called it moralistic. If the adjective implies that he is narrow and conventional in his judgments, it is ill chosen. It is not narrowminded to deplore fratricide and incest. The trouble lies elsewhere. Quinn[38] has correctly diagnosed the weakness of the passage. Catullus' denunciation of the age is too direct, too abstract, too unqualified, too heavy-handed. Any opposition of shining virtue to conscienceless depravity is bound to seem melodramatic and Catullus has not managed to escape this trap. Furthermore, one is disturbed by the lack of any rational analysis of the problem. The poet points with alarm, wrings his hands, but goes no further. What has caused this hideous falling away into vice? Is it the fault of the Parcae? Or does time by its very nature mar and degrade the original harmony? What, if anything, can be done to halt and reverse the downward spiral? No answer is given; perhaps no one knows.[39]

*

Alexandrian in form,[40] no. 64 is no mere literary exercise. It is typically Catullan in its approaches, attitudes and preoccupations. An astonishing number of themes taken from the shorter poems are incorporated into its substance. The so-called moral epilogue denounces vices similar to those attacked in the invective poems. The mythical material introduces dramatic conflicts and expressions of hope and fear analogous to those which we have met in the Lesbia cycle. Ariadne consumed by passion and forsaken by her faithless lover is undoubtedly a surrogate for the poet himself. He takes her part, identifies with her, can see himself in her. Her lyric lament expresses a despair which reminds us of his own anguished disillusionment with Lesbia. Likewise he is personally involved in the story of Peleus and Thetis. The mythical pair represent what he had once hoped for in his relationship with Lesbia, at a time when she still seemed to him to be a goddess on earth. In brief, no. 64 recapitulates and expands most of the major themes which appear elsewhere in the body of his poetry. It is so thoroughly Catullan in spirit, so intimately related to his other writings and to his life experience, that it is difficult to see why it was once regarded as a translation from the Greek. Klingner is unquestionably right in regarding it as his greatest achievement, the crown of his literary career.[41]

CHAPTER TEN

Some Conclusions

As we have mentioned several times in this book, Catullus was one of the New Poets, a prominent member of that band of brilliant young men who, in the course of a single generation, succeeded in transforming Latin poetry. Until they made their influence felt, the dominant poetic genre at Rome had been the Ennian epic, heavy and long-winded, preoccupied with nationalistic themes, historically oriented and thoroughly impersonal. Departing from this tradition, the young innovators turned to Alexandria for their models and brought over into Latin literature the dominant forms of Hellenistic verse: miniature epic, elegy, and "lyric," i.e. the independent short poem. One of their chief aims was to master the literary erudition and concentrated brevity characteristic of the best Alexandrian writers. Along with high standards of craftsmanship in language and versification, they cultivated a new sophistication of outlook and a new ironic wit. Even more important, they initiated a shift from the state-centered values of their Roman predecessors to a new individualism and a new concern for the subjective and personal. In brief, the New Poets effected a radical change in the Roman literary sensibility and gave a different direction to the development of Latin poetry. The effect of their work on subsequent writers was lasting and profound.

It is easy to exaggerate the influence of the Alexandrians on the New Poets and in particular their influence on Catullus. Certainly he was no slavish imitator of the Greeks. He recognized an obligation to "make it new," in Ezra Pound's phrase. He realized that he had to move beyond his models, adapt the tradition to his own talent, carry it forward. To his short poems he brought an intimate and vivid personalism that marks an enormous advance upon the elegant, evasive conventionality of the Hellenistic epigram[1] and has no discernible parallel in Greek literature after early iambic and melic verse (e.g., Archilochus, Sappho, Alcaeus, Ibycus and Anacreon). His literary raw materials are purportedly taken from real life experience in the contemporary world. The experience par excellence is of course the madness or disease of passionate love, which strikes arbitrarily and irresistibly and makes its victim *miser*, pitiable, a pathos figure in the fullest sense of

the word. In language that often seems to approximate
ordinary colloquial usage, Catullus dramatizes the whole
course of his affair with Lesbia from its anxious beginnings to its acrid end.[2] It is this series of some two
dozen love poems (all short, except for no. 68 and no.
76) that, in the opinion of most modern readers, consti-
tutes his most creative innovation and his chief title
to literary fame.

     Yet his longer poems must not be underestimated.
Formerly dismissed as stuffy Alexandrian exercises, they
are now recognized as being no less innovative than the
Lesbia lyrics. In two of them, nos. 64 and 68, Catullus
introduces mythological subject matter and adopts a more
elevated style to match. The invocation of the heroes
in no. 64, 22-30 suggests that mythology offered him an
escape from his corrupt present into the ideal splendor
of an imagined past. More important than this rather
literary nostalgia is his technique of blending myth
with autobiography, a procedure that apparently was unknown to the Alexandrian Greeks. Peleus' marriage to
Thetis marks the fulfillment of a bliss that Catullus
had fleetingly and imperfectly experienced at the house
of Allius. Our author repeatedly identifies with the
passionate and suffering heroines of legend.[3] He sees
correspondences between his own pathos experience and
that of an Ariadne, overwhelmed by passion and abandoned
by her false lover. He empathizes with the ardent and
devoted Laodamia, who lost her irreplaceable Protesilaus
at Troy, the very place where his own brother was
buried. The interrelation of personal experience with
mythical paradigms in no. 68 foreshadows Augustan practice, expecially that of Propertius; for this reason
among many others, this poem has been called the proto-
type of Roman "subjective" love-elegy.

     These are fundamental innovations. Taken collec-
tively they make up the essence of what has been called
the "Catullan Revolution."[4] That revolution marks an
important advance over Alexandrian precedent, a broad-
ening of the classical sensibility, and a shift in the
whole direction of the Graeco-Roman literary tradition.
Nevertheless, it does not signal a complete break with
the past,[5] and therefore the term "revolution" is perhaps somewhat misleading. Radical discontinuities are
hard to find in literary history; probably they do not
exist. In many important ways Catullus is linked to
his predecessors and is plainly a continuator of established poetic practice. To call him a Romantic,[6] as
if he had somehow miraculously anticipated the European
literature of the Nineteenth Century, seems to me to be

a serious anachronism. Catullus is no Romantic. He is
an essentially classical author and by that very fact a
literary traditionalist.[7]

He is typically classical in his respect for the
exemplaria Graeca, the tested and approved models, both
Hellenistic and earlier. His debt to Sappho as a mono-
dist and as a composer of wedding-songs is already familiar to us and need not be rehearsed here: the very
name Lesbia, "girl of Lesbos," bears witness to his de-
pendence. His invective poems are based not only on
Archilochus, Hipponax and other Greeks but on the work
of his Roman predecessors in the comic-satiric tradition.[8] Ross has shown that most of the short elegiac
pieces are written in the style of pre-neoteric, old-
Roman epigram.[9] His close relationship with the Alexandrians, especially Callimachus, requires no further
documentation at this point. As a literary traditionalist he accepts without cavil the received genres of
classical poetry. He is familiar with the rhetoric
taught in the schools of his day and makes expert use
of it. In poetic diction, imagery and versification he
shows no significant break with established practice.
Like all other Latin authors he takes it for granted that
the correct method of literary composition is by
imitatio:[10] the poet's proper task is not to strive for
absolute originality but to rival and if possible to
excel the form and style of the recognized classics, the
great models of achievement in each kind. In addition,
he accepts the classical principle of decorum, which
prescribes that the style of any given poem must be appropriate to the presumed speaker, the circumstances and
the literary genre. This is strikingly evident in the
hymn to Diana, no. 34, but may be observed throughout
his writings.

Later Roman authors like to call Catullus *doctus,*
"polished," "accomplished."[11] For him as for the Alexandrians before him poetry is above all an art.
Ingenium, "innate talent," is of course indispensable;
so too is that strange subconscious impulse that we call
inspiration. All the same, poetry remains *ars,* an acquired skill. Skill is developed by study. We learn
from lines 31-36 of no. 68 that one needs a whole library of books in order to write a large-scale work.
No. 1 with its references to polish and pumice gives
us some idea of the importance Catullus attaches to
exact and discriminating craftsmanship. In no. 95 he
expresses his admiration for Cinna's ultra-Alexandrian
Zmyrna, an epyllion that was nine years in the writing.

Significantly, the Muses connote to our author not inspiration but technical expertise. They are *doctae
virgines*, "accomplished maidens" (no. 65, v. 2). He con-
fides his thoughts to them; they put his ideas into
memorable form and pass the result on to his readers
(no. 68, 41-50). So intent was Catullus upon mastering
the technical secrets of earlier writers that he even
deigned to compose verse translations of Callimachus
(the *Coma Berenices*, no. 66), of Sappho (no. 51) and
Theocritus (the *Pharmaceutria;* this version has not come
down to us, but it is referred to by the elder Pliny,
H.N. 28, 19). Such exercises no doubt helped him to acquire his distilled and concentrated style. The informal, colloquial manner that he deliberately adopts in
so many of the shorter poems must not be mistaken for
artless spontaneity; it is evidence for his skill in the
difficult art of concealing art. Even the least ambitious poems are workmanlike, competently constructed
and not devoid of artifice. We do not regret that they
have been preserved.[12]

The average emotional temperature of Catullus'
writings is high; hyperbole and rhetorical questions
abound. Nevertheless, the artist is invariably in control of his art. He is not thrown off balance by sheer
passion.[13] Even when he is in the grip of vehement love
or hate, he never dreams of rejecting or undervaluing
reason. On the other hand, lyric poetry that is bereft
of feeling is a contradiction in terms. Many of
Catullus' most unforgettable poems combine intense personal involvement with rational and artistic detachment.
The writer is at once the observer and the observed;
thought and emotion are intertwined. A similar combination of emotion and unfaltering insight has often
been discerned in Sappho.[14]

Non-Sapphic, however, is Catullus' technique of
dramatizing inner division by self-address. We have
called attention to several poems in which he apostrophizes himself by name: *Catulle, miser Catulle.*[15] Naturally these vocatives are associated with imperatives,
jussives or rhetorical questions. They are spoken by a
superior self who analyzes and understands to an (un-
replying) inferior self who agonizes or endures or is
simply unaware.[16] The superior self exhorts, arouses,
encourages or warns the inferior self. We are not always sure that he wins out, but he never gives up hope,
never stops trying.

Catullus did not write to please a literary patron;

he had no need of one. He wrote to please himself and a small circle of like-minded friends. His primary audience was therefore a lettered elite. Wheeler[17] is no doubt correct in supposing that the poems were at first passed around from hand to hand and only at a later date made available to a wider readership. The general public, when they read his published work, found themselves treated as semi-outsiders, not fully informed about what was going on. They were allowed only to overhear the poet's words. Probably they missed many of the elliptical and half-hidden allusions. So do we; it is just this semi-private quality that obscures the meaning of many of the occasional pieces to this very day. Barring the unlikely event of new information turning up, the ultimate intention of many passages will in all probability never be recovered.

Hand in hand with his literary traditionalism goes a distinct conservatism in morals and religion.[18] Unlike his many false friends, Catullus honors the virtues of *fides*, "good faith," and *pietas*, "responsibility." He insists upon loyalty and integrity in personal relationships. He naively expects men and women to stand by their sworn word and to show gratitude for benefits received. In time of crisis he turns to the just and merciful gods in prayer (no. 76). He writes a hymn to Diana, perhaps with a view to public presentation at a religious festival; he prays that she may protect and preserve the people of Romulus. He even offers the archaic *inferiae* at his brother's grave in the Troad, in spite of the fact that he knows the rite is vain and ineffectual. In his wedding-songs he upholds the old-fashioned upper-class view that *par conubium*, "marriage with a fitting and proper partner," is a blessing both to family and nation; he maintains that *iustum matrimonium* is in accordance with nature, reason, law and immemorial custom, and indeed that it is the gods' best gift to the human race.

On the other hand, there is also a strain of nonconformity and rebellion in Catullus. Since he was wealthy and well-born, he could afford a certain independence of outlook. In his invectives he cuts a very different figure from the pathetic *miser* of the poems of complaint. He speaks out with republican forthrightness and blistering obscenity against Caesar and Pompey and their underlings, whom he regards as destroyers of the commonwealth, obsessively intent upon consolidating political power and appropriating the spoils that belong by right to the state. Few would

157

have dared to say so much so openly. Yet he attacks politicians on personal rather than ideological grounds: probably he did not understand the realities of politics very well. Certainly his attitude toward Rome's exploitation of conquered peoples is unenlightened and unreflective. Like the vast majority of his contemporaries, he takes it for granted that the empire exists for the economic advantage of the ruling class.

He is exceptional in his rejection of normal Roman career objectives. Apart from his year in Bithynia, he lived a life of *otium*. He manifested no interest in entering politics, law, the army or public administration. The central concerns of his life were poetry and love; in both areas he was a pioneer. Before his time, writers had regarded love as a youthful aberration to be presented in the comic or satiric mode. Catullus insisted upon taking love seriously. At the beginning of the affair, Lesbia was his *domina* and he her servant; or even more hyperbolically, she was his radiant goddess and he her worshipper. Later he dreamt of a perfect relationship with her, grounded in physical passion to be sure, but sanctioned by oaths and marked by *bene velle* and *consensio* on both sides; it was to be a companionship of kindred spirits. He said that he felt for her a responsible and protective affection such as fathers feel for their sons and for their daughters' husbands. Yet in spite of these idealistic yearnings he openly admitted that he was carrying on a love affair with a married woman. How could he square this conduct with his vaunted *pietas* is a puzzling question.

His main concern is with man, not nature. Nature for its own sake does not interest him very much. Of course, he often describes the world around him, but these descriptions serve either as a basis for comparisons (e.g., the mountain cascade in no. 68, 57-62) or as a significant background for human speech and action (e.g., the seascapes of no. 64).[19] Like most Latin authors, he is repelled by wild and desolate scenery. The remote woodlands of the Diana hymn inspire a certain awe, but he shudders at the dark snow-clad forests of Cybele's sinister mountain. Even well-cultivated farmland subdued by human labor and ministering to human needs (which Ruskin[20] regarded as the favorite Roman landscape) fails to excite his admiration. We recall how, in his spring poem (no. 46), he flees the rich plowland of sweltering Nicaea for the shining cities of Asia. He simply does not share Horace's enthusiasm for the country life or Virgil's passion for agriculture. It is true that Sirmio appeals to him partly because of its natural beauty, but he values even more the security it affords and the opportunity for repose after the hardships of travel abroad. Rome, not Sirmio, was his usual place of residence; the metropolis was more attractive than the countryside. At times he seems to sense that nature is positively alien to man. It has no kinship with us. In our sufferings the elements mock us by their indifference, and the endless cycles of the external world taunt our ephemeral hold on existence. Man is not fully at home in his world.

Catullus has a favorable opinion of himself. Notwithstanding his occasional excursions into mild self-mockery, he is not troubled by feelings of inadequacy or inferiority. He readily assumes the role of an urbane arbiter of social behavior, and passes confident judgment on the gaucheries and ineptitudes of his acquaintances. He girds against his *saeclum insapiens et infacetum,* his "witless, tasteless generation" (no. 43, 8). He retaliates against his rivals with scathing invective. In some respects he believes he stands far above other men. Especially does he praise himself as a faithful lover. He compares his love for Lesbia to a beautiful but defenseless flower, nicked and destroyed by the plow of her *culpa.* The world has never seen a *fides* to equal his, nor will it ever again.[21] No one can be his parallel.

Despite this conviction of personal uniqueness, the modern reader ordinarily has little difficulty identifying with him. All poetry worthy of the name fuses the particular with the universal. His thoughts, experiences and emotions are widely shared,[22] especially by young people. Betrayal and rejection are common experiences. Disillusionment is nothing new. Many youthful idealists (Hamlet was not the first) have discovered to their pain that reality does not live up to their expectations, that ingratitude is pandemic, that society is sometimes foolish but more often corrupt, that the flower of love is callously destroyed, that death is final, that this world can show itself a god-forsaken hell, that there are innumerable reasons for pessimism and despair. But Catullus is not always sad. He knows the joy of homecomings, the delight of reunions, the solid satisfactions of true friendship, the sweetness of laughter and kisses, and the exhilaration that comes from plenty of good wine. Excellence does not belong entirely to the past. The wedding songs celebrate fruitfulness, concord and fidelity, happiness in love and in the ongoing continuity of the family. In sum, whether he praises or finds fault, he thinks and feels as many of us still do. He bears witness to the unchanging substratum of human nature. If he did not do so, his poetry would not be classical.

Many classical writers think of man as a paradoxical blend of grandeur and misery. Man is magnificent in his capacity for heroic achievement but pitiable because of the manifold limitations under which life must be lived. Catullus does not altogether accept this formula. He does not deny the possibility of heroism but sees it as belonging to the remote past (Peleus) and as often flawed or spurious even then (Theseus, Achilles). On the other hand, he has a thoroughly classical awareness of human finitude. In his view, our freedom is compromised in a minor sense by other men but in a major sense by time, fortune, fate (the Parcae) and the gods. Against the depredations of the first three he sees no appeal; the gods, however, are ambivalent. He holds that they punish the guilty, but they do not always protect the innocent. At their best they impose obligations of *fides* and *pietas* ; if we live up to these obligations we are entitled to call upon them in prayer when trouble comes. Usually we do not live up to them, and therefore the world has become a moral waste land in which even the holiest bonds of affection are regularly dishonored. At their worst they smite us with passion (Venus and Cupid) or inexplicable madness (Cybele). Really, the cards are stacked against us. Man is born to trouble as the sparks fly upward. To live is to suffer, either through our own fault or that of others or through the very structure of reality; and the end of all is total extinction, *nox perpetua*.

This is a dark picture, but I repeat that Catullus is far from being a total pessimist. Life does offer major consolations, though the sort that most men value are vain. Catullus does not believe in transcendence through responsible and devoted service to the commonwealth, as many Romans of his class and status did; or through conversion to philosophy, whether Stoic or Epicurean, with its notorious devaluation of the affective life; or through initiation into one or another of the many oriental mystery cults. He certainly does not believe man can save himself through the pursuit of power, wealth and status. Crass hedonism does not seriously tempt him. Depressed by the decadence of the contemporary world, he has no hopes the process may be reversed and a better age be at hand; he dreamed of no new *saeclorum ordo* such as Virgil foresaw in his Fourth

Eclogue. For Catullus, the major sources of satisfaction are true friends (especially fellow poets), conviviality, love in its glorious beginnings, familiar and beloved surroundings (e.g., Sirmio), the joys of a clear conscience, and above all his art.

Not that he believed in art for art's sake.[23] Poetry to Catullus is a *source* of good, both to his readers and to himself. To his readers it is valuable not only because of the pure pleasure it gives but also because of the wisdom it imparts. Poetry can be a way of teaching, advising, exhorting and consoling. As vicarious experience it enhances our understanding of the human predicament. To the poet, his poetry is even more. It is self-expression first, a kind of safety valve for the pent-up emotions. Further it confers power: power to celebrate whatever may merit praise; power to punish the wicked, to expose the inept, to defend the helpless and to retaliate upon the ungrateful. Even more important it is a way to self-understanding. One of the best ways to sort out one's experience, to make sense of one's existence, is to try to write a good poem about it. And finally if the *patrona virgo* grants her favor, it is a way to create a series of artifacts which, in a qualified sense at least, will escape the destructive power of time and last *plus uno saeclo* : down through the years.

F I N I S

NOTES TO CHAPTER ONE

In the footnotes, books and articles on Catullus are referred to by the author's name, date and page number(s) only: for further information consult the *List of Works Cited*, pp. 182 below.

1. Poem 11, 10-12 alludes to Caesar's crossing of the Rhine in the summer of 55 B.C.; poem 45, 22 refers to war preparations against Britain and the east, under way in 55 B.C.; poem 55, 6 mentions Pompey's portico, perhaps dedicated in 55 B.C.; poem 113, 2 speaks of Pompey's second consulship, also 55 B.C.
2. I do not insist upon these dates; Bardon 1970, 5-8 indicates how shaky they are.
3. There is no direct evidence of this, but it seems a reasonable assumption: see Kroll 1968, v.
4. Whether the New Poets (sometimes called the "Neoterics") constituded a "school" in the modern sense is a matter of debate. For a fuller assessment of the movement see Quinn 1959, esp. 44-48; Newman 1967, esp. 52-60; Ross 1975, 3-8; Schmidt 1975, 1630-1631; Granarolo 1973, 278-360; and Lyne 1978, 167-187.
5. Literally, "girl of Lesbos." Catullus thinks of her as comparable to the girls addressed by Sappho (7th/6th century B.C.) in her love poems, and of himself therefore as a second Sappho, Roman and male. See Lieberg 1962, 92-95 and the literature there cited; also Bayet 1956, 47-48.
6. The evidence for this identification is set forth by C. Deroux 1973, 390-416 (with an abundant bibliography).
7. For details about the nickname *Quadrantaria* see Austin 1952, 124-125.
8. Or perhaps "explained himself"; see Granarolo 1958, 66.
9. But as we shall see in Chapter Three the praise is very probably ironic.
10. Lindsay 1948, 90; Wilder 1963, 142.
11. As is pointed out by Levens 1968, 361-2; Bardon 1970, 8; and others. Only some twenty poems are roughly datable: see Quinn 1959, 102. The attempts of Maas 1942, 81ff. and Stoessl 1977 to establish a full and exact chronology for the poems have not won a favorable reception. Stoessl's book has been subjected to a thorough and stinging review by Wiseman 1979. The reconstructions of Quinn 1972 are by the author's own admission extremely speculative.
12. Levy 1968, 249-53 supports Tenny Frank's theory that the discoverer of the MS was Benvenuto's patron Cangrande della Scala, overlord of Verona from 1311 to 1339. In line 3 of the epigram Benvenuto derives the first element of Cangrande's name from the Old French *cane*, "reed," equivalent to the Latin *calamus*.

Line 4 perhaps alludes to an equestrian statue of Cangrande at Verona (see Levy's photograph, p. 252); the overlord gazes down at the "transient throng" with an air of amused astonishment; Skutsch 1976, 18, however, holds that this statue was erected after Benvenuto's death.

13. But see Clausen 1976, 43 and Skutsch 1969, 148.
14. Wheeler 1934, 23 and 30. On the arrangement and publication of Catullus' poems see Fordyce 1961, 409-10. Fordyce's views, which follow Ellis 1878, xlvi-1 and Wheeler's first chapter, have recently been endorsed by Wilkinson 1974, 84. Clausen 1976, 37-43 accepts Wheeler's conclusions in essence. For opposing theories see Segal 1968, 300-301; Wiseman 1969, 1-31; Quinn 1972, 9-20, 52-53; Giardina 1974, 224-35; and Granarolo 1973-74, 61-62. A summary bibliography on the question is provided by Vretska 1964 I, 1090; Granarolo 1973-74, 49-62 is fuller.
15. It is only fair to note that several recent investigators part company with Wheeler here, holding that the *polymetra* (or most of them) were published in the present order by Catullus himself: consult Wiseman 1969, 1-6; Quinn 1972, 17; Van Sickle 1981, 69. In addition, some argue that the elegiacs, nos. 65 to 116, might also have formed a separate book; see Quinn 1972, 12-15.
16. Buchheit 1959, 320, quoting Knoche, *Gymnasium* 1958, 155ff.
17. Despite Elder 1966, 148.
18. According to Catullus. Fraenkel 1962, 259 holds (with Jacoby) that Cornelius merely translated, for Greek history, the *Chronica* of Apollodorus.
19. Gow-Page 1965, II 459 and the references there cited; Loomis 1972, 34-62.
20. Bowra 1961, 391-6.
21. Herzog 1936, 338-41 tries to combine 14b with 2b to form a single whole. The resulting "poem" is even more cryptic than its constituent parts.

NOTES TO CHAPTER TWO

1. Fraenkel 1950, II, 395-6 and references there cited; Finley 1965, 103-9.
2. Veranius turns up in three other poems of Catullus. According to no. 12, 15-16 he had been in Spain with another friend of the poet, Fabullus. Both are mentioned in nos. 28 and 47 as members of the retinue of a provincial governor named Piso.
3. It is only partially synonymous with *vultus*, which means "face" with especial reference to the eyes; see Ernout-Meillet 1959-1960, 469 and 751.
4. On Fabullus see note 2 above.
5. We should not conclude from this vividly hyperbolic image that Catullus is a bohemian starving in a garret. He is simply (as

we should say) a young man between allowance checks.

6. Witke 1980 rebuts recent attempts to interpret the *unguentum* of this poem in an obscene sense.
7. Vessey 1971, 48.
8. But see Cairns 1975, 27-29.
9. Some other renderings: "here is Bacchus undiluted" (Quinn 1970 *ad loc*): "I am Bacchus' man, through and through" (Bolton 1967, 12).
10. Wiseman 1969, 7-8 fancifully supposes that "bitterer cups" (v. 2) is programmatic, announcing the harsh invective wit of the poems which follow (e.g., nos. 28 and 29).
11. This Caelius is sometimes identified with the M. Caelius Rufus whom we have referred to in Chapter One, but the Caelius of no. 100 is a Veronese (v. 2) and Caelius Rufus was not.
12. Quinn 1959, 80.
13. Granarolo 1967, 119.
14. For two versions of what actually happened see Tanner 1972, 506 and Fehling 1974, 376.
15. Croce 1943, 67-68; similarly Kroll 1968, vii in an oft-quoted phrase called him an *urwüchsiger Naturbursche*, a "primitive child of nature." Both judgments are seriously misleading.
16. For another view of no. 35 see Khan 1974. Khan regards the poem as an example of Catullus' consummate tact; he is giving Caecilius an excuse for turning down his invitation on the ground that the Cybele poem has made an irresistible impression on the bluestocking girlfriend.
17. Otis 1966, 226 and 391-392 for further details and a partial reconstruction.
18. Klingner 1964, 157.
19. Fraenkel 1962, 263, following Jachmann; for a brief defense of the unity of no. 95 see Elder 1966, 148, n. 7.
20. Murray 1927, 112. For details on Catullus' use of this meter consult Sedgwick 1950, 64-69; West 1957, 98-102; Duhigg 1971, 57-61; and especially Patzer 1955, 77-95.
21. Klingner 1956, 202-204 is excellent on this aspect of Catullus' elegiac epigrams.
22. Ross 1969, 115-139.
23. Discussed in Chapter Six below.
24. In no. 50, *otium* is praised: we shall meet another view of *otium* in no. 51 (Chapter Three).
25. Quinn 1970, 237.
26. Wilkinson 1974, 82 (following Macnaghten and Ramsay) sees a similar shyness in no. 51.
27. Buchheit 1976 goes farther; in his view, no. 50 expresses Catullus' total commitment to poetry as a special, quasi-Dionysian way of life. This article is an extension of Segal 1970.
28. Frazer 1959, 559-562.
29. This is the interpretation of Fraenkel 1956, 278ff. It has not gone unchallenged. Davis 1971, 297-302, following Tränkle

1967, 93-99, holds that Quintilia was Calvus' mistress, not his wife, and that there is no indication that he was unfaithful to her; in v. 4 *missas* means "long departed" or "gone," not "rejected."

30. So taken by Fraenkel 1956, 288, with Ferrero, and by Bardon 1970, 115.
31. So taken by Quinn 1963, 81 and Granarolo 1967, 30-32.
32. Williams, 1968, 189 thinks the *si* marks an acceptance of the terms in which Calvus wrote his own elegy on Quintilia.
33. Line 6 is thought to echo a line from Calvus' elegy, *frag.* 16B (Morel): *forsitan hoc etiam gaudeat ipsa cinis,* "perhaps even the ashes may still rejoice in this."
34. Copley 1956, 125-9 along with most interpreters believes this is a serious poem. Ross 1969, 101 thinks Catullus is not in earnest: the reference to Simonides is "playful."
35. Quinn 1959, 41-42 and 1970, 417; against him see Forsyth 1975.
36. According to Frank 1928, 65 this is P. Alfenus Varus the jurist, later *legatus* of Octavian and *consul suffectus* in 39 B.C. He may be identical with the Varus of nos. 10 and 22.
37. On this metre see Loomis 1972, 145-149.
38. Vessey 1971, 54-55 conjectures that Catullus and Alfenus had a homosexual relationship; Witke 1967 attempts to revive the theory that Alfenus had lured Catullus into intimacy with Lesbia; but it is improbable that *amorem* in v. 8 refers to anything other than friendship with Alfenus.
39. As Neudling 1955, 37f. argues.
40. Granarolo's splendid analysis (1967, 310-372) of the expressive question in Catullus is highly instructive and deserves a careful reading; notice especially p. 355, on the present passage.
41. Kroll 1968 *ad loc.*
42. Baehrens 1893 *ad loc.*
43. No. 78b, sometimes connected with 77, seems to be a separate fragment; Kroll 1968 *ad loc.* believes it is the remnant of an attack on Clodia's brother, P. Clodius Pulcer, who is also assailed in the following epigram, no. 79.
44. Ross 1969, 118-119, following D.L. West, sees Catullan elision as conveying emotional intensity. I would definitely agree; no. 9, v. 6 has already supplied an instance.
45. Weinreich 1969, 51.
46. *Rhet.* II, 4, 21.

NOTES TO CHAPTER THREE

1. Murray 1927, 255.
2. Maybe more; see Quinn 1972, 72.
3. For a judicious interpretation of Sappho's poem, accompanied by full bibliography, see Kirkwood 1974, 120-122 and 255-60.
4. Kidd 1963, 298-308 offers a detailed analysis of Catullus'

departure from his model.

5. This is the current consensus. Wilkinson 1974, 82-5 states the case for regarding it as a separate poem, but I cannot accept his conclusions. Richmond 1970, 197-204 and Clausen 1976, 40 also separate the last stanza from what precedes.

6. *Otium* in this poem is interpreted in a variety of ways; for some sample opinions consult Lattimore 1944, 184-7; Fraenkel 1957, 212; Kidd 1963, 304; Frank 1968, 237. My view is closest to that of Woodman 1966, 217-226.

7. Grimaldi 1965, 87-95 and Commager 1965, 83-110 have excellent remarks on this aspect of Catullus' art; it is also touched upon by Kidd 1963, 299-300.

8. Recently interpreted (together with nos. 43 and 51) by Rankin 1976.

9. He does not catalogue her charms. As has often been noted, the only physical attribute he singles out for special mention is her foot (no. 68, 70-72).

10. Cicero would not have disagreed with this assessment. He writes of him (*Att.* 1, 18, 1), "Metellus is no human being, only sand, air, pure desolation."

11. Khan 1971, 165.

12. On these two poems consult Segal 1968, 284-301. I am conscious of a special debt to this excellent article.

13. Wilder 1963, 148 imagines Clodia as a person who is very good at mathematics and who knows "all about the stars and what they do." This pleasing fancy gives added point not only to nos. 5 and 7 but perhaps also to the *Coma Berenices*, no. 66.

14. Mynors regards 2b as a fragment of another poem and not part of no. 2. This must be correct; the indicative of v. 11 does not square with the subjunctive of line 9. For an ingenious but finally unconvincing attempt to join 2 and 2b see Lieberg 1962, 99-110. I have already mentioned (Chapter One, note 21) Herzog's endeavor to combine 2b with 14b.

15. Poeschl 1960, 17.

16. The curious reader may wish to consult Dorothy Parker's acid sequel to this poem in which Lesbia says, "I called it sweet and made believe I cried:/the stupid fool! I've always hated birds." (*Collected Poems*, p. 181).

17. It has not always been taken in this way. E.P. Morris (commended by Wheeler 1934, 228-30) regarded the poem as a humorous portrayal of Catullus "in the character of a lover trying to touch her heart by the vain threat of leaving her." Recently this idea has been revived and extended by Skinner 1971, 298ff., who holds that the speaker is so inconsistent that Catullus must be dramatizing himself as a comic lover. The tone is one of self-mockery; the poet stands aside to contemplate his own folly with detached and sardonic irony; this is his defense against self pity. Perhaps, but I doubt that Catullus' sense of tragicomedy reached that far. My own interpretation is modelled in general upon that of Rowland 1966, 15-21. Connor 1974 sees no. 8 as moving from good-humored

cajolery in the opening lines to a new mood of blustering attack at the close.

18. Baehrens 1893, *ad loc.* (p. 109).

19. No. 8 is the first poem written in scazons, i.e. five iambs followed by a trochee. On this metre see Loomis 1972, 102-18. It will recur in nos. 72, 31, 37, 39, 44, 59, 60.

20. We have already noted similar deficiencies in no. 73 (Chapter Two).

21. It is generally assumed that she must be the *puella* of lines 2 and 9, but her name does not appear in the text; so too in no. 8.

22. That the *Annales* are "monstrous" is implied in line 8: portents and prodigies were destroyed in a fire of wood from "sterile" (*infelicibus*) trees.

23. The revisionist interpretation of Österud 1978, according to which the "hymn" to Venus is seriously intended and poem no. 36 itself constitues the sacrifice offered to her, I find singularly unpersuasive.

24. The meaning of *foedus amicitiae* (v. 6) is highly controversial. McGushin 1967, 91 tries to show that it virtually equals marriage. Although it is true that in no. 96, 4 *amicitia* is used in apparent reference to the marriage of Calvus and Quintilia, McGushin's interpretation makes Catullus' attitude toward Lesbia seem much more commonplace than it probably was. Ross 1969, 80-95 and 1975, 9-15, following Reitzenstein, holds that in no. 109, 6 and in other similar contexts (e.g. no. 72, 4 and 76, 1-6) the poet regards his relationship with Lesbia as metaphorically equivalent to a Roman political "friendship." In my view, it is improbable that the idealistic and unpolitical Catullus would allow his conception of love to be colored by the utilitarian conventions of party politics. It is much more likely that the *foedus amicitiae* of no. 109, 6 represents a conflation of traditional Roman social and religious conceptions with the theories of *philia* (love and/or friendship) set forth by certain Greek writers, especially the sources utilized by Cicero in his *de Amicitia*. Catullus may also be thinking of the *philia* of Hellenistic love epigram.

25. The verb that she uses in line 1 is *nubere*, lit. "to take the marriage veil," but this is probably just a euphemism for "to make love": see Lieberg 1962, 264n.3. There is no solid evidence to show that Lesbia ever contemplated actual marriage to Catullus.

26. Copley 1949, 33-35 thinks that Catullus is torn by guilt feelings over wanting someone whom he does not love, but this interpretation introduces religious scruples foreign to Romans of Catullus' generation, as Elder 1951, 128 rightly objects.

27. As is pointed out by Hallet 1973, 110, the paterfamilias would choose his sons-in-law with great care, take pride in them, hold them in the highest esteem, assure them of his unqualified support and backing.

28. *Odi* and *amo*, though transitive verbs, are not supplied with

direct objects, and a certain elliptical ambiguity results. Does the poet mean that he loves certain qualities in her but hates certain others? Or does he simultaneously love and hate the same qualities? Although the latter is more likely to tear one in two, the former must be meant: he hates her behavior but "loves" her *venustas*.

29. Weinreich 1969, 51. He also calls attention to the super-abundance of verbs in no. 8.
30. Weinreich 1959, 75-90, followed by Lieberg 1962, 276-277. The attempt of Schaefer 1966, 63-68 to rebut Weinreich I find unconvincing.
31. The phrasing of Ross 1969, 172 can scarcely be bettered: "The request has precedent, is within the gods' power, and the recipient is worthy."
32. We reserve discussion of the religious aspects of no. 76 for Chapter Eight below. The long elegy, no. 68, will be taken up in Chapter Seven.
33. It will be recalled that no. 77 (Chapter Two) is also addressed to a certain Rufus; he may be identical with the addressee of the present poem. See Neudling 1955, 37f.
34. For a recent interpretation consult Penella 1976.
35. See the arguments of Friedrich, 1908 *ad loc.*
36. Wilamowitz 1924, II 307. For an able statement of the opposing view (the poem is friendly to Furius and Aurelius) see Kinsey 1965, 537-44.
37. Wilder 1963, 50 explains this hostility by the hypothesis that while still a child she had been violated by her uncle. This is sheer fiction but psychologically plausible.
38. Fraenkel 1955, 5f. Putnam 1974 discusses the implications of the flower-image in detail.
39. For an extension of my remarks in this paragraph see Burck 1952, 166-7 and Klingner 1956, 107.
40. C.S. Lewis 1936, 5.
41. Commager 1965, 103.
42. We shall discuss the invectives against Lesbia in greater detail in Chapter Four.

NOTES TO CHAPTER FOUR

1. Wheeler 1934, 44.
2. Tennyson called Catullus "tenderest of Roman poets." That is as may be (No. 61, 216-20 may supply an example), but he was not always tender.
3. It is not easy to bring these terms over into believable English. A man who is *lepidus* is sparkling and smart in speech, graceful in utterance and action. A *venustus* is a man of finer feeling. An *urbanus* is polished and sophisticated. A *facetus* is a man of ironic wit. Additional implications emerge in special contexts.

4. It is not so loutish, however, as that of no. 69 (on the body-odor of Rufus) or no. 23 (on Furius' constipation problem) or no. 97 (on Aemilius' foul breath).

5. In fact it has been plausibly conjectured that sexual jealousy is the ultimate motive behind his satiric attacks on a number of adversaries, named or anonymous, whose personal relations with the poet are otherwise obscure: for example, no. 97 against Aemilius; no. 98 against Victius; no. 69 against Rufus; and nos. 71 and 78b against unnamed enemies. These epigrams are conspicuous for their violence and grotesque obscenity.

6. A pun, conscious or unconscious, may be involved: Ravidus sounds like *rabidus*, "madman."

7. Obscenity is simply the violation of a linguistic taboo. It is traditional and expected in Latin invective verse. Neverthe-less it provides a good clue to the author's tone of voice, signalling anger, disgust or contempt. It is often associated with a kind of macho self-affirmation. Scholars have long shied away from the topic but they are beginning to pluck up courage; see Granarolo 1967, 162-177; Bardon 1970, 65-74; Lateiner 1977.

8. On these poems consult Bardon 1970, 81-83 with the literature there cited; also Schaefer 1966, 28-33; Forsyth 1972/73, 175-177; Stoessl 1972, 408; and Macleod 1973, 304.

9. For further details on no. 116 see Forsyth 1977.

10. The reader will pardon the anachronism involved in this trans-lation.

11. It is precisely defined (in Latin) by Kroll 1968, 35; for further comment consult Housman 1931, 408 and Richlin 1981.

12. Baehrens 1893, 219.

13. On the theme of incest in Catullus see Rankin 1976.

14. Ferrero 1955, 201.

15. See however the full discussion in Williams 1968, 550-556. It must be conceded that in poem no. 16 (discussed below) Catullus seems to deny that the Juventius poems have a basis in actual experience; see Schaefer 1966, 12.

16. For fuller discussion see Neudling 1955, 19-20 and 94-96.

17. For evidence that the rival attacked in nos. 24 and 81 is actually Furius see Schaefer 1966, 26, who extends the argu-ments of Kroll 1968 *ad locc.*

18. As was pointed out in the preceding chapter, there is scholarly disagreement about Catullus' attitude toward Furius and Aurelius. In most of the poems addressed to them the tone seems extremely abusive. Nevertheless Quinn 1959, 107 and 1972, 164ff. argues that in Catullus' society such abuse does not necessarily signal enmity. Kinsey 1965, 537-538 and Macleod 1973, 294-303 endorse this view. Though tempted by their arguments, I have elected to follow Richardson 1963, 93-106 in taking Catullus' abusive language seriously.

19. Rankin 1976 gives a clear and persuasive account of this poem.

20. For a full discussion of *sal* and *lepos* in this poem see Buchheit 1976.

21. Ferrero 1955, 95-102, esp. 100.
22. Taylor 1949, 145.
23. Most recently Fredricksmeyer 1973.
24. No. 68, 135-40 is his nearest approach to it.
25. Pascal 1916, 136-139.
26. On Catullus' political poems Deroux 1970, 608-631 is useful.
27. This partisan of Caesar had been prosecuted by Calvus in a notable series of orations alluded to in nos. 14, 3 and 53, 2-3.
28. No. 52 (along with no. 29 and no. 4) is written in iambic trimeters: on this metre see Loomis 1972, 87-101.
29. This is the superbly Lawrentian rendition of James Michie 1969, 205 (and elsewhere).
30. For a recent analysis of the Ameana poems see Skinner 1978-9.
31. See Granarolo 1958, 292 for an illuminating discussion of the word *cinaedus*. Some hold that *Romulus* (v. 5) designates Pompey or the typical Roman citizen rather than Caesar: most recently, Cameron 1976.
32. Bickel 1949, 15.
33. *Jul.* 73, quoted earlier (Chapter One).
34. On the *clementia Caesaris* see Taylor 1949, 165.
35. Two further poems of self-criticism, nos. 10 and 28, will be taken up in the next chapter.
36. Aufilena, who according to no. 100 was once loved by Quintius of Verona (cf. no. 82), is vigorously attacked in nos. 110 and 111. In no. 110 she accepts money from Catullus and then reneges on her promises; in no. 111 she is accused of incest with her uncle. For a recent discussion of these epigrams see Stoessl 1973, 450-456.
37. This is a parody of *flagitatio*, a recognized method of recovering stolen property; consult Williams 1968, 197-198 and Fraenkel 1961, 49-51.
38. So Quinn 1969, 24 and 1970, 145.
39. On the metre of no. 17 ("priapean") see Loomis 1972, 70-72.
40. Mynors' reading *attigerit*, v. 20, offers grammatical difficulties; one is tempted to accept the Renaissance conjecture *attigerat*. I follow the reconstruction of the story given by Kroll 1968 and Quinn 1970; for some other versions see Lenchantin 1928, 203-207; Copley 1949, 245ff.; Neudling 1955, 22; and Richardson 1967, 423-42. Scholarly disagreement continues.
41. Dryden, *A Discourse Concerning the Original and Progress of Satire*, 1693.
42. Notably Baker 1958, 110-112 and Ross 1965, 256-259; they were anticipated by Croce 1943, 70. For another view see Nielsen 1977.
43. Aristotle *Rhetoric* II, 8, 9 (a passage of great interest for Juvenal criticism).
44. Willey, 1940, 106-107.

1. Wheeler 1934, 95-96 and 256; Quinn 1972, 155-157.
2. Frank 1928, 104 and 1933, 249-256. His arguments are by no means conclusive. Williams 1968, 716 says that no convincing connection between Catullus and Lucretius can be established: "their relationship, if any, is totally uncertain."
3. According to Wheeler 1934, 96 (following Ellis and Kroll); but Neudling 1955, 178 thinks that Catullus visited his brother's grave and wrote the poem in the course of his journey back to Italy.
4. See for example Odyssey XI, 216-24 and the remarks of Stanford 1947, 381.
5. Granarolo 1967, 314 n. 3 calls this a *question angoisée*. See note 40, Chapter Two (above).
6. For an analysis of this simile see Fraenkel 1921, 82-83.
7. Granarolo 1967, 300-302. (Catullus is not referring to literary compositions.)
8. Bardon 1970, 84 remarks that "chaque fois qu'il fait allusion à son frere, il s'adresse à lui."
9. So Baehrens 1893, *ad loc.*
10. See the classic account of these rites in Fustel de Coulanges 1956, 21-25.
11. My account of no. 46 is derived in part from Wilhelm 1965, 304. There is a useful discussion of this poem, along with no. 31, in Schaefer 1966, 33-37.
12. Baehrens 1893, 245-6 (on vv. 4 and 6).
13. An epigram of Cinna (fr. xi Morel) suggests that he may have made the voyage back along with Catullus.
14. Most recently discussed by Moore-Blunt 1974.
15. This point is stressed by Musurillo 1961.
16. The technique of no. 50 (Chapter Two) is similar.
17. See note 11, Chapter Four.
18. Presumably the father of Caesar's last wife Calpurnia, whom he married in 59 B.C. See the discussion in Neudling 1955, 42-45. He was impeached by Cicero in 55 B.C.
19. Frank 1938, 83.

NOTES TO CHAPTER SIX

1. Although it is rather brief and technically one of the *polymetra*, the hymn to Diana will be bracketed with the longer poems because of its choral character. No. 67, the address to the door, although one of the longer poems, has already taken up in the discussion of satire and comedy, Chapter Four.
2. Stigers 1977 is outstandingly excellent on this poem.
3. On amoebaean song see Gow 1950, II 92-94; Merkelbach 1956,

97-113.

4. See the remarks of Fraenkel 1955, 6-8 and Granarolo 1967, 306 n. 1, 309.

5. Wilamowitz 1924, II 280 calls it "ein Wettsingen zwischen [Catull] und Sappho, sozusagen eine Tenzone."

6. Bowra 1961, 3-13, but note the qualifications of Kirkwood 1974, 10.

7. I follow the view of comedy developed by Northrop Frye 1957, 163-186.

8. Brilliantly sketched by Fustel de Coulanges, 1956, 42-48.

9. I assume that this is a medieval conception; see Highet 1949, 57-58.

10. P. Fedeli, 1972 devotes an entire monograph to the analysis and interpretation of this poem.

11. The pattern is $\times\times - \cup\cup -\cup\times$ (glyconic), $\times\times-\cup\cup-\times$ (pherecratic). For a full discussion of this metre consult Loomis 1972, 63-86.

12. Wheeler 1934, 201-205.

13. Four times it occurs with a repeated *O* in the form *O Hymenaee Hymen/Hymen O Hymenaee,* but eleven times (during the procession, vv. 114-183) in the fuller and more excited form, with *io* repeated: *io Hymen Hymenaee io/io Hymen Hymenaee.*

14. On this type of imagery consult Luck 1969, 134-136.

15. This burning torch, repeatedly mentioned, is emblematic of the proper moment for marriage, which takes place in the early evening (recall the refrain *sed abit dies,* "but daylight fades"). Surprisingly, the torch is absent from no. 62 and from the epithalamium in no. 64 (but cf. the figurative use in v. 25). In no. 62 its place is taken by six references to the rising of the fiery evening star, which has much the same symbolic meaning. The evening star is not mentioned in no. 61 but is alluded to once in no. 64 (v. 329).

16. This is stressed later on: note *puellula,* "little girl," vv. 175 and 181.

17. Perhaps the modern larkspur, considered to be the tallest and most beautiful of the Roman garden flowers.

18. Not, however, to his face; Manlius is not present at the *Fescennina iocatio* but waiting at home (according to the fiction of the poem).

19. This imagined blush is intended as a humorous compliment to Junia. We moderns are annoyed when we are caught blushing; to the Romans the blush was a sign of good character, or at least of a soul not yet lost to shame: see Seneca, *Epistulae Morales* xi.

20. Granarolo 1967, 304.

21. "On the Poetry of Catullus" in *The Complete Works,* ed. T. Earle Welby, XI p. 209.

22. Tufte 1970, 22.

23. It is misleading to call them "The Fates." Fate usually means cosmic necessity, i.e., the fundamentally mysterious power,

173

above and beyond the gods themselves, whereby things inevitably come to be as they are. The Parcae do not represent this cosmic necessity but only a small part of it. They spin the course of our lives into existence. This spinning precedes birth and even conception; according to Onians 1951, 335 this is the normal view.

24. The argument of Giangrande 1972, 135-147 that Catullus actually endorses and admires Achilles' conduct will not convince many readers.

25. This is the divine name of Queen Arsinoe, late wife of Ptolemy II.

26. One thinks of Alexander Pope's lines on "the conqu'ring force of unresisted steel," *Rape of Lock* iii, 171-178. For a discussion of Pope's debt to the *Coma Berenices* see McPeek 1939, 140-143.

27. Some scholars (e.g., Putnam 1960, 223-228 and Granarolo 1967, 129-130) have found this passage so Catullan in ethos that they regard it as an addition to the Greek original, composed by Catullus. This is not impossible, but the objective evidence in support of the theory is inconclusive. It is true that these lines are not contained in our Callimachus papyrus, but they may derive from a second edition of Callimachus' poems; so Trypanis 1958, 85; Fordyce 1961, 328; and Pfeiffer 1965, I, 121.

28. For what it is worth, I record the fact that Wilamowitz 1924, II, 286 supported hypothesis no. 2 above, whereas Granarolo 1972, 332 argues in behalf of no. 3. I myself confess a subjective inclination in favor of no. 4 and have tentatively advanced it in Chapter Three. Nos. 1 and 2 I regard as flagrantly cynical, but they are not to be excluded solely on that account.

NOTES TO CHAPTER SEVEN

1. For *munus* see vv. 10, 32, 149; for *domus*, vv. 68, 156; for *officium*, vv. 12, 42, 150; for *hospes*, vv. 12 and 68.

2. *Mani* is the conjecture of Lachmann; the MSS. give *Mali* or *Malli*.

3. With MSS. variations: at 41 and 150 *Allius* is the conjecture of Scaliger.

4. Some scholars raise the objection that Catullus nowhere else addresses any of his friends solely by the *praenomen*. Nevertheless (as Fraenkel 1962, 262 observes) this usage was always possible among intimates, and Mynors has evidently accepted Lachmann's conjecture *Mani* on that basis.

5. Note *utriusque*, v. 39, on which consult Prescott 1940, 479 and 487.

6. Fordyce 1961, 345, following Kroll *ad loc.*

7. Jachmann 1925, 211; approved by Fraenkel 1962, 262, Williams 1968, 231, and most recently by Skinner 1972, 500. I take this opportunity to record a special obligation to Skinner's lucid article, even though I do not accept her principal conclusions.
8. In v. 12, *hospitis officium* means "the duty of a guest toward a host"; *hospitis* is used in two senses and the genitive in two constructions.
9. Heine 1975, 166-186 is a noteworthy exception.
10. Lenchantin 1966, 213.
11. Skinner 1972, 504, following Fraenkel.
12. I follow Weinreich 1969, 244 in the main. Many other arrangements have been proposed: Witke 1968, 31; Luck 1969, 65; Williams 1968, 233; Quinn 1972, 181-2; Kroll 1968, 219; Fordyce 1961, 344; Wiseman 1974, 75. But they differ only in monor detail. For the similar pyramidal structure of poem no. 64 consult Murley 1937, 305ff.
13. Klingner in Bayet 1953, 517; Offermann 1975, 61 resists Klingner's analysis, unsuccessfully in my opinion. The passage is analyzed in detail by Phillips 1976.
14. Baker 1960, 171-173.
15. Poeschl 1960, 18.
16. If we accept Mynors' text of v. 68; on the difficulties of this line see Wilkinson 1970, 290 and Baker 1975.
17. The prayer to Nemesis, vv. 77-78, shows that as yet Catullus is conscious of no personal offense against the gods; see Schaefer 1966, 82 and 83 n. 1, rebutting Lieberg 1962, 239ff.
18. For a full discussion of this point see Macleod 1974, 82-88.
19. Lieberg 1962, 224 sees an allusion here to Laodamia's suicide; loving Protesilaus more than life itself she died by her own hand, thus following him to the grave.
20. Cf. Witke 1968, 41 and Friedrich 1908, *ad loc.*; for a full discussion of the passage, diverging in some respects from my interpretation, see Offermann 1975, 63-66.
21. Elder 1951, 103.
22. Granarolo 1967, 122; Quinn 1972, 188.
23. Almost, because Lesbia was in sober fact only an ordinary mortal, whereas Laodamia was a heroine and lived in a better time (the heroic age); so Lieberg 1962, 228.
24. Despite the objections of Schaefer 1966, 83-84.
25. Lieberg 1962, 249f.
26. In line 135 he refers to himself by name; this strikes a note of pathos and is uncharacteristically self-effacing (So Kroll 1968 *ad loc.*).
27. Quinn 1970, 374; full discussion in 1972, 190-201.
28. Elder 1951, 127 writes, "Subconsciously Catullus transferred his love for his brother to Lesbia...hence his rather pathetic attempts to make (her) appear less faithless than he undoubtedly knew she was." Witke 1968, 49 accepts this idea. Thomson 1961, 57 goes further: "In poem 68 the hope that Lesbia will replace his brother is so strong that he is pre-

pared to be magnanimous about her temporary lapses into faith-
lessness."

29. Luck 1969, 58.
30. Frank 1928, 46-47.
31. Booth 1961, 135.
32. On the origins of this form consult Day 1938 *passim*; also
    Butler and Barber 1933, xxxv - lxvi.
33. The poem in question is the so-called "Alexandrian Erotic
    Fragment." On this fragment and on the whole question of
    servitium amoris consult Copley 1947, 285-300, esp. 289; also
    Lilja 1965, 76-89.
34. Klingner 1956, 208.
35. This theme is exhaustively studied in the monograph of Lieberg
    1962; cf. Lilja 1965, 186-191.
36. Wheeler 1934, 178.
37. Wilkinson in Rostagni 1953, 85.
38. Luck 1969, 66 citing Butler and Barber 1933, lix; Bardon 1970,
    150 takes a similar view. Schaefer 1966, 73, 78, 94-95, 109 is
    less circumspect: for him no. 68 is *die erste Römische Elegie*
    because of the sense of dependency (*Sich-abhängig-Finden*)
    which pervades the poem. Day 1938, 106-111 and Frank 1928, 61
    express similar opinions.
39. Ross 1975, 1, 56, 101-102. Chapters Three and Five of Ross'
    book attempt a reconstruction of Gallus' poetry. Some new
    fragments have lately been discovered; consult Van Sickle 1981,
    72-75.

NOTES TO CHAPTER EIGHT

1. Elsewhere (no. 68, 17-18, 51-52; no. 64, 71-72, 94-98) Catullus
   attributes the onset of passion to Venus and Cupid, who are
   emphatically not just or benevolent (although there is also a
   bona Venus; see no. 61, 44 and 195) and whose fires strike
   arbitrarily and unjustly; but no. 76 takes no notice of Venus
   and Cupid.
2. On this metaphor see La Penna 1951, 206-208.
3. It will be recalled that she was the subject of a poem by
   Catullus' friend Caecilius (no. 35, 14 and 18).
4. Elder 1940, xxxiv holds that he had seen in Bithynia the
   effects of religious frenzy upon Cybele's worshippers, which
   seems a reasonable inference; so, too, Weinreich 1936, 466.
5. In the cult (as distinguished from Catullus' poem) the purpose
   of the mutilation was to insure the perfect continence necessary to the proper performance of sacerdotal duties: see Nock
   1925, 27.
6. A tonic accent on the second *breve* in the final series of
   short syllables is extremely helpful in reading the lines
   aloud, but it is omitted by many authorities. For an extended

discussion of the galliambic see Loomis 1972, 119-136.

7. Quinn 1972, 250-251, hazards a curious (and unpersuasive) psychological explanation.
8. On this see Dodds 1960, xiii-xvi.
9. See Dodds 1940, 155-176; Fitten 1973, 262-263; and Nietzsche, *Birth of Tragedy*, section 1.
10. Guthrie 1954, 157ff. refers to the Mevlevi dervishes who dance to cymbals and drums until they imagine they are turning on the axis of the universe, or drive needles through their cheeks without feeling pain or shedding blood. These rites continue in Anatolia to the present day. Also Anatolian in origin were the Montanist ecstatics of the second century A.D.; on them consult Schepelern 1929.
11. On the shift in gender see Weinreich 1936, 472 and 481-483; his text differs in some particulars from that of Mynors.
12. Nock 1925, 26 and 33. By the change of clothes the Gallus wished to show publicly that he had renounced all the active functions of the male sex.
13. In line 36, *sine Cerere* might simply mean that the Gallae were too boneweary to eat before going to sleep (Weinreich 1936, 499). However, "Ceres" is a metonymy for bread, the food of civilized man; one doubts that Attis' followers carried rations up the mountain.
14. Schaefer 1966, 98, 100 has a valuable discussion of light/dark imagery in this poem.
15. On the aubade or dawn song in classical and medieval verse see the brilliant study of Saville 1972, esp. 173-177.
16. Fedeli 1978 studies in detail the contrast between these two speeches.
17. Schaefer 1966, 97.
18. The theme of *amechania* is analyzed by Snell, 1953, chapt. 3, and Versenyi, 1974, chapt. 3. On the lyric quality of Attis' lament see Schaefer 1966, 102-103.
19. Unlike Catullus, Virgil and Lucretius (*Aen.* IX, 82ff., X, 220 ff.; *de R.N.* II 600ff.) make Cybele a goddess of cities (cities are built on sacred hills). Her mural crown shows that she is a protectress of walled areas, especially in time of war.
20. Dionysus the blond, long-haired dancer is pitted against the short-haired, dark, athletic Pentheus who admires wrestling (v. 455) and is in all likelihood a wrestler himself.
21. Dodds 1960, 77; Frazer 1955, I, 277-278.
22. Fraenkel 1962, 259; also 1950, III, 740-741. His views seem to be based on Weinreich 1936, 489-495.
23. Highet 1957, 26; Harkins 1959, 104-111; Bagg 1965, 83-87; Whigham 1966, 43; Rubino 1974, 152ff. and 1975, 295-298. For an acute criticism of the theory consult Schaefer 1966, 104-105. Forsyth 1976 has some common-sense remarks on this subject.
24. No. 11, 20 is sometimes cited in support of this interpretation, but the line has nothing to do with castration.

25. Highet 1957, 26.
26. Bardon 1970, 96 agrees with the authors cited in note 23 above that no. 63 renders a deep psychological conflict in symbolic form, but he refrains from equating Cybele with Lesbia. According to his theory Catullus desires castration as a purification or a punishment, yet simultaneously fears it as entailing loss of selfhood. In the end, fear wins out over desire, and Catullus resolves the conflict by accepting himself as he is. I believe Bardon's formulation is not altogether imcompatible with the view I espouse in the next paragraph.
27. Weinreich 1936, 496 moves in this direction: "perhaps in a corner of his soul he was not wholly insensitive to (a deity such as Cybele)." Granarolo 1967, 54 quotes Weinreich with what seems to be grudging concurrence, but refrains from developing the idea.
28. On decorum see D'Alton 1931, 115-131; Brink 1963, 228-230; Wimsatt and Brooks 1957, 80-91.
29. Bowra 1961, 200-201.
30. Henry 1950, 53.
31. Weinreich 1969, 39 resists this view.
32. Cf. Chapter Six, footnote 11.
33. He is not excessively solemn about them, however, and in two cases invokes them in comic or jocular contexts; see no. 14, 12 and no. 53, 5. Marmoreale 1952, 77, who believes Catullus underwent a radical conversion to the mysteries of Dionysus toward the end of his life, would regard these as early poems. But the conversion theory has won few adherents. Consult Traina 1954, 358ff. for a devastating critique.

NOTES TO CHAPTER NINE

1. On the epyllion as a literary form see Vessey 1970, 38-43 with the literature there cited.
2. Putnam 1961, 199. I am deeply indebted to this excellent monograph. Also helpful is Konstan 1977.
3. Klingner 1964, 167-168.
4. Harmon 1973, 314.
5. Harkins 1959, 113; Putnam 1961, 167; Kinsey 1965, 911-912 is skeptical.
6. Otis 1964, 100.
7. Lieberg 1958, 32-33; also Putnam 1961, 169-170.
8. There is an apparent contradiction here. In line 11 Catullus told us that the Argo was the first ship; now we are informed that (apparently in an earlier time) Theseus had sailed from Piraeus to Crete and back again. The usual explanation (in my view rather lame) is that a small boat sufficed for the short voyage to Crete, whereas a much larger vessel was needed for the long haul to Colchis. Granarolo 1967, 155 has proposed another solution to the problem; he assumes that the scenes

depicted on the crimson coverlet are anticipatory, not a representation of past action; the Argonauts therefore antedate Theseus, and the Argo is indeed the first ship. Granarolo's theory has not won acceptance, chiefly because there is no indication in the text of the poem that the coverlet is prophetic, i.e., that it had been woven by or at the direction of a divine being. Consequently, it is safer to adhere to the traditional view of the chronology and either (a) to swallow the feeble explanation of the discrepancy mentioned above, or (b) to accept the readings of MS O for vs. 11, according to which the line merely means that the Argo was the first ship launched by Athena; so Lenchantin 1966, 143 and Quinn 1970, 302; or (c) adopt the view of Giangrande 1972, 124-126, who dates the Theseus-Ariadne story after the betrothal of Peleus to Thetis (vv. 19-21) but before their wedding (v. 31ff.), which took place much later (cf. vv. 294-297).

9. This is suggested by the loosened state of her clothing, emphasized in lines 63-67; Ovid is more explicit: *Heroides* xi, 9-14.
10. Segal 1969, 72 speaks of "an interpenetration of the literal seething of the sea and the metaphorical seething of Ariadne's passion"; human experience and the natural world are mysteriously connected.
11. Klingner 1964, 216-217.
12. Putnam 1961, 170; Klingner 1964, 200-201.
13. Kinsey 1965, 919; Harmon 1973, 319. According to Giangrande 1972, 127 Theseus forgets Ariadne and abandons her not deliberately but by divine intervention; Bacchus smites him with amnesia. However, Catullus makes no allusion to this version of the myth in the text of the poem.
14. According to Kinsey 1965, 916 the coverlet *indicat*, "reveals" or "gives evidence of" the *heroum virtutes*; by providing an outstanding instance in Theseus' career, the embroidered figures reveal the essence of all heroism.
15. Harmon 1973, 318-319.
16. According to Aegeus (vv. 228-30). However, Catullus nowhere states that she intervenes in Theseus' behalf.
17. Williams 1968, 708.
18. *Sicine* is used with similar effect in no. 77, 3 (the reproach to Rufus).
19. This is explicitly stated earlier in line 55.
20. Putnam 1961, 182-4, pointing to similarities of phraseology between the present passage and nos. 101 and 65, believes Catullus saw an analogy between Aegeus' loss of Theseus and his own loss of his brother.
21. In line 20 of no. 4 "Jupiter" is a metonymy for "wind."
22. Kinsey 1965, 919. How the Furies, invoked at v. 193, are involved in the matter, we are not told.
23. The subject of a celebrated painting by Titian; cf. Thompson 1956, 259ff.

24. Finley 1966, 66-67.
25. He is following a version of the myth according to which Dionysus had seen her in Crete and fallen in love with her there: Lenchantin 1966 *ad loc.*
26. Preller-Robert 1964, I, 680-682.
27. Klingner 1956, 217 and 1964, 206-208.
28. Marmoreale 1952, 198 theorizes that Catullus was actually a Bacchic initiate. I do not wish to go that far: see footnote 33 in the preceding chapter.
29. Clearly explicated by Quinn 1962, 53-54.
30. *Iliad* XVI, 143.
31. This point is made by Bramble 1970, 30-31.
32. Merrill 1893, 155.
33. On the color imagery of the poem see Harmon 1973, especially p. 324.
34. Dover 1963, 200-201.
35. Early societies believe that music has the power to compel. That is why song is used in magic. One recalls that the English word "charm" is derived from the Latin *carmen*, "song."
36. The relation of their decrees to the will of Jupiter and the rest of the Olympians is left shadowy and undefined, and the question of human free will is not raised.
37. Quinn 1972, 262.
38. 1972, 263-264.
39. Catullus' contemporary the historian Sallust devotes chapters 10-13 of his *Bellum Catilinae* to an analysis of the degeneracy of his times. He limits his observations, however, to Rome, and, as a historian should, he ignores the gods and gives believable reasons for what happened; consult Earle 1961 chapter iv and Syme 1964, 66ff., 136, and 238.
40. The pyramidal structure has frequently been diagrammed; see footnote 12 to Chapter Seven.
41. Klingner 1956, 220: "Krone eines einheitlichen Lebenswerkes." Putnam 1961, 199 says that no. 64 is "the copestone of Catullus' genius." Ferrero 1953, 383ff. and Granarolo 1968, 2⁻ reach similar conclusions.

NOTES TO CHAPTER TEN

1. Garrison 1978.
2. Otis 1964, 102 and 105.
3. Some have sought psychological reasons for this (e.g., Bagg 1965, 77 and 87-88 and Putnam 1961, 194-195). I agree with Schaefer 1966, 69-72 that such explanations are superfluous; Catullus does not suffer from a heroine identification complex. The outstanding examples of the pathos experience in mythology happen to be female rather than male (Klingner 1956, 207-208). Why this should be so is an interesting question that goes far

beyond the scope of the present book.

4. Quinn 1959, especially p. 26; the expression had been used earlier by Reitzenstein 1935, 64-65 and Havelock 1939, 132, 162 and 167. Lyne 1978, 176 would restrict the "Revolution" to the Lesbia poems.

5. Crowther 1971, 246-249 argues that Catullus and the New Poets did not fundamentally change the traditions of poetry but brought to prominence what in many cases had existed earlier.

6. As is done by Herescu 1957, 433-455 and Blaiklock 1959, among others; Grimaldi 1965, 87-95 provides an excellent rebuttal of their views.

7. This is of course the principal thesis of Wheeler 1934.

8. Granarolo 1967, 174-175; Quinn 1959, 10-12, 17; Crowther 1971, 246-249; Granarolo 1971, esp. 385-403.

9. Ross 1969, esp. 137, 151 and 167.

10. On *imitatio* see Quintilian X, 2; Guillemin 1924, 35-57 (also 1930, 153-211, 296-325).

11. The exact meaning of this term is a matter of debate. I take it as referring both to literary erudition and mastery of technique; see Fordyce 1961, xxi-xxii.

12. Quinn 1959, 22-34.

13. At the end of no. 8 he seems to come perilously close to it.

14. Kirkwood 1974, 120; for examples of the same phenomenon in other authors see Kidd 1963, 300.

15. No. 8, 1 and 19; no. 46, 4; no. 51, 13; no. 52, 1 and 4; no. 76, 5.

16. This usage is mostly confined to direct address, but in no. 7, 10 the inferior self appears in the dative case (*vesano... Catullo*); here the adjective implies a rational censor who is passing judgment on the "mad" lover.

17. 1934, 21-26.

18. Well brought out by Granarolo 1967, 52-107.

19. Here again he resembles Sappho; see Bowra 1961, 233.

20. Consult the chapter "Classical Landscape" in his *Modern Painters*.

21. Recall no. 8, 5; no. 37, 12; no. 58, 3; no. 87, 1-4.

22. Copley 1969, 71 puts it well: "He has a depth of mind and breadth of heart that enables him to trace in himself the feelings of all men."

23. This famous phrase is of course subject to various interpretations. I assume that it means that the end of poetry is not to reveal nor even to please but simply to exist and to be beautiful. This type of aestheticism is post-classical.

LIST OF WORKS CITED

This list is limited to the books and articles mentioned in the footnotes. For fuller bibliography to Catullus, the reader is referred to the following (in addition to Marouzeau's *L'Année Philologique*):

Leon, H. J. "A Quarter Century of Catullan Scholarship (1934-1959)" *Classical World* 53 (1960) 104-113, 141-148, 173-180, 281-282

Kroyman, J. "Bibliographie zu Catull für die Jahre 1929-1967" in Kroll, W. *C. Valerius Catullus*[5] (Stuttgart 1968) 301-318

Thomson, D. F. S. "Recent Scholarship on Catullus (1960-69)" *Classical World* 65 (1971) 116-126

Granarolo, J. "Catulle 1948-1973" *Lustrum* 17 (1973-1974) 27-70

Stoessl, F. *C. Valerius Catullus: Mensch, Leben, Dichtung* (Meisenheim am Glan 1977)

Harrauer, H. *A Bibliography to Catullus* (Hildesheim 1979)

*

Austin, R. G. *M. Tulli Ciceronis pro M. Caelio Oratio*[2] (Oxford 1952)

Baehrens, A. *Catulli Veronensis Liber*[2] (Leipzig 1893)

Bagg, R. "Some Versions of Lyric Impasse in Shakespeare and Catullus" *Arion* 4 (1965) 64-95

Baker, R. J. "*Domina* at Catullus 68, 68: Mistress or Chatelaine?" *Rheinisches Museum* 118 (1975) 124-129

Baker, S. "The Irony of Catullus' 'Septimius and Acme'" *Classical Philology* 53 (1958) 110-112

Baker, S. "Lesbia's Foot" *Classical Philology* 55 (1960) 171-173

Bardon, H. *Propositions sur Catulle*, Collection Latomus vol. 118 (1970)

Bayet, J. "Catulle, la Grèce et Rome" in *L'Influence Grecque sur la Poésie Latine de Catulle à Ovide* (Entretiens II 1953, Fondation Hardt) 3-55

Bickel, E. "Catulli in Caesarem Carmina" *Rheinisches Museum* 93 (1949) 1-23

Blaiklock, E. M. "The Romanticism of Catullus" *University of Auckland Bulletin* 53 Classical Series 1 1959

Bolton, J. D. P. "Merus Thyonianus" *Classical Review* 17 (1967) 12

Booth, W. C. *The Rhetoric of Fiction* (Chicago 1961)

Bowra, C. M. *Greek Lyric Poetry*[2] (Oxford 1961)

Bramble, J. C. "Structure and Ambiguity in Catullus 64" *Proceedings of the Cambridge Philological Society* 16 (1970) 22-41

Brink, C. O. *Horace on Poetry: Prolegomena to the Literary Epistles* (Cambridge 1963)

Buchheit, V. "Catulls Dichterkritik in C. 36" *Hermes* 87 (1959) 309-327

Buchheit, V. "Catull c. 50 als Programm und Bekenntnis" *Rheinisches Museum* 119 (1976) 162-180

Buchheit, V. "*Sal et Lepos Versiculorum* (Catull c. 16)" *Hermes* 104 (1976) 331-347

Burck, E. "Römische Wesenszüge der Augusteischen Liebeselegie" *Hermes* 80 (1952) 163-200

Butler, H. E. and Barber, E. A. *The Elegies of Propertius* (Oxford 1933)

Cairns, F. "Catullus 27" *Mnemosyne* 28 (1975) 24-29

Cameron, A. "Catullus 27" *Hermes* 104 (1976) 155-163

Clausen, W. "Catulli Veronensis Liber" *Classical Philology* 71 (1976) 37-41

Commager, S. "Notes on Some Poems of Catullus" *Harvard Studies in Classical Philology* 70 (1965) 83-110

Connor, P. J. "Catullus 8: the Lovers' Conflict" *Antichthon* 8 (1974) 93-96

Copley, F. O. "Servitium Amoris in the Roman Elegists" *Transactions and Proceedings of the American Philological Association* 78 (1947) 285-300

Copley, F. O. "The 'Riddle' of Catullus 67" *Transactions and Proceedings of the American Philological Association* 80 (1949) 245-253

Copley, F. O. "Emotional Conflict and its Significance in the Lesbia Poems of Catullus" *American Journal of Philology* 70 (1949) 22-40

Copley, F. O. "Catullus c. 38" *Transactions and Proceedings of the American Philological Association* 87 (1956) 125-129

Copley, F. O. *Latin Literature* (Ann Arbor 1969)

Croce, B. *Poesia Antica e Moderna*2 (Bari 1943)

Crowther, N. B. "Catullus and the Traditions of Latin Poetry" *Classical Philology* 66 (1971) 246-249

D'Alton, J. F. *Roman Literary Theory and Criticism* (London 1931)

Davis, J. T. "*Quo Desiderio:* the Structure of Catullus 96" *Hermes* 99 (1971) 297-302

Day, A. A. *The Origins of Latin Love-Elegy* (Oxford 1938)

Deroux, C. "À propos de l'Attitude Politique de Catulle" *Latomus* 29 (1970) 608-631

Deroux, C. "L'Identité de Lesbie" *Aufstieg und Niedergang der Römischen Welt* ed. H. Temporini (Berlin 1973) I 3, 390-416

Dodds, E. R. "Maenadism in the Bacchae" *Harvard Theological Review* 33 (1940) 155-176

Dodds, E. R. *The Greeks and the Irrational* Sather Classical Lectures 25 (Berkeley 1951)

Dodds, E. R. *Euripides: Bacchae*2 (Oxford 1960)

Dover, K. J. "The Poetry of Archilochus" in *Archiloque* (Entretiens X 1963, Fondation Hardt) 183-222

Duhigg, J. "The Elegiac Metre of Catullus" *Antichthon* 5 (1971) 57-67

Earl, D. C. *The Political Thought of Sallust* (Cambridge 1961)

Elder, J. P. "The Art of Catullus' Attis" *Transactions and Proceedings of the American Philological Association* 71 (1940) xxxiii-xxxiv

Elder, J. P. "Notes on Some Conscious and Subconscious Elements in Catullus' Poetry" *Harvard Studies in Classical Philology* 60 (1951) 101-136

Elder, J. P. "Catullus I, His Poetic Creed, and Nepos" *Harvard Studies in Classical Philology* 71 (1966) 143-149

Ellis, R. *Catulli Veronensis Liber*[2] (Oxford 1878)

Ernout A. and Meillet A. *Dictionnaire Étymologique de la Langue Latine*[4] (Paris 1959-1960)

Fedeli, P. *Il Carme 61 di Catullo* (Friburgo Svizzera 1972)

Fedeli, P. "Struttura e Stile dei Monologhi di Attis nel Carme 63 di Catullo" *Rivista di Filologia e di Istruzione Classica* 106 (1978) 39-52

Fehling, D. "Gegen die neueste Äusserung zu Cat. 56" *Hermes* 102 (1974) 376

Ferrero, L. *Un' Introduzione a Catullo* (Turin 1955)

Finley, J. H. *Four Stages of Greek Thought* (Stanford 1966)

Finley, M. I. *The World of Odysseus* (New York 1965)

Fitton, J. W. "Greek Dance" *Classical Quarterly* 23 (1973) 254-274

Fordyce, C. J. *Catullus* (Oxford 1961)

Forsyth, P. Y. "The Gellius Cycle of Catullus" *Classical Journal* 68 (1972) 175-177

Forsyth, P. Y. "Catullus 82" *Classical Journal* 70 (1975) 33-35

Forsyth, P. Y. "Catullus: the Mythic Persona" *Latomus* 35 (1976) 555-566

Forsyth, P. Y. "Comments on Catullus 116" *Classical Quarterly* 27 (1977) 352-353

Fraenkel, E. *Aeschylus: Agamemnon* (Oxford 1950)

Fraenkel, E. *"Vesper Adest"* *Journal of Roman Studies* 45 (1955) 1-8

Fraenkel, E. "Catulls Trostgedicht für Calvus" *Wiener Studien* 69 (1956) 278-288

Fraenkel, E. *Horace* (Oxford 1957)
185

Fraenkel, E. "Two Poems of Catullus" *Journal of Roman Studies* 51 (1961) 46-53

Fraenkel, E. (review of C. J. Fordyce *Catullus* 1961) *Gnomon* 34 (1962) 253-263

Fraenkel, H. *Die Homerischen Gleichnisse* (Göttingen 1921)

Frank, R. I. "Catullus 51: *Otium* versus *Virtus*" *Transactions and Proceedings of the American Philological Association* 99 (1968) 233-239

Frank, T. *Catullus and Horace* (New York 1928)

Frazer, Sir J. G. *The New Golden Bough* ed. T. H. Gaster (New York 1959)

Frazer, Sir J. G. *Adonis, Attis, Osiris*³ (London 1955)

Fredricksmeyer, E. A. "Catullus 49, Cicero and Caesar" *Classical Philology* 68 (1973) 268-278

Friedrich, G. *Catulli Veronensis Liber* (Leipzig 1908)

Frye, N. *Anatomy of Criticism* (Princeton 1957)

Fustel de Coulanges, N. D. *The Ancient City* trans. Willard Small (Garden City 1956)

Garrison, D. H. *Mild Frenzy* Hermes Einzelschriften 41 (Wiesbaden 1978)

Giangrande, G. "Das Epyllion Catulls im Lichte der Hellenistischen Epik" *L'Antiquité Classique* 41 (1972) 123-147

Giardina, G. C. "La Composizione del *Liber* e L'Itinerario Poetico di Catullo" *Philologus* 118 (1974) 224-235

Gow, A. S. F. *Theocritus* (Cambridge 1950)

Gow, A. S. F. and Page D. L. *The Greek Anthology: Hellenistic Epigrams* (Cambridge 1965)

Granarolo, J. "Où en Sont nos Connaissances sur Catulle?" *L'Information Littéraire* 8 (1956) 56-65

Granarolo, J. "L'heure de la Vérité pour Tallus le Cinède" *Revue des Études Anciennes* 60 (1958) 290-306

Granarolo, J. "Catulle et César" *Annales de la Faculté des Lettres d'Aix* 32 (1958) 53-73

Granarolo J. *L'Oeuvre de Catulle* (Paris 1967)

Granarolo, J. *D'Ennius à Catulle* (Paris 1971)

Granarolo, J. (review of P. Fideli *Il Carme 61 di Catullo*) *Revue des Études Latines* 50 (1972) 330-332

Granarolo, J. "L'époque Néotérique" in *Aufstieg und Niedergang der Römischen Welt* ed. H. Temporini (Berlin 1973) I 3, 278-360

Grimaldi, W. M. A. "The Lesbia Love Lyrics" *Classical Philology* 60 (1965) 87-95

Guillemin, A. "L'Imitation dans les Littératures Antiques" *Revue des Études Latines* 2 (1924) 35-57

Guillemin, A. "L'Originalité de Virgile" *Revue des Études Latines* 8 (1930) 153-211 and 296-325

Guthrie, W. K. C. *The Greeks and their Gods* (Boston 1954)

Hallett, J. P. "The Role of Women in Roman Elegy" *Arethusa* 6 (1973) 103-124

Halporn, J. W., Ostwald, M. and Rosenmeyer, T. G. *The Meters of Greek and Latin Poetry* (Indianapolis 1963)

Harkins, P. W. "Autoallegory in Catullus 63 and 64" *Transactions and Proceedings of the American Philological Association* 90 (1959) 102-116

Harmon, D. P. "Nostalgia for the Age of Heroes in Catullus 64" *Latomus* 32 (1973) 311-331

Havelock, E. A. *The Lyric Genius of Catullus* (Oxford 1939)

Heine, R. "Zu Catull c. 68" *Latomus* 34 (1975) 166-186

Henry, R. M. "Pietas and Fides in Catullus" *Hermathena* 75-76 (1950) 63-68, 48-57

Herescu, N. I. "Catulle et le Romantisme" *Latomus* 16 (1957) 433-445

Herzog, R. "Catulliana" *Hermes* 71 (1936) 338-350

Highet, G. *The Classical Tradition* (New York 1949)

Highet, G. *Poets in a Landscape* (New York 1957)

Housman, A. E. *"Praefanda" Hermes* 66 (1931) 408

Jachmann, G. (review of W. Kroll *C. Valerius Catullus*) *Gnomon* 1 (1925) 200-214

Khan, H. A. "Observations on Two Poems of Catullus" *Rheinisches Museum* 114 (1971) 159-178

Khan, H. A. "Catullus 35--and the Things Poetry Can Do to You" *Hermes* 102 (1974)

Kidd, D. A. "The Unity of Catullus 51" *Journal of the Australasian Universities Language and Literature Association* 20 (1963) 298-308

Kinsey, T. E. "Catullus 11" *Latomus* 24 (1965) 537-544

Kinsey, T. E. "Irony and Structure in Catullus 64" *Latomus* 24 (1965) 911-931

Kirkwood, G. M. *Early Greek Monody* Cornell Studies in Classical Philology 37 (Ithaca 1974)

Klingner, F. *Römische Geisteswelt*[3] (Munich 1956)

Klingner, F. "Catulls Peleus-Epos" *Studien zur Griechischen und Römischen Literatur* (Zürich 1964) 156-224

Konstan, D. *Catullus' Indictment of Rome: the Meaning of Catullus 64* (Amsterdam 1977)

Kroll, W. *C. Valerius Catullus*[5] (Stuttgart 1968)

La Penna, A. "Note sul Linguaggio Erotico dell' Elegia Latina" *Maia* 4 (1951) 187-209

Lateiner, D. "Obscenity in Catullus" *Ramus* 6 (1977) 15-29

Lattimore, R. "Sappho 2 and Catullus 51" *Classical Philology* 39 (1944) 184-187

Lenchantin de Gubernatis, M. *Il Libro di Catullo* (Turin 1966)

Levens, R. G. C. "Catullus" in *Fifty Years (and Twelve) of Classical Scholarship* ed. M. Platnauer (Oxford 1968)

Levy, H. L. "Catullus and Cangrande della Scala" *Transactions and Proceedings of the American Philological Association* 99 (1968) 249-253

Lewis, C. S. *The Allegory of Love* (Oxford 1936)

Lieberg, G. "L'Ordinamento ed i Reciproci Rapporti dei Carmi Maggiori di Catullo" *Rivista di Filologia e di Istruzione Classica* 36 (1958) 23-47

Lieberg, G. *Puella Divina* (Amsterdam 1962)

Lilja, S. *The Roman Elegists' Attitude to Women* Annales Academiae Scientiarum Fennicae B 135, 1 (Helsinki 1965)

Lindsay, J. *Catullus: the Complete Poems* (London 1948)

Loomis, J. W. *Studies in Catullan Verse* (Leiden 1972)

Luck, G. *The Latin Love Elegy*[2] (London 1969)

Lyne, R. O. A. M. "The Neoteric Poets" *Classical Quarterly* 28 (1978) 167-187

Maas, P. "The Chronology of the Poems of Catullus" *Classical Quarterly* 36 (1942) 79-82

Macleod, C. W. "Parody and Personalities in Catullus" *Classical Quarterly* 23 (1973) 294-303

Macleod, C. W. "Catullus 116" *Classical Quarterly* 23 (1973) 304-309

Macleod, C. W. "A Use of Myth in Ancient Poetry" *Classical Quarterly* 24 (1974) 82-88

Marmoreale, E. V. *L'Ultimo Catullo* (Naples 1952)

McGushin, P. "Catullus' *Sanctae Foedus Amicitiae*" *Classical Philology* 62 (1967) 85-93

McPeek, J. A. S. *Catullus in Strange and Distant Britain* Harvard Studies in Comparative Literature 15 (Cambridge Mass. 1939)

Merkelbach, R. "*Boukoliastai*: Der Wettgesang der Hirten" *Rheinisches Museum* 99 (1956) 97-133

Merrill, E. T. *Catullus* (Boston 1893)

Michie, J. *The Poems of Catullus* (New York 1969)

Moore-Blunt, J. "Catullus 31 and Ancient Generic Composition" *Eranos* 72 (1974) 106-118

Murley, C. J. "The Structure and Proportion of Catullus 64" *Transactions and Proceedings of the American Philological Association* 68 (1937) 305-317

Murray, G. *The Classical Tradition in Poetry* (Cambridge Mass. 1927)

Musurillo, H. A. *Symbol and Myth in Ancient Poetry* (New York 1961)

Mynors, R. A. B. *C. Valerii Catulli Carmina* (Oxford 1960)

Neudling, C. L. *A Prosopography to Catullus* Iowa Studies in Classical Philology XII (Oxford 1955)

Newman, J. K. *Augustus and the New Poetry* Collection Latomus vol. 88 (1967)

Nielsen, R. M. "Catullus 45 and Horace Odes 3, 9: The Glass House" *Ramus* 6 (1977) 132-138

Nock, A. D. "Eunuchs in Ancient Religion" *Archiv für Religionswissenschaft* 23 (1925) 25-33

Offermann, H. "Der Flussvergleich bei Catull c. 68, 57 ff." *Philologus* 119 (1975) 57-69

Onians, R. B. *The Origins of European Thought* (Cambridge 1951)

Österud, S. "Sacrifice and Book Burning in Catullus' Poem 36" *Hermes* 106 (1978) 138-155

Otis, B. *Virgil: a Study in Civilized Poetry* (Oxford 1964)

Otis, B. *Ovid as an Epic Poet* (Cambridge 1966)

Pascal, C. *Poeti e Personaggi Catulliani* (Catania 1916)

Penella, R. J. "A Note on *(De)glubere*" *Hermes* 104 (1976) 120-122

Pfeiffer, R. *Callimachus* (Oxford 1965)

Phillips, J. E. "The Pattern of Images in Catullus 68, 51-62" *American Journal of Philology* 97 (1976) 340-343

Poeschl, V. *Catull* (Heidelberg 1960)

Preller, L. and Robert, C. *Griechische Mythologie*[5] (Berlin 1964-1967)

Prescott, H. W. "The Unity of Catullus 68" *Transactions and*

Proceedings of the American Philological Association 71 (1940) 473-500

Putnam, M. C. J. "Catullus 66, 75-88" *Classical Philology* 55 (1960) 223-228

Putnam, M. C. J. "The Art of Catullus 64" *Harvard Studies in Classical Philology* 65 (1961) 165-205

Putnam, M. C. J. "Catullus 11: the Ironies of Integrity" *Ramus* 3 (1974) 70-86

Quinn, K. *The Catullan Revolution* (Melbourne 1959)

Quinn, K. *Latin Explorations* (London 1963)

Quinn, K. "Practical Criticism: a Reading of Propertius 1, 21 and Catullus 17" *Greece and Rome 16* (1969) 19-29

Quinn, K. *Catullus: the Poems* (London 1970)

Quinn, K. *Catullus: An Interpretation* (London 1972)

Rankin, H. D. "Catullus and the 'Beauty' of Lesbia" *Latomus* 35 (1976) 3-11

Rankin, H. D. "Catullus and Incest" *Eranos* 74 (1976) 113-121

Rankin, H. D. "Poem 16 of Catullus" *Symbolae Osloenses* 51 (1976) 87-94

Reitzenstein, E. "Das Neue Kunstwollen in den *Amores* Ovids" *Rheinisches Museum* 84 (1935) 62-88

Richardson, L. Jr. *"Furi et Aureli, Comites Catulli"* *Classical Philology* 58 (1963) 93-106

Richardson, L. Jr. "Catullus 67: Interpretation and Form" *American Journal of Philology* 88 (1967) 423-433

Richlin, A. "The Meaning of *Irrumare* in Catullus and Martial" *Classical Philology* 76 (1981) 40-46

Richmond, J. A. "Horace's Mottoes and Catullus 51" *Rheinisches Museum* 113 (1970) 197-204

Ross, D. O. "Style and Content in Catullus 45" *Classical Philology* 60 (1965) 256-259

Ross, D. O. *Style and Tradition in Catullus* (Cambridge Mass. 1969)

Ross, D. O. *Backgrounds to Augustan Poetry: Gallus, Elegy and Rome* (Cambridge 1975)

Rostagni, A. "L'Influenza Greca sulle Origini dell' Elegia Erotica Latina" in *L'Influence Grecque sur la Poésie Latine de Catulle a Ovide* (Entretiens II 1953, Fondation Hardt) 59-90

Rowland, R. L. "*Miser Catulle*: an Interpretation of the Eighth Poem of Catullus" *Greece and Rome* 13 (1966) 15-21

Rubino "Myth and Meditation in the Attis Poem of Catullus" *Ramus* 3 (1974) 152-175

Rubino, C. A. "The Erotic World of Catullus" *Classical World* 68 (1975) 289-298

Saville, J. *The Medieval Erotic Alba* (New York 1972)

Schaefer, E. *Das Verhältnis von Erlebnis und Kunstgestalt bei Catull* Hermes Einzelscriften 18 (Wiesbaden 1966)

Schepelern, W. *Der Montanismus und die Phrygischen Kulte* trans. W. Baur (Tübingen 1929)

Schmidt, P. L. "Neoteriker" in *Der Kleine Pauly* ed. K. Ziegler, W. Sontheimer and H. Gärtner (Munich 1975) V, 1630-1631

Sedgwick, W. B. "Catullus' Elegiacs" *Mnemosyne* 3 (1950) 64-69

Segal, C. P. "Catullus 5 and 7, a Study in Complementaries" *American Journal of Philology* 89 (1968) 284-301

Segal, C. P. *Landscape in Ovid's Metamorphoses* Hermes Einzelschriften 23 (Wiesbaden 1969)

Segal, C. P. "Catullan *Otiosi*" *Greece and Rome* 17 (1970) 25-31

Skinner, M. B. "Catullus 8: the Comic Amator as *Eiron*" *Classical Journal* 66 (1971) 298-309

Skinner, M. B. "The Unity of Catullus 68: the Structure of 68a" *Transactions and Proceedings of the American Philological Association* 103 (1972) 495-512

Skinner, M. B. "*Ameana Puella Defututa*" *Classical Journal* 74 (1978-9) 110-114

Skutsch, O. "The Book and the Bushel" *University of London Institute of Classical Studies Bulletin* 16 (1969) 148

Skutsch, O. "Notes on Catullus" *University of London Institute of Classical Studies Bulletin* 23 (1976) 18-22

Snell, B. *The Discovery of the Mind* trans. T. G. Rosenmeyer (Oxford 1953)

Stanford, W. B. *The Odyssey of Homer* (London 1947)

Stigers, E. S. "Retreat from the Male: Catullus 62 and Sappho's Erotic Flowers" *Ramus* 6 (1977) 83-102

Stoessl, F. "Catulls Gelliusepigramme" *Wiener Studien* Beiheft 5 (1972) 408-424

Stoessl, F. "Aus Catulls Frühzeit" *Hermes* 101 (1973) 442-463

Stoessl, F. *C. Valerius Catullus: Mensch, Leben, Dichtung* (Meisenheim am Glan 1977)

Syme, Sir R. *Sallust* Sather Classical Lectures 33 (Berkeley 1964)

Tanner, R. G. "Catullus 56" *Hermes* 100 (1972) 506-508

Taylor, L. R. *Party Politics in the Age of Caesar* Sather Classical Lectures 22 (Berkeley 1949)

Thompson, G. H. "The Literary Sources of Titian's Bacchus and Ariadne" *Classical Journal* 51 (1956) 259-264

Thomson, D. F. S. "Aspects of Unity in Catullus 64" *Classical Journal* 57 (1961) 165-205

Traenkle, H. "Neoterische Kleinigkeiten" *Museum Helveticum* 24 (1967) 87-103

Traina, A. "Catullo e gli Dèi" *Convivium* 1 (1954) 358-368

Trypanis, C. A. *Callimachus* Loeb Classical Library (Cambridge Mass. 1958)

Tufte, V. *The Poetry of Marriage* University of Southern California Studies in Comparative Literature 2 (Los Angeles 1970)

Van Sickle, J. "Poetics of Opening and Closure in Meleager, Catullus, and Gallus" *Classical World* 75 (1981) 65-75

Versényi, L. *Man's Measure* (Albany 1974)

Vessey, D. W. T. C. "Thoughts on the Epyllion" *Classical Journal* 66 (1970) 38-43

Vessey, D. W. T. C. "Thoughts on Two Poems of Catullus: 13 and 30" *Latomus* 30 (1971) 45-55

Vretska, K. "Catullus" in *Der Kleine Pauly* ed. K. Ziegler and W. Sontheimer (Stuttgart 1964) I 1089-1092

Weinreich, O. "Catulls Attisgedicht" *Annuaire de L'Institut de Philologie et d'Histoire Orientales et Slaves* (*Mélanges Franz Cumont*) 4 (1936) 463-500

Weinreich, O. "Catull c. 60" *Hermes* 87 (1959) 75-90

Weinreich, O. *Catull: Sämtliche Gedichte* (Zurich 1969)

West, D. A. "The Metre of Catullus' Elegiacs" *Classical Quarterly* 51 (1957) 98-102

Wheeler, A. L. *Catullus and the Traditions of Ancient Poetry* Sather Classical Lectures 9 (Berkeley 1934)

Whigham, P. *The Poems of Catullus* (Baltimore 1966)

Wilamowitz-Moellendorff, U. von *Hellenistische Dichtung* (Berlin 1924)

Wilder, T. *The Ides of March* (New York 1963)

Wilhelm, J. J. *The Cruelest Month* (New Haven 1965)

Wilkinson, L. P. "*Domina* in Catullus 68" *Classical Review* 20 (1970) 290

Wilkinson, L. P. "Catullus 51 Again" *Greece and Rome* 21 (1974) 82-85

Willey, B. *The Eighteenth Century Background* (London 1940)

Williams, G. W. *Tradition and Originality in Roman Poetry* (Oxford 1968)

Wimsatt, W. K. and Brooks, C. *Literary Criticism: a Short History* (New York 1957)

Wiseman, T. P. *Catullan Questions* (Leicester 1969)

Wiseman, T. P. *Cinna the Poet* (Leicester 1974)

Wiseman, T. P. "Catullus, His Life and Times" *Journal of Roman Studies* 69 (1979) 161-168

Witke, C. *Enarratio Catulliana* (Leiden 1968)

Witke, C. "Catullus 13: a Reexamination" *Classical Philology* 75 (1980) 325-331

INDEX OF POEMS

No. 86: 31, 37, 59   No. 113: 17

87: 37, 39, 42   114: 59

88: 52   115: 59

89: 52, 53   116: 52-53

90: 52

91: 52, 53

92: 31

93: 62

94: 59

95: 17-19, 36, 135, 155

95B: 18

96: 20, 23-24, 73

97: 170

98: 170

99: 55

100: 14, 25

101: 23, 72-73, 74-75, 76,
78-79, 133, 157

104: 37-38

105: 59

107: 36

108: 57-58

109: 28, 37-38, 94

110: 171

111: 171